CIVIL WAR

CIVIL WAR

ANCESTRAL BONZ III

CARROLL SILVERA

ISBN: 978-1-942451-98-3
Civil War: Ancestral Bonz III
Copyright © by Carroll Silvera

All rights reserved.

No part of this publication may be reproduced, distributed, or transmitted in any form or by any means, including photocopying, recording, or other electronic or mechanical methods, without the prior written permission of the publisher, except in the case of brief quotations embodied in critical reviews and certain other noncommercial uses permitted by copyright law.

For permission requests, write to the publisher at the address below.

Yorkshire Publishing
3207 South Norwood Avenue
Tulsa, Oklahoma 74135
www.YorkshirePublishing.com
918.394.2665

There are few who can succeed without
someone who believes in them.
For me, that person has always been
Sally Jeanne Silvera.

Author's Note

The Civil War was in many respects the first *modern war*. Its scope was unprecedented. During the long hours of research, I found this to be the most compelling of stories—both from the viewpoint of the North as well as that of the South, as well as the families throughout this land of America that it touched, and more often than not—*destroyed!*

One out of every twelve adult American males served in the war, and few families were unaffected by the event. Over 620,000 Americans died in conflict, 150 *percent* more than in World War II.

Because battlefield surgeons were consistently overworked and frequently lacked equipment, supplies and knowledge, nearly all stomach or head wounds proved fatal, and gangrene was rampant.

Fifty thousand of the survivors returned home with one or more limbs amputated. Disease, however, was the greatest of threats to the soldiers, killing twice as many as were lost in battle.

The Civil War was not neatly self-contained; it was a total war, fought not solely by professional armies but by and against whole societies. Farms became battlefields, cities were transformed into armed encampments, and homes were commandeered for field hospitals.

After one battle a woman recalled that *"wounded men were brought into our house and laid side by side in our halls and first-story rooms…carpets were so saturated with blood as to be unfit for further use."*

The Civil War was also *modern* in that much of the killing was distant and impersonal, mechanical. The opposing forces used an array of new weapons and instruments of war; artillery were "rifled" or had grooved barrels for greater accuracy, repeating rifles, ironclad ships, observation balloons, and wire entanglements. During this time, the telegraph was invented and used most by those in the North. Men were killed without knowing who had fired the shot that felled them.

The historical content of this book is accurate—those persons depicted are fictional—yet based on my own *ancestral bones*.

The debate over why the North won and the South lost the Civil War will likely never end.

Lee's own explanation of the Confederate defeat retains an enduring legitimacy: "After five years of arduous service marked by unsurpassed courage and fortitude, the Army of Northern Virginia has been compelled to yield to overwhelming numbers and resources."

Acknowledgments

To Sally Silvera, my most avid fan. She read each and every page, offering support on a daily basis, and the invaluable insight of her costume designs. To all my avid fans who find history as interesting as I do.

To Toni David, I give my profound thanks for so diligently compiling a family tree that goes back beyond the year 1152. To Linda Glaz of Hartline, who encouraged me. Heartfelt thanks to all the curators of The Stones River Battlefield, the Battle at Franklin, and the curators of the plantations that were saved from the devastation of the War. To Robert Moon who so generously gave me mementos he had found on the battlefields and to Carey Latham who made it possible for me to visit plantations that have survived.

To all at Tate who diligently worked to publish this. To Gregory, my not-so-silent partner, without him there would be no books, stories perhaps, but no books.

From the bottom of my heart, I thank you all!

Contents

Fall 1862	13
Man and War	24
Bozeman Trail	30
Synchronicity of Hearts	36
Crevasse of Azure	41
The Celestials	45
The Railroad	49
Elisabeth	56
Joseph	64
The Rusteaters	70
Omaha	78
Love at First Sight	88
Joy	96
The Cradle	102
Time	115
The Child	120
Intuition	127
The Hunt	136
Eleanor's Visit	147
Most Bizarre—AKASA	164
Letters	173
Gettysburg	184

The Waiting	190
Home	197
The Gathering	205
Men	218
Josiah and Sally Susanne	227
Agnes	235
Respite	240
The Decision	248
Southern Gentlemen	264
Inside Andersonville	273
Initiation	278
William Tecumseh Sherman	288
Jeremiah	298
Spring 1865	309
Sikes Plantation	317
Rebels Not Yanks	323
Miss. Abigail	334
Jonas	345
Diagnoses	352
James Martin Prescott	361
Revelation	370
Jamie's Last Letter	376

Fall 1862

Jamie looked at Mack's burnished hair as it caught the last of the rays of the sun. It hung as long as his own thick, onyx head of hair but was wiry and a coppery red, Mack's beard offered a continuous effort to maintain the look of a large grizzly. His massive chest and shoulders were ensconced in belts of ammunition, much like that of Juan Alvarado as they had rode from the King Ranch in Texas.

At his left rode Micah Parsons's, usually talkative, the young man had been silent for most of the afternoon. His brother Tommy rode next to him. A grave mistake, Jamie thought, the Parsons had lost so many children... *God, save these two.* He thought of Micah's words as he had caught up to Jamie this morning, that "he'd be fightin' fer the Confederates—them there, they be my folks."

Damn, he hoped like hell he would never be in a position to kill the boy. Or Tommy for that fact, it might be worth losing *his* life rather than to have to do that. An image of Elisabeth rose before him, and he smiled. He was damn sure she would not share that same opinion. However, he knew she would not want to know, should such a decision be necessary.

She had always said she would go with him to war.

He thought of his spunky wife and was not surprised to find he thought she was as good or better at war than that of the men he traveled with, although perhaps not as good as the great Scotsman. His mind wandered to the cattle drive from the King

Ranch. A tumultuous set of emotions besieged him, guilt that he had let her down, pride in what she had done. Her bravery, her strength, the fear that had clutched at his heart...*he had thought he had lost her.*

"'Copper fer yer thoughts, lad...' the lilted Gaelic speech of Mack Mackenzie stirred him from his reverie.

Jamie looked over into the clear blue eyes of Mack—*Ian MacKenzie* in point of fact. Why, this giant of a man could be the archangel Michael. He thought of the words of wisdom he had imparted over the years they had known one another, the kindness he had shown to each and every person he had come in contact with, the gentleness with which he cared for his family, his peaceful ability to just let things be...as Jamie thought all of these fine things—the sight of Mack swinging his Claymore charged through his mind, as quickly, the sound of Mack's mellifluous voice given up in song. He looked at his friend and thought, *I'll be damned, the man is a world unto his own.* Jamie shrugged his shoulders, grinning at Mack. "More than likely the same as you."

"*The lass.* Aye, meself as well, me own Ilene...God rest her soul. An' me boy. May the Lord be lookin' after 'em whilst I be helpin' Him." Mack was quiet for a time. "How long do ya think Jamie? Fer the war?"

"I don't know, thought it would be over by now. I think we all did. What a damnable mess, they should have never let them bring slaves here."

"Aye, but it be profitable an' we all be knowin' what thet' wee tinge o' power an' wealth brings ta ya now. It happened in Scotland...'tis like a wee snowball, my friend. An aphrodisiac... once you be feelin' thet' power over yer kind, 'tis a mighty man thet' kin' give it up. 'Tis not jus' the work they be doin' there in the south, 'tis the power thet' give 'em thet' claims ta own 'em."

"I know. I know. After all, they keep bills of lading on them. '*Certificates of Breeding.*' Do you think it will actually stop, should Lincoln win this war?"

"I dunno'…anythin' thet' is profitable…man is, well, Jamie lad, man is a greedy bugger. Ya give him three squares a day an' soon he be wantin' dessert. Makes me think of me Lassie all over again… my God, the woman kin' cook. Jus' ya think, even the Indian's be not threatin' her, so long as she kin' make donuts fer 'em." He laughed his great laugh, stopping to gaze off into the distance. Turning to Jamie, "What do you think, they be fine, our ladies, yes?"

"Lord, I pray so. Joseph said he'd check on them. Charlie and Albee are there, Swede and Juan, although I think Swede will be apt to follow us. Then of course, there is *Jeff*." Jamie looked to see the scowl that crossed Mack's features.

"Harumph" was the only sound that came from the big Scotsman.

Jamie looked over at Micah and Tommy. He was always shocked by how very much Micah resembled his father. The same dome-shaped head, although Micah had a thick head of mousy, blond hair. Pa's pate was without nary a hair…then there were those ears, like sails on a boat, it must have been love on Ma's part. Jamie didn't know if he'd have married a homely person, what of the next generation; he smiled to himself, thinking of Pa. Pa Parsons was a fine man; he recalled the sound of his laughter, his quiet ways, the pipe that was his steady companion, the smoke curling around his face at most hours of the day. He heard that same chuckle now and turned to find it was Micah. *So…seemed he sounded like his sire as well.*

"D'ya think the train'll be there, Jamie? What iffin' we git on the wrong one?"

Jamie looked over at Micah and wondered at the courage it took to ask those questions, to admit fear and angst as a grown man. It took a great sense of self and knowledge of your own worth. His thoughts ran immediately to Jeff Tallman, certainly those attributes were lacking.

"Not to worry, Josiah sent this missive"—he patted his breast pocket—"with the name and time…they have a troop train that runs from Fort Fetterman. It is just for us." He found it distasteful to not tell them the truth. He had heard from Josiah just last week. But would it make a difference? He sincerely doubted it, and to be honest, he knew from experience few things would be as they had thought. He hadn't found the opportunity to speak with them, but then, he had made no effort to do so.

James Martin Prescott was near blind in his patriotism; he thought every able-bodied man should fight for his country. Truth be told, he was angry with his brother Joseph, some of his hired hands, and most assuredly, Jeff Tallman for not joining. He knew this was not the Revolutionary War, but…*Hell, there was no reason to try and justify his actions, he had simply not told them.*

They rode on in silence. The coming adventure of war and vibrant patriotism having left them as the day had given way to heat and wind, to thirst and weariness. Like small boys, the farther from home they rode, the less the thrill of war appeared. Reality was indeed a sobering state.

They were to have connected with the train at Fort Laramie, riding with the others that had opted to join in the fight; *Lincoln's War*…James Martin Prescott was not surprised to find the train had not yet come to Fort Laramie.

Josiah would be waiting for him in Omaha of that he was certain, the man being stalwart in his honesty and friendship. He had called for Jamie as he had said he would. Jamie would join as a commissioned officer, Josiah Piedmont and Stephen Douglas—although not a Whig—would see to that. Beyond that, he had no idea of what lay ahead for him.

Jamie had thought it would be over by now. *This war of Lincoln's*…his heart lurched momentarily as he acknowledged—*he was pleased it was not.*

What was there about men and battle, the call to battle had always held sway to a mysterious longing within him. He had traveled from Maine to the land of the Arabs to fight as a mercenary, to travel on a camel in the abysmal heat, to thrust a knife into the heart of a person he knew nothing of…in a cause of which he had no interest. He knew most would anticipate that he hand done so for the money. But in fact, he had gone for the adventure, the victory, the desire to test life and limb. To challenge the most inner workings of his faith and his physical attributes, his prowess.

Today he rode to war for a different reason; he would fight to the death if need be, for this, his country, this country that had promised life, liberty, and the pursuit of happiness. To say what you wish, to worship as you pleased, to have the right of free enterprise, of free speech.

He reached down and patted Danny's neck, wondering all the while how many had forgotten what that meant. The nation was, after all, over a hundred years old, how many generations knew nothing else?

James Prescott looked at the big Scotsman that rode beside him and wondered at the Claymore that was slung next to his rifle. Did he have a kilt in his bedroll? He had watched this giant bear of a man slice the head off more than one enemy. Jamie remembered the war cry of Mack's people in the highlands of Scotland and stood in awe of this fine man's strength. He touched the sword that hung at his side, a sword that Mack had forged for him, one he had yet to use. Mack was a good friend, and Jamie was a bit surprised to find he would leave Ilene behind. Although he was as certain that Mack, too, wondered at his leaving Elisabeth behind.

His heart heaved and he swallowed hard, remembering the sight of the back of his wife as she had turned and gone into the house, a small pang of guilt rose in him. He could feel the smallness of her body as she had leaned into him. He again felt the swelling of their child that grew within her, sense the fragrance of her hair, hair of ebony that blended with his own. The fragrances that mingled with the crisp autumn air, heard the rustle of gold and burnished copper leaves that danced from limbs that would soon be barren, the odor of chimney smoke as it curled skyward into the lazy clouds of fall. They had said nothing. They had said it all. It had been weeks since Josiah had sent his messenger. He had crooked his finger beneath her chin, raising her lovely face to look upon his, the emerald of her eyes had sparkled with tears unshed, a single solitary tear had taken flight upon the cheek of her sun bronzed, ivory skin.

He had sat upon Danny, looking back at their home, the land they had claimed, the house and barns he had built with his bare hands. He had waited for her to turn to wave good-bye.

She had not.

Would Mack be thinking the same? Jamie knew Mack trusted Duncan to look after his mother and the land, but Duncan was very young, albeit the image of his father. Duncan, at fifteen, stood as tall as his father and nearly as thick of arms and chest—still, he was but a boy.

Iridescent bubbles of pink lay upon stratus clouds of rose that scooted thick and graceful across the backdrop of a powdered-blue sky, clouds long and angular at the base, bubbling with brilliant hues of color. Softer shades of pink-tinged edges along heavy voluminous clouds floated in the front, traveling above the emerald green of the forests, their darkness calling the evening to a close. To the south, the sky hung with ominous, thick, steel thunderclouds, burgeoning in their fullness, their edges gilded in gold that faded to the softness of ivory. The backdrop, the ever big blue sky they had learned to associate with the Montana Territory. Tomorrow promised a day of sunshine and heat, perhaps it would rain late tonight. He could taste the moisture in the air.

James Prescott's philosophical concept of war was simple and straightforward, and he'd seen plenty of them. War was a passionate expression of an intellectual concept against moral turpitude. Each side thinking the other to be in the throws of evil and hatred, of vile, disgusting un-evolved, uneducated behavior. He thought that sounded fine. He could hear the sounds of that new song in his mind. What was it called…"The Battle Hymn of the Republic"! He liked it.

> *He is wisdom to the mighty He is honor to the brave*
> *So the world shall be his footstool and the soul of wrong his slave…*

So neither side was right. He smiled, a soft chuckle escaping. Applied to this war, that seemed ridiculous, slavery was wrong!

Once more, his mind and ears tuned into the enthusiastic chatter from Tommy Parsons, proclaiming his enthusiasm for both the train ride and the war.

"You ain't laughin' at me, are ya, Mr. Prescott?"

"No. No, Tommy. Just thinking of the complexities and obscenity of wars. But yes, we are headed for Fort Fetterman."

"Why that's right close ta Fort Laramie, ain't it?" Tommy said with all the eagerness of a fifteen-year-old. "An' we jus' ride the horses on?"

"That's it." Jamie looked at young Tom Parsons and wondered if he was really fifteen years old. He was taller than Micah and broader…guess it was not his business.

"How long fer we git there?"

"Where are you planning to get off, or have you changed your mind and decided to fight for the Union?" Jamie chided young Tommy Parsons

"Naw. Naw, Kintucky. Pa says it's not really a Confederate State, but…best we fight with the rest o' our kin'. Pa, he said it wouldn't be proper not."

"And what of your mother, what does she say?" Jamie felt certain *Kintucky* was in the Confederacy…but it didn't really matter, it *was* a slave state.

"Ah, y'all know Ma, she don' wan' us goin' ta war no way. She says we jus' got here an' she dun' lost 'nough chil'rin."

"And did the two of you think of that? What of your ma?" Jamie suddenly felt old and fatherly, he felt the excitement rise in his chest…soon he *would* be a father. The thought, the very fact was a miracle! All this time he had thought Elisabeth to be barren. He smiled to himself, thinking of Elisabeth and the child, the fact that *he* would be father; he simply found it hard to imagine! All the while listening, as Micah interrupted his younger brother to answer Jamie's question.

"Guess we'll be gitin' off at Sedalia, Ben an' me we figur' Tommy n' me kin' ride ta where Lee be. Thought I'd be makin' a special request ta have Tommy here, an' me in the same…what d'ya call it?"

"Regiment?" Jamie answered him.

"Yeah, regiment."

"I don't know if that such a good idea, at least not for your folks, you would both be in danger at the same time."

"But I could look after Tommy here…"

Jamie heard the low chuckle of the younger boy and looked over to see a larger, more physical young man. Tommy resembled Ben more than that of Micah. Where Micah took after Pa, lean and wiry, Tommy, at fifteen, was a big, strapping boy, handsome and level-headed, not unlike their older brother Ben. Jamie thought of the Oregon Trail and the constant bickering and teasing between Tommy and their younger brother, Davy, and smiled.

"Think I kin' look after myself, Micah…"

Jamie looked at Micah and, hoping to derail this line of conversation, asked, "Who is looking after your mining, Micah?"

"Got Pa an' Davy ta do that, an Ben, he'll see ta it they do the right thing. Then, 'course got some fellas from down ta Butte, ya know ta do the diggin'. I figure I won't be gone all that long. 'Member they all got a share, I been workin' Ma and Pa's claim too. What about you fellas, gonna look fer gold on yer land?"

"Maybe, I've been so busy with the stock and building that I've not given it much thought. What about you, Mack?"

"Aye, when I've the time…seems ta be the least o' my concerns now, I be more'n happy just to have a steady pace o' the work an time ta see to buildin' a weapon ya would no be havein' ta reload evera' time."

Jamie's admiration of the man's skill with weapons was unsurpassed. "Perhaps the government can see the necessity of that. At a time like this, I would think that those with ingenuity and money would take this opportunity to see to it we have more efficient weaponry."

"Aye, Jamie lad, I'd be lovin' ta make it me own, but I'd be pleased to have the convenience should another be discoverin' it. I be readin' the papers and got me own monies on the Smith an' Wesson fellas, may be that Remington fella as well."

It was Tommy's voice that broke the silence. "Where's yer brother, Mr. Prescott? Thought fer sure he'd be comin'."

"No, he is needed at home." His voice sounded clipped and short, and to be sure, that *had not been* his intention. Jamie had thought he'd be coming too. He wondered if Joseph resented not being able to come. Strange how life worked its way through the lives of people. It had not been but two, perhaps three, years ago that Jamie had thought Joseph *had it all.* That perhaps his own ambitions and connections—*his high-faluten education,* as his big, burly, younger brother had termed it—along with his stint with the French Foreign Legion, the trip into the desert sands of the Arabs had been just a fluke. Joseph had married a levelheaded conservative girl he had known his entire life, one who had no qualms in milking cows and pitching hay, gathering eggs, and helping his family as well as that of her own.

Many a night, Jamie had lain and looked up at the Southern Cross and thought that was what *he should be doing.* Life was damned strange. Just didn't seem right, his brother Joseph, sitting at home, playing nursemaid to a woman who was for all intents and purposes damn near mad. *Crazy!* Of course, they had all known about her mother but—*sweet Jesus!* Why Joseph? Big, kind, easy going Joseph! He felt the irregular rhythm of his heart. Truth be known, it made him angry with Eleanor, that and the way she had treated Elisabeth. Elisabeth had nursed her, cared for her, *delivered her child*—what thanks did she get? Jealousy or not, it was damned spiteful of Eleanor. Eleanor and *Agnes Corrigan*. Now there was a woman he didn't understand...best not to think of those things. Not a thing you can do about another man's life and his whims. Joseph loved Eleanor and was determined to see to it she regained her health. Although after the last child, Jamie doubted that would happen. The last time he had seen her, she looked more like an Indian squaw than that of Joseph's wife from Maine.

One thing at a time, he thought. Best not to get wrapped up in the emotional turmoil of his brother's life. He felt the missive from Josiah in his breast pocket. *The last missive.* The letter that said there would be *no train.*

Guilt raised its ugly head and nausea rushed up into his throat. He had only received the missive two days ago; he thought it too late to make changes. Preparations had been made by the four of them, and well, he guessed he had a million excuses, all of them lacked the integrity he tried to live by. There would be no railroad to ride on; it seemed that the Congress just could not put it together. James thought of the information the missive held from Josiah Piedmont.

Jamie could see Josiah's words as they were sprawled across the pages; having read the letter so many times, it seemed to be imprinted upon his mind. *The Unionist and the Confederates each had lost over two thousand men in Maryland, hardly a conclusive battle.*

What the hell they were doing up there was beyond him; Jamie knew Maryland to be a slave state, but its size alone made it rather insignificant. The whole of the war seemed to play out in his mind. Josiah seemed concerned about Grant. "Seems ta be in his cups a great deal of the time, Lincoln still thinks we can use him." Josiah had gone on to say, "The good news, if you can call it that, was that on September 22, Lincoln announced that the slaves in territories that were presently in rebellion would be freed on January 1, 1863."

Jamie thought it strange Lincoln didn't free the slaves in the North. It was not a secret that slaves were held in the North as well.

The whole damned war could be over by the time they arrived! Particularly, should they find they had to ride all the way, and with the damnable pack animals. Josiah had said there would be a Wells Fargo Stage waiting for them at Fort Fetterman. Lord he hoped that to be true. Although he thought he'd sooner ride Danny than sit in the confines of a stage day and night.

He would tell them tonight. They could go home it they were of a mind.

Man and War

"So, Tommy, you up for the first watch?" Jamie thought he could see the boy's chest swell with pride. First watch would be more than likely safe. Mack and Micah could get some sleep and Jamie could catnap by the fire, keeping watch on Tommy. Young as he was, a watch in the middle of the night was iffy business.

The fire burned low, the coals still holding a red orange glow to them, their stomachs full. Micah had killed a lone deer that would serve them for the next few days. It hung now, high in the branches of the gray and white, blotchy, leafless limbs of a Birch.

Having finally told them of the letter from Josiah, and offering each the opportunity to return home should that be their wish, Jamie felt some relief. They were but a day's ride from home, albeit a *long* day. He was not surprised to find Tommy to be the most disappointed. *They were all disappointed*. Riding a train would have been easy. He should have known it was too damn good to be true.

"Aw, an' I was wantin' ta ride thet train! But I'm still goin', I done made up my mind an' I'm goin', what about you, Micah, ya still goin'?"

"'Sure 'nough. Ain't lookin' forward ta crossin' them mountains again though."

"Mack?" Jamie looked at the Scotsman, knowing he had made the most sacrifice having left his family.

"Naw, lad, should ye be tellin' me afore, 't wo'ld be the same, me mind too, bein' fixed. I'll no be turnin' back."

"Good! Good. Josiah has made his instruction clear: 'We are to take the Bozeman Tail to Fort Fetterman and follow the Platte onto Chicago, should the Wells Fargo not be there we ride on.'"

"Chicago, where the hell is that? Ain't never been there." Excitement and fear mingled in the words of Micah.

"It's north of the Oregon Trail, right at the base of the Great Lakes. It's where they are gathering their headquarters. The Union Pacific railroad is under construction—*of a sorts*. Josiah said, 'He didn't hold much faith in what stage of construction.' Those that were in control couldn't seem to be in agreement, if it were indeed operational, it will make our traveling less difficult. He'll meet us in Chicago if at all possible, but when we arrive in Omaha, he asks that we telegraph him and he will take leave to meet us."

Jamie did not tell them of Josiah's plan to "brief James and see to it that he was up to date."

Jamie was not at all certain where he would deposit the Parsons brothers; would they go to Chicago with he and Mack, or go off on their own down to Kentucky? He would have to speak to Micah about that, or perhaps Josiah. There was ample time to decide; it was some twelve hundred miles to Chicago. His best guess was that it would take them two, three weeks—that was providing they had no trouble with Indians. His hope was that the train would be up and running in January; he had promised Elisabeth he would be home for the birth of their first child. He was certain there'd be hell to pay if he was not. A flash of fear ran through him as he thought of Elisabeth giving birth, and he quickly pushed it aside; it served no purpose. There was nothing he could do even if he had stayed home.

His mind wandered from the newspapers, again to Josiah's letters. He had to admit he had been bowled over by the response of the Confederates to the Union. To be honest, when he examined all that had transpired, he was not only surprised but somewhat in awe. It had taken a great deal of spunk and courage to stand up to the newly elected president of the United States and simply excuse yourselves from participating. To elect a president and form a Confederacy for those that believed in the southern way of life—to *act* on that belief. The newspapers had reported that they had instituted a constitution. Certainly they had shown they held the courage of their convictions. Eleven of the Southern states had seceded, Virginia had split itself in half… they had elected Jefferson Davis as president of those states and had promptly fired upon Fort Sumter on the twelfth of April— two days later, capturing it. No grass was growing under their feet! Although from what Josiah had said, Lincoln had set them up "to fire the first shot."

Upon that first shot, Lincoln had called for seventy-five thousand volunteers the very next day. Jamie could not wait to hear what had come of that! The Battle of Bull Run had then taken place. This had taken place in Virginia and had been the first major land battle between the armies.

Jamie turned over—the heat of the campfire now at his back. He knew he needed to sleep, yet to still his mind was difficult, as battles and the war waged on within his thoughts. He thought of the newspaper accounts of the Battle of Bull Run. On July 16, 1861, the untried Union Army under Brigadier General Irvin McDowell marched from Washington against the Confederate Army, which was drawn up behind Bull Run beyond Centreville. On the twenty-first, McDowell crossed at Sudley Ford and attacked the Confederates' left flank on Matthew Hill. The papers had said the fighting had raged throughout the day as the Confederate forces were driven back to Henry Hill. Late in the afternoon, Confederate reinforcements extended and broke the Union right flank. The Union retreat rapidly deteriorated into a rout. Thomas J. Jackson earned the nom de guerre "Stonewall." Jamie smiled at that; he had been known by *Stonewall* since Jamie had known him.

He turned over yet again, adjusting the saddle that he rested his head on. The facts, if you could believe the journalists, busied themselves in his mind, making him think of Ezra Gilky, my God, if this is the stuff that ran through Ezra's head all the time… He wondered if Ezra had gone too. *Now* he couldn't remember where he was to go. Sighing deeply, he laced his fingers behind his head. Might as well give up on the idea of sleeping. Besides, he needed to sort out what was going on. It could well be a matter of life and death, his own and those of his comrades.

His thoughts ran to the report of July 22, the shattered Union army returned to the safety of Washington; Richard King flashed in his mind, and he thought of the big man's determination and his convictions…

Despite their genteel outward behavior, the Southerners had shown themselves to be men of steel. He had not, however, been surprised by the convictions of Lincoln; to shut down the ports of the South was a gutsy move, proving once and for all he meant business. Not that he doubted Lincoln, having heard him speak in Cincinnati, he knew he was a man not to be trifled with, which led his thoughts to the battle at Antietam.

The Army of the Potomac, under the command of George McClellan, mounted a series of powerful assaults against Robert E. Lee's force near Sharpsburg, Maryland, on September 17—*that had shocked him!* What the hell were they doing up there again? Again, the Confederates had driven the army of the Potomac back. The bloodiest single day in American military history had ended in a draw, yet the fact that the Confederates had retreated gave Abraham Lincoln the "victory" he desired before issuing the Emancipation Proclamation.

Jamie would have thought the war would be on Southern soil, not on the soils of the north. Remembering that they had tried to keep the slave states and the free states equal throughout the nation…with California's disappointment at not being counted as a slave state—or was it the Confederates that were disappointed.

He hadn't paid much attention at the time, however it was shortly after this that Josiah had written. He knew Josiah would not have called for him should he not have thought the *war* "was to wear on."

Jamie again snuggled down into his bedroll, his immediate thoughts were of Elisabeth, the bedroll was new, and there was room for only the likes of him. He couldn't remember when last he had slept in a bedroll without Elisabeth at his side. He sat up and whispered to Tommy, "Tommy, are you awake, you all right there?"

"Yes, sir. I'm jus' dandy. Shucks, I kin' do this, Mr. Prescott. I kin', I ain't no kid no more, ya know."

"I know that, Tommy. Wake me if you need and remember to wake Micah for the next watch. Too, remind him to wake me for the third watch." He lay down and started to pull the bedroll up. Turning toward Tommy, he rose on his elbow. "Tommy, call me Jamie, makes me feel old, you calling me Mr. Prescott." Jamie heard a soft chuckle and Tommy's whispered "Yes, sir."

"Hell's fire, that's not much better." Jamie pulled the watch fob from his pocket and opened it, the firelight just enough to discern the contents, therein lay a small likeness of he and Elisabeth on their wedding day—as well as a lock of her hair. She had placed it there yesterday morning, cutting a piece of his for herself. He held it to his nose and breathed deeply. *The fragrance that was Elisabeth suffused his soul.* He felt his heart race and his loins heat...hoping the scent of her would stay with him all the while he was gone. A despicable choice a man must make—between the love of a woman and the love of his country.

Jamie remembered the warmth of the African plains as he had lain upon them, the sight of the Southern Cross against the blackness of the night skies, the seasickness that had engulfed his body on the boat to France...the thrill of the city of Paris, the light, the energy...something difficult to put into words, *ineffable to be sure.* It now seemed a lifetime ago. *Young men were fearless in their quest for adventure.* He sighed and looked up at the night skies of Montana; crystal clear and alive with the stars of the heavens, the deep apricot gold of a harvest moon hung regal against its blackness. A harvest moon…all things lead his thoughts to Elisabeth. He could see a vision of her now as she picked corn, green and lima beans, cabbages and tomatoes, dug potatoes, storing them in the cellar he had built. He could smell the scent of hay and oats he, Mack, and Joseph had cut, piling them with care in the barns. Jeff Tallman once more entered his mind—*damned hardheaded fool of a man* refused to be a part in the joint effort of planting and harvesting.

Danny stood not ten feet away, tethered to his arm. Tethered to Danny was one of the four-pack mules they had brought with them. Jamie felt the lumps of rifles, pistols, and boots that lay within his bedroll, a moment of deja vu swept over him. Once again, he looked over at Tommy. He sat with his back to the fire, pistol in one hand, rifle only inches from the other. His broad, young back alert and ready. Jamie thought of himself at that age and knew they would be safe for the watch of Thomas Parsons.

Jamie sighed deeply and heard the resonant sound of snoring from the gentle giant that lay next to him. Snores that would certainly keep the Indians at bay. *Might as well, bring a grizzly into mate.* He chuckled softly to himself, it had been a long day filled with the grief of leaving as well the excitement of going to war. A strange emotional coupling. Man is indeed an inexplicable animal. At long last, he slept.

Bozeman Trail

Jamie woke to the sound and smells of the fire smoke and fresh brewed coffee, having slept but another two hours from his early morning watch. Mack knelt before the fire. "We be blest with doughnuts and fresh coffee—best we get up an' movin'."

Micah was up and ready, Tommy lolled in his bedroll, finally having fallen asleep long after Jamie had taken watch. Excitement and trepidation—Jamie was certain to be the cause.

"Morning, Mack, see we made it through the night." He looked up at the big Scot and watched as his finger pointed out to the west. A large herd of buffalo sauntered through the gold of waving plains grasses, the morning light just initiating its appearance, the world quiet and renewed. The autumn of the year was a favorite time of his, the slow dying and resting of the world as it came to terms with the cycle of life. The shedding of the old to bring upon it the new. The crisp coolness of the air—the vibrant colors of Mother Nature. He watched the soft floating lace of dandelions as they drifted aimlessly to their new resting place. The buffalo with their huge heads and shaggy chocolate coats reminded him of the Indians in the valley near Scotts Bluff as they had traveled on the Oregon trail. The beauty and symmetry executed within the brutality of the stalk and the kill—the sanctity of the native peoples as they had slain the great buffalo. He heard Mack's voice.

"Makes ya wish ta kneel and pray do it now."

"It does. Indeed it does."

"Jamie lad, er' ya ready?" Mack glanced at the mountains to the east of them. "Will no be easier fer the waitin'."

"You're right, I was thinking about it last night. Without wagons, herds of animals, women, and children, we should be able to do it in one day. What do you think?"

"Ay, I think we go 'til we get on the other side. I've no great love o' this mountain, lad."

"Micah, Tommy, you fellas grab a bite, get some coffee, and we move out. Mack and I think we can get over this mountain today."

"Sure 'nough," came the sleepy reply of Tommy.

"Micah?"

"Ready, boss."

The eastern skies held the swelling of the morning sun, the blue of Montana's skies still a remarkable sight after over two years. Large cottony puffs floated in ephemeral laziness above the sharp white peaks of the mountains. The Bozeman Trail lay before them in all its gore and glory. Thoughts of the Bozeman Trail gave way to flashes of fear in his gut. The Rocky Mountains ran three thousand miles north and south, with its highest peak straight in front of them. Likened to the same Continental Divide in the east, the rivers ran to the west on the western side and east on the eastern side. Jamie thought of all that water and wondered at the dryness of the Plains; surely, the waters ran beneath the ground. He damn sure didn't relish crossing them—*the mountains or the plains*. It had nearly killed all of them coming here, and it was nearly three months later in the year now than when they had crossed them previously. Although today they had excellent mounts, no wagons, no weary children or women, no herds of taciturn starving animals. They all wore bishops—or as Pa would say, *long johns*. He thought of Pa and their young Olivia; would Tommy remember? He knew for certain Micah would.

"Are we loaded, your powder dry, got a tight lead on those mules?" Jamie looked at his friends for confirmation. "Good, doesn't appear to be snow, the skies up there are clear. Let's move on out, get this over with!"

They could smell it, taste it. The sleet, the ice…long before it became visible, as if there were signs of danger that skulked with the mountain itself.

Jamie pulled his hat down close over his head, pulling a woolen scarf around his mouth and nose. The men that rode at his side, emulating his actions. The travelers were now adrift in the snow from previous days—previous months and years. Danny's hooves often dropping three or four feet to meet the crusted ice below. How many feet of snow actually existed on this mountain? Some said as much as 130 feet of ice and snowpack lay beneath them.

The wind came at them from the northwest, beating the icy pellets against their backs. They were above the tree line now, nothing but glacial ice and howling wind and sleet greeted them.

They had all done this once before—fear mounting within each of them. The wind at your back was far better than the icy pellets of wind against your face, blinding you and freezing your extremities. The higher they climbed into the mountainous terrain, the more ominous the sleet and snow became and the more they were blinded by the whiteout. Knowing the disorientation it caused, they stopped and tied a rope between each of them, with Mack behind Jamie and the mules between them, then Micah and Tommy. Jamie tugged on the rope now, feeling the tug from the man behind him. *Mack*, he thought with relief. They would each continue to send along a tug every few minutes. To backtrack and search for someone after they had been missing for an hour or more would lead to certain death.

Hour after ominous hour, they trudged deliberately through banks of glacial ice and snow. Jamie often sensing the hesitancy of Danny's footing, stopping to find that nothing at all lay in front of them, only a sheer mountain cliff. Had they lost their way? He thought of Lawrence O'Quinn, who had had the horrendous responsibility of moving the pioneers over this treacherous Bozeman Trail.

He tugged at the rope and backed Danny up to then traverse what looked to be more solid footing, fighting all the while the panic that stirred within him. It had been nearly eight hours that they had been riding, the sunlight but a glimmer at what appeared to be the base of the mountain. They hadn't seen sunlight all day, yet there was no indication that they were even halfway down the mountain. He felt a wrenching feeling of fear in his gut. What if he had taken yet another wrong turn? Again, the thought of O'Quinn shot through his mind. *Next time he saw him, he would humbly apologize*, for he had been more than a little peeved each time Lawrence had had the wagons veer back on the trail. The thought of traveling across the top of this mountain for days on end—more frightening than anything he could think of at this moment—they would never survive! *God, let that not be the case.*

The sound of a large booming noise suddenly rose up the side of the mountain; his first thoughts—*an avalanche!* He tugged on the rope that held them captive to one another.

Boom!

The sound again echoed throughout the mountain, coming from a great distance, yet shattering the quiet. They now stood on the crusted snow, each covered in a blanket of snow and ice, the rope hanging between them. Jamie looked back at Mack and saw only the glitter of clear blue eyes, lashes ensconced in white crystals of ice, his red beard glazed in place, sparkling of white, glistening lace. The snow lay deep on his shoulders and the brim of his hat. The grim line of his mouth evidenced that he, too, thought it to be an avalanche. Nearly in unison, they looked back up the mountainside. There appeared to be no avalanche coming toward them. Again, their eyes locked.

Boom! Again. The noise seemed to be coming from below them. Was it rifles? Jesus! *That was all they needed now was to have to fight the Cheyenne.* Jamie's better sense told him no Indian in his right mind would be up here on this mountain in this weather. He knew for certain it would not be the Flatheads or the Lakota.

Boom! There it was again!

Jamie coaxed Danny tremulously back to where Mack stood, the horse snorting great clouds of vapor, his eyes large and white with horror. Jamie leaned in close to Mack, the wind whistled, swirling the ice crystals of snow about them, nearly shouting to make himself heard. "Do you hear that?"

"Aye, I do," his voice as muffled as Jamie's own.

"What do you think it is?"

"Aye, an avalanche on the far side o' the mountain, ya kin'?"

"I think it's dynamite."

"*Dynamite! Holy Mary Mother of God*, thet be bad as an avalanche, could be causin' one."

"Indeed it could, we have to get off this mountain! Tommy, Micah, mount up!" Danny began to prance; his ears laid back, his eyes wide with fear at the alarm he sensed within Jamie.

"Who'd be usin' the dynamite, James lad?" Mack hollering to make himself heard, his tongue pink in the otherwise white of his face.

"The railroad! Josiah said he thought they would be down there." Jamie watched as Mack nodded his head in understanding. He raised his arm to the Parsons boys and mouthed his words to "follow him." *May the hand of God help us*, he prayed. He could see the tree line below them. The emerald color of evergreens, a whisper through their snow-covered branches, the trees stunted and short in their courageous effort at growth as they struggled to find nutrients in the granite home they had chosen. Jamie set his course for that same tree line—urging Danny down with perseverance and determination, hoping against hope that his decision for them to follow in Danny's wake would not put them in more danger. How much stress could the mountain absorb?

Once they reached the tree line, an avalanche was less likely to kill them. *Trees meant they were off the mountain!* If they could just keep moving, they would soon be at the base. The thought of the railroad men being there—more encouraging than he had thought possible.

The wind had turned and now swirled about them, unable to make up its mind which direction to travel. Large intricate flakes of lace like ice came in a lazy waltz of eloquence; thick and blinding it floated about them with a beauty that was dazzling and *deadly*!

Boom! He felt the tremor that came from deep within the glacial ice of the great mountain. He shuddered! *Boom!* Jamie felt Danny struggle as his hooves fought for purchase—felt the shifting of Danny's footing as they slid below him.

Crack! A deafening noise came through the silent earth and with the sound, the earth opened wide! The breach of the ice and snow shuddered as it grew wider and ever deeper, its interior one of stunning beauty, showing the soft eerie glow of turquoise.

Jamie felt paralytic fear as it raced through his mind—his body! Pulling at the reins, he shouted, "Back! Back, Danny! Back!" He looked back at Mack, for the first time seeing fear dart from his eyes.

The deep mouth of blue continued in its quest to swallow them, as the earth trembled and shook.

He felt the tautness of the lifeline as it shifted between them—without a moment between—glimpsed the blur of brown that slid past the open mouth of the mountain! His chest tightened; fear clutched his heart.

This was a fight he would not win; Mother Nature always stacked the cards! Weapons, brute strength—none of it mattered. *She* was always in control!

He thought of Elisabeth.

Synchronicity of Hearts

The spoon dropped to the floor from the pan of cornstarch pudding she had been stirring. A lump rose in her throat—*the only thing that kept her from screaming.* Fear engulfed her. *Jamie is in danger!* She sensed it; she could feel it as if it were *her*! She watched as if in slow motion; the splattering of milk and eggs as they flew across the golden pine of the floors. Her hand flew to cover her mouth, the other clutching at the mound of the child that she carried within her.

"'Lisobet'! Mz.'Lisobet', you good? It is el niño?" Alarm filled Maria's voice as she ran to her.

"No. No, Maria. Yes, yes…I am fine…Just, it's Jamie. *Something has happened!*"

"Oh no, Mz. 'Lisobet', he be fine, big strong hombre, he be fine. Sit. Sit, rest. I finish you flan. Sit."

She did need to sit; her knees were weak and queasy, her hands clammy with fear. She reached for the stove to steady herself, thinking better of it. The flatiron stove gave out more heat than a bonfire. She heard the scrapping of the chair across the floor as Maria deposited it directly at her knees, a timely gesture indeed, as she sat down hard, that familiar surreal feeling encompassing her.

She watched as Maria stooped to clean the pudding from the sparkling floors.

With elbows on knees, she placed her head in her hands. *Breath deeply*, she told herself. Knowing there was naught else to do. She didn't even know where he would be now.

In the mountains! Oh, God. *The mountain!*

She thought of their crossing over the Bozeman Trail, and again, the nausea pushed up to her mouth, causing her to retch.

The *mountain!*

She thought of Ilene and she walking next to one another, of the ice and snow making it impossible to see one another, though they were but two feet apart. She saw in her mind the cattle dying from the ice and snow in their nostrils.

The child that Pa carried. *Olivia! Purple and stiff—in death.*

She could feel Maria's hand on her back, patting her, seeing the basin she held before her. *Please, God, be with him.* The prayer was a silent one as she vomited into the basin. She wiped her mouth and tried to stand, her knees wobbly and weak, her entire body left chilled and moist.

"Sit, missus. Sit. You wish médico come?"

She reached up and patted Maria's hand. "No. No, Maria. Thank you, thank you, I shall be fine." She breathed deeply and tried in vain to shake the feeling, to break the tie that bound the two of them, knowing this was not good for their child, this feeling of fear and helplessness. *Where was he?*

She thought of the hours, the days he had been gone, little more than two days had passed, it had to be *"the mountain."* She thought of Mack Mackenzie and breathed a sigh of relief; she had nearly as much respect for Mack's strength and courage as she held for her husbands. They were both strong, intelligent men, and they would be able to handle anything; she wondered if Ilene had felt it too. *The fear. The danger.* She thought of Ilene's belief in the "wee ones" and her habit of going to what she had deemed to be a *"sacred place."*

She smiled as she thought of how long it had taken Ilene to find such a place here in Montana, the "wee ones be ever'where in Scotlan'," she had told Elisabeth. "No here. Meself be thinkin' I no be findin' such a place."

Lord, what she would give to talk to Sally Susanne; she perhaps could get a better feel for it. She would be more objective. "Silly of me. Maria, please I'm fine now. Thank you, thank you."

What would she do without Maria? What a wonderful gift God had given her in this woman; Richard and Henrietta King must surely miss her and Juan. She thought of how much Juan and Maria Alvarado had given up to come all the way to Montana with them, in Texas, on the King Ranch they had had their own home; here they had shared a room in the bunk house until less than a month ago when Jamie and the hired hands had finished a small room on the back of her and Jamie's home.

"Perhaps some fresh air is what I need, really, I am fine. Truly, Maria, I'm fine." She opened the great, lavishly ornate door of their log home and smiled at the wonder of it, of the trouble Jamie had gone to, simply to surprise her.

She stood now on the stoop. Before her, the world lay at her feet, resplendent in its golden cloak of autumn. The river rushed by, huge waves of white water against the ever-changing colors of the river, a cold, steel gray, shading to hues of azure blue. Great billowy puffs of clouds scudded quickly beneath and between the sun to cross Montana's great blue skies. It was remarkable, the difference one tiny moment made. The wind swept noisily through the valley, giving rise to the roaring of the waters. She listened to the sounds of hundreds of small birds as they screeched through the air, moving to the Southern climates. She did not remember what these birds were, perhaps starlings, and from here, she could not distinguish them. She knew without question the lone bald eagle that soared above the treetops, catching the updraft of the wind.

From her home, perched on this small hillock, she could watch the herds of animals as they sought safety and feeding grounds for the winter, a season that loomed bleakly before them. Her vegetable garden hung in brown and withered shrouds of death and dormancy. She heard the sound of cracking, sharp and lurid, the noise coming in bits and pieces, as if she could bear witness to the breaking of Mother Nature's creations. A tree was about to fall. She had watched as they had cracked and spilt into sections. She watched in awe as they had moved gracefully from the main trunk of the tree itself in deceptive slowness, falling to the ground as straight as if they remained one tree, often driving themselves deeply into the ground to stand beside the tree that had nurtured them, gradually giving in and thudding with poise and dignity to the ground. Ground that moved greatly at the impact, providing a resting place for the dying of the tree.

She hoped this tree would be so; Charlie and Little Flower lived within the copse of the forest just down from their house. She thought of the cabin he had built for them, nearly as nice as her own home. Again, a prayer rose to her mind, *That Charlie's house not be the depository of the tree.*

She watched as the red-gold leaves circled, as if choreographed, to the ground, the earth now blanketed with the gold of autumn. She took a deep breath, finding she indeed felt better.

How very different she was now, how her life had changed... Lord, there was no comparing the child-woman who had run off with James Martin Prescott and the woman who stood here on the steps of a home made with logs from a nearby forest and mud from the river below.

She felt the stirrings of the child she carried and smiled at the thought of Jamie thinking she was barren. She had put great effort into *not having a child.*

Would this child ever know the privileged society that Elisabeth Parthena Bunyan—now Prescott—knew? She doubted it.

She had knowledge now and foresight given to those who had endured much. She knew this child would have to work from sunup to sundown, be it male or female. Had she any right to bring this child into a world of such grave hardship? She knew that her wisdom here was limited. For she loved this child more than anything she had thought possible. More than even Jamie, or perhaps, she loved Jamie in a different manner. Ma Parsons was right; there "was no explainin' the love a mother had fer her chil'." She thought of her mama and wondered at that. Of her grandmère... *Lord how she missed them*!

Elisabeth took a deep breath and envisioned Jamie surrounded by white light, safe and sound, strong and confident. Would she ever see him again, and should she not, what in the world would she do?

She looked at the vastness of the land, the cattle and horses that dotted the pastures, and for a brief moment, she was overwhelmed. All of this he had left in her care... She simply would not think of that.

She turned and walked back into the cozy warmth of the house, filled with the gifts of comfort he had provided her. The table Jamie had built for them the first Christmas, the bed he had had sent from the east as a surprise for her, the glazing in the windows, the great ornate door. *All for the love of her.*

She wondered; would he be living still in the lean-to should it not be for her? More than likely, he would be living in the bunkhouse with the hired hands or in the barn with his treasured horses. She smiled, grateful the fearful feeling had passed. It now seemed to have been but a slight rift within her emotions.

He was, as Maria had said, *a great, strong man*. The thought of the great strong man sent a slight shiver through her body, warmth that traveled to, and stayed, in the nether parts of her. Parts, it would be best she learn to forget, at least until such a time as he returned.

Would he be home for the birth of this child as he had promised? Somehow she doubted it.

Crevasse of Azure

Jamie felt the thunder as the ground rocked beneath Danny's hooves, the sounds of the glacial ice—a roar in his ears. The blur of brown, one of the pack mules appeared to fly inches from the ground. The rope tethered to the animal skipped with a whiplash effect across the white of the snow, flying in slow motion just beyond the azure blue of the crevasse. The world around him stood in silence as he watched, a remarkable sphere of silence and time held him in abeyance.

He felt the depth of pain, of loss. How would he tell Ma her sons were gone! The clutching pangs of remorse at his involvement in the dreadful scene enveloped him. This was entirely his fault! He had spoke of little else but the war and Lincoln since first they had begun the trip on the Oregon Trail. Was it any wonder these two young men would think it the most common, the most righteous path to follow?

His eyes darted up the mountain to where the Parsons boys sat upon their mounts, the lifeline pulled taunt from Tommy's pommel, the boys' hazel eyes wide with abject terror, his horse lathered in the icy cold of the mountain as he fought for foothold. He looked into the eyes of Mack—eyes the color of the glacial cavity that was opening around them.

The mule appeared to be descending more rapidly now. The brown of the mule elongated, now but an illusion before his eyes. Jamie's hands were cold and stiff.

Perhaps a bullet... The ground quaked again, and he thought better of that. The world seemed to swirl in activity, without his cooperation or involvement. In his peripheral vision, he saw Mack raise his pistol. He heard the coldness of his own voice, the echo as it bounced across the mountain's surface. He felt his hand instinctively move to his side. "No! The noise!"

He felt the pommel of the knife in his hand, watching with detached fascination as the glint of meager sunlight hit the blade of his Bowie knife as it flew from his hand through the air. With a lurid leisureliness, the knife seemed to float across the snow-covered mountain, landing upon the tautness of the rope. He heard the ping as the tightness of the rope snapped; it slowly curled like that of a pig's tail and lazily fanned its way back up the hill. He watched the rapid descent of the pack mule as it headed down into the blue of the fissure.

Tommy halted his horse but yards above the fissure. Jamie saw the wild look in the boy's eyes—*excitement, only excitement* rested there, the previous terror no longer visible. Jamie felt the ice crystals on his face, heard the sound of Mack's voice, felt the prancing of Danny beneath him—heard the snort of his horse and reality seemed to bound toward him.

"Verra well done! *'Mo dheirfear!'* 'Near shet me britches, I did. Er' ye be fine?"

He looked at Mack; in the anxiety of the moment, Mack had lapsed into a thick Gaelic brogue. Jamie felt a surge of emotion for Ian Mackenzie. He was honored to be called 'his friend.' "Think I'll be needing a new knife, Mack."

"Aye, lad, aye. But we have the lads...'tis all thet matters."

"Micah, Tommy, you fellas, follow me. Let's get off this mountain before we become permanent residents." He hoped the blasting would stop for the day; the daylight hour's diminishing rapidly. Would that keep them from blasting, or were they driven by a harsh taskmaster?

Jamie had made a fine "deal" to supply beef to the Union Pacific crews, by way of a scoundrel by the name of "Durant." He had no idea that they would have completed the railroad to this point. Perhaps this was the other line, coming from the eastern side, or to the south. The railroads were many and charted to traverse the nation.

Danny picked his way gently through the thick, glacial mounds of snow and ice. The wet snows of cold, high mountain peaks was not light and feathery, but more like mortar, as it lay on the ice from ages long gone.

The men stopped to gather supplies that had careened from within the mules' packs, and Jamie pulled out a new rope. They *would* have a rope tied to them until they got off this mountain.

"No, I ain't tying no damn rope t' me. I ain't! That near scared the piss outta me!" Micah and his horse were backing up the mountain in an effort to establish the vehemence of his statement.

"Fine. Do whatever you wish. You get lost in this snow and fog, or get taken by a grizzly, don't scream for help 'cause we won't know where to look for you." Jamie watched as Tommy rode to where Micah stood. He and Mack went about the business of tying the lifeline to the animals once more. Suddenly, Micah stood before him. Without acknowledgment, Jamie threw him the rope. A man surely had the right to make his own decisions, but he did not savor telling Ma Parsons another of her boys died before they even got to the battle.

Jamie pondered how much more time they had before those at the base of the mountain would begin blasting again and looked at his watch, perhaps an hour of sunlight—if you could call this sunlight. A white fog of mist and ice shadowed them—even from themselves. The denseness of it seemed to cling to the ground, hanging as a curtain from the sky. Trees shrouded in mystery, a blanket that kept sounds around them filtered, a small envelope of a world that seemed to move about them as they slowly zigzagged down the mountainside. He could see the small tracks of fox and rabbits, the small skittering of a lone squirrel. Signs of the bark scraped from the trunk of smaller deciduous trees. Was it deer scraping the velvet from their antlers, or the marking of the grizzly? At this moment he cared not.

Jamie had no idea how long it had taken to ride down off the mountain. His thoughts, *only that they do.* Suddenly, he heard the sharp scrape of Danny's hoof on the granite that lay beneath the snow. He turned to Mack and, pulling the scarf from his face, grinned.

The Celestials

Before them lay a veritable city of people, a tent city to be sure, with wagons stacked high with timber, blazing campfires, the smell of meat cooking, the fragrance of strong, bitter coffee that had set all day, drifted to where they stood.

A profusion of mules stood tethered about other wagons loaded with explosives. All surrounded by men armed with rifles and pistols; *de bandelarios* slung across their chests. They watched the coolie hats of Asians as they scurried swiftly in that floating ease that was remarkable to their kind, billowy gowns of gray ensconcing their small energetic bodies. The smatterings of mandarin rose among the wafting smoke of fires and the drift of the stench of man, all far too rapidly for Jamie to decipher it. The pristine air of the mountain—now but a distant memory.

He turned to Mack. "What do you say? Want to introduce ourselves and see what's going on? Better the devil we know than the devil we don't."

"Aye, 'tis that."

The man in charge was set off from the others, his small tent worn. A makeshift desk piled with papers and maps of all sort. His head bent over it in consternation… He looked up from the desk, an eye patch covering his left eye, as Jamie and Mack lifted the flap to the tent and stood within the confines of the cluttered tent that was obviously the man's home. "Who the hell are you, and what the hell do you want?" His voice gruff, filling the small space.

"James Martin Prescott at you service, sir. Ian Mackenzie here, Micah and Tommy Parsons." Jamie stretched his hand out over the piled sheaf of papers and rolled maps, rulers, squares, and compasses. "And you, sir, are?"

"James Harvey Strobridge…what the hell do you want, and where the hell did ya come from?"

Jamie felt Mack at his side, felt the tension rise in the big man's frame, watching as Strobridge reached for his pistol.

Ever the diplomat, Jamie set about as if no threat existed. "Just passing through on our way to the Omaha and Chicago. *General James Prescott at your service.*"

"That, well, that's none of my concern. Can't say I give a diddly wink about the plight of the damn niggers, seems a waste of valuable time ta me, and I might add, money." Strobridge rose from his chair, towering over the desk. For an instant, he stood sizing up the men who stood before him. "What can I help you with? As you can see, I'm damned busy here."

"I can see that. We would like to spend the night here. We shall be gone early of a morning 'be no bother to you or your crew. 'You working for Charlie Crocker?"

"I am, and jus' how would you know that?"

"I sold him some beef cattle not long ago, thought you'd be on the other side of the mountain."

"Ah, I heard about you. Yeh, thought we would too, but here we are. Hell's fire, it's fine with me should ya stay the night. There's women out there, food, such as it is. Yer welcome ta anything but the firewater, as the injuns call it. Damn stuff causes more trouble than I intend ta contend with. Stay away from the 'Celestials.' They're easily put off, keep mostly to themselves."

"I saw them. Do you have many Chinese working for you?"

"Yeah, little fuckers don't look like much, but they're hellava workers. Don't cause no problems. More'n I can say for the other brutes." James Harvey Strobridge reached out and pleasantly shook the four men's hands, his eye patch giving him a look of menace. He turned back to his desk. It was obvious they had been dismissed.

"You talk One-Eyed Bossy Man?" Jamie looked down and saw the flat features of the Chinese, his pigtails covered by a conical straw hat, gray blue pajamas floating about his frail sinewy form.

"Is there some place we can eat and sleep for the night?"

"Yes. Yes, follow..." They followed the little man to the bonfire that burned hot and bright. A side of beef stretched across it on a skewer of pine. The little Chinaman tapped at the arm of a tall, thin man. "Mista, Mista One-Eyed Bossy Man say feed men."

The Irish lit of Lawrence O'Quinn escaped from the man who turned to them. "An' who might you be?"

The crew that made up the railroad party was comprised of mainly Irish immigrants, Chinese, disgruntled gold diggers, with whom Tommy and Micah spent the evening, and some soldiers that had been in battle. They hadn't really left their posts but had told their commanding officers that they "would much rather do this than stand, run, and hide while someone was shooting at them."

Jamie sensed someone standing behind him as he sat sopping up beans with flatbread, a pile of what was sure to be his own beef piled before him. Looking up, he saw that Mack, too, had a visitor.

The women were comely, although reeking of an odor that made him swallow hard. Hair piled high on their heads, the dark circles of exhaustion, showed as bruising, beneath weary eyes. They smiled through chapped lips, teeth yellowed and stained—those that were not missing. Their skin displayed pustules and blackheads. Great long earrings dangled from their ears, and the *lady* who had stood behind Jamie now stood before him and opened her great canvas coat.

Black net stockings rose thigh high, revealing creamy white skin, a very healthy muff of curls, covering her netherlands, a corset of red bound her waist small and tight. Her bosom pushed up and billowing over the black lace that made every attempt at support. A black onyx necklace lay heavy between her breasts. She reached down to touch his hair, and he smiled up at her.

"Not tonight, sweetheart. Maybe tomorrow." He'd be long gone come daybreak. Jamie knew this was not a life these women had particularly chosen; he had seen it often. This was the only way in which a woman could survive without marriage—that or pretend to be a man. He had seen it while on the continent, had heard about the women other men had brought out to the gold fields in California, promising them money, husbands, anything to get them to come willingly. Often kidnapping them. *Women*—always a commodity that was in demand. He looked over at Mack as the young lady disappeared among the many bodies, the firelight catching her matted locks of hair.

"Aye, I be wonderin' how long it be afore I take up with the likes o' that?" Mack was laughing out loud and clapping his hand on his knee.

"More than likely before we get back home, I fear."

"Ay, t'would be fine ta be a faithful husband, the Lord seemed ta not make it an easy thing fer a man."

Jamie thought of the vermin and the disease that came with the likes of such "pleasure" and shuddered.

The Railroad

They had spread their bedrolls at the edge of the railroad camp. Taking their chances with the likes of animals and Indians rather than that of the rough "rust-eaters"—as they called themselves. To the east, the skyline showed the faintest glimmer of dawn. The air was bitter cold—a "norther"—came off the mountains. He hadn't heard the Parsons boys come back to where they had lain their bedrolls, but now he looked over to see them curled tightly together in warmth, and more than likely, drunken stupor. It had been his intention to stop at Fort Laramie and visit with O'Shaunesey for a bit but now thought better of it. If the railroad was laid here, perhaps Fort Laramie lay to the west and north of them. Damn, he hated to be so disorientated by his surroundings. The blizzard in the mountains had caused them to come down off the mountain much farther east and south than he had planned.

He reached over to wake Mack. "Aye, I be awake, are ya ready ta go, man?"

"I think it best. We don't know what we shall encounter between here and Omaha. These railroad fellows look to be a motley bunch."

He heard the soft chuckle of Mack. "Ay, thet they do."

He and Mack had taken turns during the night watching the animals and their own lives. The ruckus that seemed to emanate from the railroad workers going long into the early morning hours, with Tommy and Micah apparently enjoying the company of both the women and the drink of the men, leaving Jamie to speculate at how the railroad workers functioned during the day. The work was difficult and dangerous, and them without sleep. He found it difficult to believe One-Eyed Bossy Man to allow such dilly-dallying.

The small, yellow-skinned Celestials, however, lay sleeping and quiet throughout the night. Now, in the early dawn of morning, they scurried silently to and fro, from the fires to their common camp.

"Tea, mista, tea?" The same small man came to stand before James and Mack. In his hand, he held two steaming cups of liquid.

"Thank you. Thank you." Jamie, by now having pulled his boots on and donned his hat and weapons, was awake and alert, reaching out for the cup. "Thank you."

The small, slight person before him bowed and smiled. "We have rice, you hungry?"

"Yes, thank you." He poked the forms of the sleeping Parsons boys with the toe of his boot. "Come on, you fellas. Up and at 'em. Breakfast is served." He watched as Mack jabbed the sides of meat on the pack animals and heard him declare.

"Still froze solid."

Jamie thought, *Would be a nice gesture to offer the little Celestials food.* Looking at the numbers that lay on the ground sleeping, remembering all the cattle he had sold them, he thought better of it. Too, he had heard they ate a diet that consisted mainly of rice, cuttlefish, bamboo shoots, and mushrooms. He wondered where in the world they found those things here. Indeed, he wondered how they had arrived here. "Think I'll look in on Strobridge, show my appreciation, and say good-bye. Maybe he can give me some idea of what lies ahead."

"Good idea, I'll have me some rice with the wee fellas here and be readyin' these hard-headed mules."

Jamie looked over at the Parsons brothers, still sleeping. "Which of the mules are you speaking of?"

"Well, now, I no' be certain, now thet you speak o' it." The big Scotsman chuckled.

Jamie lifted the flap of the tent, looking upon James Harvey Strobridge, who was indeed up and once again sat behind his desk, his ruler in hand, his hair disheveled and looking as though he'd not yet been to his bed.

"Christ, man, nearly scared the piss outta me. What the hell you want?"

"Just thought I'd thank you for your hospitality and tell you we would be on our way. Got any sage advise. Is the railroad finished to Omaha?"

"Hell, I've no way of knowing. Damn people don't tell me a thing. Not that I care. They've no sense of what's going on. My job is to get through this damn mountain, that's all I'm concerned with at this point. You four fellas goin' ta the war in the South?" Without waiting for an answer, he proceeded, "Stupid son o' bitch Lincoln. Best ta leave sleeping dogs lie. He's a conniving one, I'll tell ya that."

"Have you met him?" Genuine interest lay in Jamie's voice.

"No, I've no need, oh, I know of him, know he don't drink, and a licensed bartender at that. If that don't beat all. I know he wheedled and wiggled his way into the presidency on his father's hard-earned money. Say he owns a distillery. An' if that don't beat all, the man has put a tax on whiskey. Shit, it jus' don't seem right. To tax a man's only comfort just ta fight a war. But that's just my opinion, and I can see ya don't share it, as yer goin' to fight for him. That right?"

"Well, as a matter of fact, we are. Prior to heading to Omaha, thought perhaps you could offer some advise as to the crews working the railroads."

"Just watch your possessions and your backs. The rust-eaters are a rough bunch of thugs, an' I got some ten thousand of the sons a' bitchin' brutes workin' for me."

As Jamie looked at the man that sat behind the desk, he thought this to be one of the few men who could handle "brutes." Nearly every other word that came out of his mouth was profanity, and it brought to mind Richard King, *and Henrietta*, her in constant vigil as to his profane language. The thought of the Kings made him smile. They were decent folks.

Jamie reached across the desk and shook the outstretched hand of James Strobridge. "Good luck, perhaps I shall see you on my return."

The man made no move to rise and merely gazed at Jamie with his one eye, the bushy brows above the dark mirthless eye one of consideration. "You're planning on returning? Huh…we'll see." With that, he resumed his work.

Again, Jamie had been duly dismissed.

As the tent flap fell behind him, Jamie heard Strobridge shout, "Oh, an' shoot any bastard that tries to fine ya for crossing railroad property." Jamie's turned and once more lifted the flap. "And exactly *what is* railroad property?"

"One hell'va lot. We got ten miles on either side of the tracks, to say nothing of the length. Just shoot 'em. Tell 'em I told ya to."

Jamie tipped his hat at the man. "Thanks, I'll tell them. See you in a month or two."

"You do that."

Jamie turned back to look at Strobridge. "Ten miles, you say? On either side?"

"That's right, that's the deal Charlie Crocker made with 'em."

"So this is to be the Central Pacific, is that right?" Jamie found he was shocked by the breadth and scope of the venture.

"Yep, got forty-eight thousand dollars to get through the Rockies and the Sierras, thirty-two thousand ta get through the Great Basin, and sixteen thousand for each twenty-mile stretch after that. Bastards don't pay though until the damn track is laid…always some shit from the government. So you can see I'm a bit under the gun—so to speak."

"I see that, and who is running the Union Pacific gang?"

"Some little pipsqueak by the name of Casement, they say— *Brigadier General John Stephen Casement*…don' know much about him. Left the army to do this. Can't say why. Seems he uses Indian women and the Irish micks. Said ta be a fairer man than myself. Not that I give a damn."

Jamie laughed. "Seems you run a tight ship here."

"That I do, that I do, I'll shoot the son of bitch that gets outta line, and they damn well know it. But you'll no doubt run into Casement if you're goin' on to Omaha and farther to the east."

"I'll tell him you said to tell him hello."

"You do that. Now I got work to do."

Jamie looked out across the expanse of the country he and Elisabeth had traveled with the others over the Oregon Trail; the desolation of the land lay unchanged. They traveled northeast to follow the Platte River, away from the railroad workers and the deafening sounds of the rust-eaters at work. The wind whipped at them as they rode head long into the rising icy winds of winter that plummeted the plains. Their hats pulled down hard upon their heads, the rawhide tied securely beneath their chins, woolen scarves secured about their necks, their Surcoats of canvas often flapping in the wind, the noise of it often heard more loudly than the wind itself. Their mounts snorting and tossing their heads as the men pushed them onward into the wind and debris the whirling gale presented.

Snow was in the air. Jamie could smell it. Glad for the absence of the mountains, the four men rode side by side, the three remaining mules tethered to them. In the words of Mack Mackenzie, "It be colder than a witches tit."

Jamie's mind wandered to his meeting with Josiah. He was anxious to see his old friend, but more than that, he wondered what part Josiah had him playing in this war. Jamie thought of his ancestry and the long history of battles that patterned who he was, his ideals. He thought of Samuel Prescott and his father,

Elisha Prescott, of William Hickling Prescott. It seemed his heritage was to serve his country. After all, if men did nothing, the country would soon not be a *free country*.

He thought of the plantation owners and their choice of Davis for president. A wise choice, he felt. Did he think they would win this fight? He wasn't sure, but to stand by and do nothing was inconceivable to him. He wondered at the number of men the other states would be volunteering. With Montana not being a state, few were required to volunteer, none expected. He thought of Strobridges' words and what he had to say, "*Lincoln was indeed a wily sort.*" Just the statehood of Ohio tended to make that apparent. He certainly would not have won the presidential election without having maneuvered Ohio into statehood. Thoughts of his and Ezra's conversations concerning Lincoln's motives clouded his mind. Could it be he was on a fool's errand, that Lincoln indeed had other reasons than slavery for this battle?

It was true, the South *had* moved away from the original colonies. They had introduced their own monetary system and elected their own president, with cabinet members as well. They had a secretary of war, and their own military commander in Robert E. Lee. Jamie had read that Davis would have a term of not four years as the president of the United States had, but of six and a half years. Ezra was right; it did seem as though the intention of the Confederate States was to govern themselves; all things considered—*it could be deemed treason.*

Indeed, it would be crucial for the Northern states to find they had to negotiate with the Southerners for supplies that only the South could provide.

Wonder what Josiah would say to all of this. On the other hand, as a country, to have the South split off would weaken the entire nation. Politically, that would be disastrous. And didn't all come down to money and power?

Perhaps those that stayed behind were right. He thought now of Elisabeth's question concerning the population of the

South versus the North. Good question. That, too, would make a significant difference in the power allotted to the United States of America. Lincoln could always offer the Negro his freedom—*if they joined forces with the Union Army.*

As darkness fell, they had neither seen nor heard other persons, nor the crews of the great "Iron Horse." With the Parsons brothers sober, they divided their watch and Jamie fell into an exhausted sleep. His last thoughts were not of Lincoln nor the Civil War, nor Josiah Piedmont, but the face of Elisabeth.

Elisabeth

Elisabeth felt the softening of her heart, the fall of her shoulders; relief swelled within her soul as the softness of unfurling gossamer ribbon. *She let go and let God.* She could not control the lives of those she loved. She sincerely wished she had not the need to try. She felt her head as it bowed involuntarily in acceptance and acknowledgment and a prayer that she remembered welled within her heart.

She had felt this on so many occasions. Yet she found she would again rise to ask God to do her biding, to intercede. To do as *she wished.*

The fields of grasses flew by her as she rode like the wind upon Mercy's back, Mercy's filly, Trésor in her wake. She had slept little and had been distraught throughout the previous night. Angst and fear had clutched at her mind, at her heart.

All for naught, as she acknowledged her lack of power. Why did she continually do this? Was it ego? It was fear. She knew that. Could she control it? It seemed not. It came on waves of an unknown future, of what lay ahead, of what had been her past. A past dotted with death and fear, of strife and decisions made with her heart and not her mind. Decisions made in danger and desire.

She thought of the man she loved, what she had done in the name of that love, what she was still willing to do.

She thought of the men she had killed; the blur of their faces rose before her eyes, and rested with a great weight upon her heart. Tears blurred her vision, now manifesting as relief and acknowledgment. Her life lay before her as if a book unwritten, the words appearing only as she turned the pages, always surprising her in its content.

She thought of all the things Sally Susanne had shown her, taught her, over the last years. Of Grandmère's words of wisdom and love, and felt the shame of her need to control and manipulate things... *That they unfold in her favor. Lord, let me remember these things. Let me acknowledge Your supremacy always.*

She reached with the back of her hand to wipe her running nose, feeling the warmth of a tear as it trickled from her eye. She felt the lightness that surrounded her in the truth of the moment. The strength and the power that surged through her in currents of stalwartness and courage. *God doesn't give you more that you can bear.* They were the words of her grandmère, and at this moment, she acknowledged the truth of them. *Take joy in the small things of life, the larger things will follow.* She had begged Him, pleaded with Him that Jamie be safe. *Demanded* he be safe, for her and for their child. Throughout the night, she had wept in utter confusion, all based on an abysmal terror—a sense of the danger she felt him to be in. She felt small and insignificant, and yet, enormously important, and could find no way to ratify these feelings that seemed to be infused within her.

She watched as the fields played in the gentle breezes of the wind that wafted from the mountain ranges, heard the sounds of the creatures of the earth, the pounding of Mercy's hooves as she flew over the earth.

Yesterday evening, she had returned to the stove, only to find Maria had finished her pudding—it was to be her supper. She smiled at the thought of pudding for supper, a child's dream to be sure. But it was what she craved. Strange things she craved—puddings, cucumbers...vegetables. The mere thought of meat repugnant. This child she carried seemed to abhor meat of any kind.

She had paced the floor, pushing aside thoughts of seeking out Ilene or Sally Susanne, both of them too far away for a ride this late of an evening.

She had turned the teacup upside down, waiting for the liquid to drain from the cup, and returned it to its upright position and saw the ice and snow…the men.

Was it her imagination, a sixth sense, or was the universe trying to tell her something! She had put the cup down, returning again to the pacing of the floor.

Perhaps she would write letters. Abandoning that thought, knowing that not to be a suitable idea. Her feelings and fears seemed to find their way to the paper through words she had *not* used. She had no desire to place fear for her safety in the hearts or minds of her parents or Grandmère.

Maria had fussed about her for a time, finally leaving her to be alone with her fears and anxieties. What was she afraid of? Being without Jamie? She *was* without Jamie. He had left her to go to fight his damnable war! Lincoln's war!

Why did that make her angry? She had always known he would do that. She had thought she would go with him. Many women went with their men into battle.

Instead, she was here on thousands of acres of land, with cattle to ship, accounts to keep, men to pay, animals to feed. She thought of Charlie; what would she do without him? And Joseph.

She looked about her now, the horse having slowed her pace to that of Elisabeth's thoughts. The terror and angst that had driven her now wearied and waning in the early morning light of day. She rode line. She had ridden line with Jamie, and now in his absence rode alone each morning. As she did now, they had looked for cattle and horses in distress, for animals that preyed upon their herds, watching for signs of birthing and of sickness among their livestock, of signs the land itself was in distress.

She thought of the first winter they had arrived here and shuddered. Only darkness and depression had lain within her heart and mind, words that she would have never thought to be connected to Elisabeth Parthena Bunyan—cold and darkness. These thoughts educed—bringing Eleanor to mind. Eleanor was a subject that Elisabeth needed to let go of, and her thoughts unfurled the golden gossamer ribbon. *Let go and let God.*

The rifle hung in the scabbard at the side of Mercy, the pistols hung on either side of her ballooning belly. She smiled at the incredulous image she must make. Buckskins and boots—the heavy surcoat of a man. Her hair piled high upon her head, the hat of the Western cowboy pushed tightly over it. She thought of the cattle drive from the King ranch and remembered thinking she would never dress this way again, yet here she was over a year later and bedecked in what continued to be appropriate for her lifestyle. She smiled at the audacity of it!

Clouds of fog came from the nostrils of Mercy, the autumn air of early morning chilled and crisp. The river birch that grew in dense forests near the river was approaching nakedness, the gold of leaves cushioning the forest floor. The wisps of curling smoke rose lazily from the chimney of Charlie's small cabin. She turned Mercy to the north and headed to the eastern corner of their property, thinking of the many stakes they had pounded into the ground to claim the vastness of this land.

A small speck of light glowed in the home of Joseph and Eleanor, or perhaps it was the barn. She wondered if indeed Eleanor was awake. Joseph would be about milking, for the moon hung low in the lightening of the morning skies. A tiny dot of light shown further to the northeast—that would be the MacKenzie's spread.

She heard the bawling of a calf and looked to see where the sound came from, only to see it standing near its mother.

She watched for the yellow-green almond eyes of the wolf, the cattle's worst predator, or at the very least, its most continuous one. She had seen none this morning, but from experience, she knew this meant nothing, as these were highly intelligent and cunning animals, able to run at a speed of perhaps thirty-five miles an hour, with their jaws capable of breaking bones and severing legs and neck alike.

Trésor ran ahead of them, and she heard the soft whinny of Mercy as she summoned her child back to within sight. The foal would be ready for genuine training soon. Elisabeth often placed a saddle on her back to accustom her to the weight; Trésor was tall like her dame, larger than that of her sire, Danny, possessing Danny's elegant lines. Prize horseflesh to be sure. Although Elisabeth found that to be something far akin to what she felt for the horse. Trésor was her child, Mercy's child. She was anything but simple horseflesh to her.

She spied the herd of Mustangs that Jamie had brought in, all fitted with halters, the Paints making her think of Josiah, of how he favored this horse with the same enthusiasm as the Indian. In truth, there were few out West that did not. Without these loyal, intelligent animals, they would be adrift, the Indian thinking the horse to indeed be a gift from God.

Ezra Gilky was the only one she could think of who seemed to feel free to wander the world on foot. Lean and tall, even gangly some might say, she had seen the man with but a mere pack on his back, a bow and quiver of arrows and a rifle as he wandered throughout the Americas and Canada. His face flashed before her now, an exquisite face. Perfect in its symmetry, soft full lips, large eyes rimmed with thick, curling lashes that exuded both intelligence and humor. Strange to think of Ezra Gilky at a time like this. She wondered how Petra endured the worry that accompanied his absence, but then he was but her brother and she had the two children, as well as her practice to concern her, to occupy her mind and heart.

Perhaps she should go into town for the winter to teach school. Where would she stay? No one really had extra rooms, perhaps the saloon? She thought of Jamie; he *would* have a fit if she stayed in the saloon, perhaps though, she would find it to be quite exciting. She felt the subtle change of a smile cross her face, felt the rub of the pommel on her belly and laughed. She could hardly be seen *as an object of desire*...although Jamie said most men had no scruples when it came to *that*. All the men she knew seemed to be quite scrupulous indeed. Well, with the exception of perhaps Jeff...and Swede, there was something about him that made her uneasy. Her mind filled with the image of Jeff and Agnes in the woods of Ash Hollow, she shuddered. *Think of something else*, she admonished herself.

In February they would brand their stock, at the same time castrating many of the new bulls. Jamie had had the blacksmith in Helena make the branding iron, a fleur-de-lis with JEP beneath it. Without thought, her mind wandered to Jamie. Jamie, what would she do without Jamie? Was he thinking of her? Was he safe? What if he wasn't home by February? She breathed deeply and marveled that every thought took her back to Jamie.

Perhaps she should have gone home, as he had wished. Thoughts of the trip *back* to Philadelphia made her feel physically ill. She could not do that again, not so soon. The Oregon Trail had been a terrifying experience, the trip south to Texas, to the King Ranch, long and hard. But the cattle drive home had left her near a broken woman, had tried her to the very depths of who she was, tried the very strength of her mind, body, and soul. *Non, elle n'a pas souhaité*. She did not wish to do that again—*not ever!*

This was her home. Strange, something more precious than costumes fashioned by *Worth*, Jupe tables, Saint Louis's Cristal and Brownstones lay within her home and her heart.

She felt the warmth of Mercy's flesh and the earth glide by beneath her hooves, and at the same time, she felt herself to be ethereal. She remembered the longing she had felt for the ritual of the church, the feelings that that longing had emanated in her. Somehow, the communion with the land, with the peace that came from the earth, had taken that need from her. Not that she would not love to kneel before the alter of St. Patrick's, but she felt that stirring within her as she knelt on the earth to pick weeds, to ride like the wind through the beauty of fields, to watch as the river rushed with enormous power over the great boulders, or the birthing of a new animal.

She looked now at Trésor as she glided over the earth's surface, every muscle and sinew defined, graceful, elegant, her mane whipping in flight, her youthful exuberance at simply being alive. She recalled the awe and delight she had felt at her birth.

Reverence filled her here continually, a reverence she received only on Sundays while she lived in her parents' home. This was *home*; this was home as much as *Jamie* was home. This land gave her peace and purpose.

Please, Lord, let me remember this moment. "Take joy in the small things of life…the larger things will follow…" always Grandmère's words, giving her peace. This winter she *would* read Grandmère's journal; she swallowed hard. It had been over two years, and she had not read it. Was it fear that keep her from opening the pages of the thick journal, fear of finding she had made an irreparable mistake? The image of the luxury and wealth that filled her family's home rose before her, the stealth with which she had left at the midnight hour just weeks after her sixteenth birthday. Left to be with a man Mama had referred to as "a scoundrel," a mere farmer. Would *she* understand? Should this child she carried commit such an act. She smiled and thought of the heartbreak that would bring to her, the smile that crossed her face, one of understanding and love. She certainly had no way of knowing, but she doubted that her mama had such an understanding. She and Papa seemed to have a quiet, comfortable acceptance of one another. She had never witnessed overt drama within their lives, only the occasional affection given a close friend, the pursed lips of her mama's disdain for an event.

She thought of their separate bedrooms and could not fathom Jamie sleeping so far from her within the same house. So very many things about her parents' relationship she had once accepted she now found strange. Again, Grandmère's journal rose within her mind... What would she find there? Grandmère seemed to have a deep understanding of Elisabeth and her feelings, her emotions, her inability to follow accepted nuances of social customs.

Enough of such as these thoughts. They only seemed to enhance her sense of loss and sadness. She would think of them tomorrow! Or...perhaps not at all!

Joseph

Elisabeth clicked her tongue and tightened her legs on Mercy and whispered, "Joseph, Mercy. Let's go to visit Joseph."

As they neared the barn, the light grew brighter, the patina of ice that coated the exterior walls of the barn giving it an ethereal glow. She pulled at the heavy door and peered in. "Joseph, are you here?" The aroma of alfalfa and straw, strong, the odor clean, although not enough that the smell of cow dung, warm and moist, didn't overpower her as she entered. The growing daylight could be seen between the logs that made up the barn. The floor, one of hard-packed dirt. Bracings and tack hung on walls, and saddles lay slung over sawhorses in the corner. The barn was twice the size of Joseph's home, stanchions going down the center, leaving two rows of milking stations. Milk cans sat clean and ready at the end of the barn. Buckets and shovels sat leaning against the wall.

Large rounds of straw piled high, keeping the barn warm and providing meager rations for the cows that they would surely require once the alfalfa was gone.

The image of the men covered in sweat rose in her mind; their sleeves rolled up, or their chests bared, rose before her, the chatter of the women as they carried water and homemade root beer to the men in the field, the pungent odor of green as they trod through the freshly cut hay. The sheen of sweat that had covered Jamie's muscled chest and arms. The salty taste of it on his lips as he had leaned down to kiss her. The sound of the sickle as it sang through the air.

It had been their first real harvest, and the sights and smells of it—the pure *joy* of it permeated her very soul. Ma, as she had kneaded bread and watched as Eleanor peeled small apples from a tree in their yard. The fragrance of summer, the sounds of children.

" Joseph...?" She found him sitting on a small three-legged stool, at least she supposed he did so, it would be hard to tell; the giant man dwarfed everything in sight. His huge hands wrapped tightly around the teat of a milk cow, one of the few cows that had survived the trip West.

His homely, joy-filled face surrounded by dust moats that rode on lantern light, the blue flame of the kerosene surrounded by an orange glow.

Some dozen cows stood ready for milking, with his hired hand, Wil, on the opposite side of Joseph. Several of the heifers had younger cows beside them. Something only Joseph would permit while trying to get the morning milking done.

She could smell the stench of feathers and chickens. Lord, how she hated the dirty chickens...

He turned to look up at her. Not stopping his milking, nor rising, his face lighting with a huge grin. He was always bemused at the sight of his brother's wife—clad in buckskins and boots. Remembering the strikingly beautiful, petite, young girl they had absconded with in the night, literally taking her from her parents' home. She had been bedecked in jewels. Finery of taffeta and furs, with white kidskin boots on her tiny feet, willing to travel to the ends of the earth for the sake of the love she felt for his handsome brother. *My, how she had changed.* He thought of the courage she had shown in the face of danger, the joy she brought to all she came in contact with. Oh, she was filled with piss and vinegar to be sure, but a lesser human being would have—

He stopped in mid thought, his Eleanor coming to mind. Who would have thought that of the two of them Eleanor would have been the more fragile?

"'Mornin', Elisabeth, you all right? Jamie?" His voice one of only slight concern; he knew she rode line each morning. "Did ya come to help me with the morning milking or to gather the eggs for me?"

She laughed at this. "Oh, Joseph, I am hardly volunteering for either of those things, but I will help if you need me too."

It was common knowledge how Elisabeth felt about milking and chickens. Dirty, dirty, dirty... She thought of their chickens this summer, feathers everywhere but on their necks and bodies. Yuck! Jamie said they were molting... Oh, it was disgusting... and the cows, poop all over their rear ends. Slobber around their mouths from chewing their cud...just disgusting. After all this time, she still found it so. She thought of young Maggie and smiled.

Yet here Joseph sat, exacting white, clean milk from this animal. She shuddered and Joseph laughed.

"Yes, I'm fine. I...I haven't heard from Jamie, of course. He said he would telegraph from Omaha in about two or three weeks, but I didn't sleep all night for worrying... I just had a dreadful feeling, but it seems to be gone. Thank goodness!"

"It was no doubt the puckish mountain. Shucks, Elisabeth, that's enough to make me cringe thinkin' about it. He's okay. Jamie, he can handle nearly anything, an' Mack too. Try not to worry." He chuckled, the milk making a loud squirting noise as it hit the tin bottom of the pail. He looked up at her now and smiled. His brown eyes round and somehow always filled with laughter, his smile a near constant condition of his face. Stubble of black dusted his face in the predawn of the day.

Lifting the teat, he aimed it her way and squirted it. Warm milk dribbled down her face, and she reached her tongue out to catch it. She laughed and sat down on the bench behind him, a bench cluttered with tack. "So, Joseph, are you ready for winter?"

"As ready as I'm ever gonna be. Got enough food and firewood. Feed for the animals, think we'll be fine. Thanks to Mack and Jamie."

"Thanks to you, too, Joseph. Mack and Jamie, and the hired hands, none of us would weather this world without the help of one another. How is Eleanor? Is she up? Have you seen Jeff or Agnes?"

She watched as his face scrunched up, his slightly bucked teeth, covered by pursed lips. "I dunno, she doesn't say much. Seems to have no interest in anything. Doesn't get dressed most days. If it weren't for Many Hands, hell, I'd be without time to sleep. Told her today she had to milk, and she rolled over and went back to sleep. It's been nearly six months, since…since, ah hell, Elisabeth, it's beyond me."

"Does she wear her spectacles?" She watched the anguish as it rushed across his face. *Dear Joseph, how she wished she could be of help.*

"No!" He laughed out loud and squirted her again, his big toothy grin, one she loved. "Think I'll hang a flag out the day she wears her spectacles."

Elisabeth laughed at that. It was common knowledge that Eleanor wore her spectacles only when she was well, meaning in Eleanor's case—"emotionally stable." Having lost two children in less than two years was a great deal to bear, quite disarming if you considered the circumstances. Elisabeth could remember every detail concerning the Indians and Henry, not something she wished to do. The last child she had lost just days prior to them returning from Texas. And Elisabeth was certain Joseph blamed himself for not being here. Eleanor, however, was difficult to help. "Is she still taking the laudanum?"

"Yeah, the thought of her not…jeez…*remember the last time.*" He shook his head at the mere thought of taking the drug from her.

Elisabeth could see him now, lying in his bedroll, his ears covered with clothing as Eleanor screamed in panic and anger hour upon hour from the inside of the prairie schooner. "I would be happy to come stay with her should you decide she is well enough to go off it, you know she will never get well as long as she takes it."

"Yeah, Elisabeth, but dammit, she likes the stuff like the Indians like their liquor. And quite frankly, I am not up to what it means. Maybe this winter."

"Is she still mad at me?" Elisabeth laughed as she asked the question, but it was truly not a laughing matter to her. Eleanor had been her friend and was her sister-in-law. She would like them to at least be able to talk things through. Mama always said there were things better left unsaid. Elisabeth sincerely doubted that; she thought things left unsaid festered in people, particularly the bad things, the anger, the pain, and the hurt. *And love*, well that—unexpressed simply found a place to hide, not healing or nurturing. A waste.

"I suppose so. Hell, she seems mad at me, or indifferent, I tell you *I think that's worse*, doesn't seem to know or care if I'm here or not."

"Oh, Joseph, I can't tell you how sorry I am."

"I know, and I appreciate you tellin' me that. Sometimes, seems a lot to suffer. But I love her, and she knows it. The hardest part is she won't let me touch her…"

Elisabeth felt her face flush, and she looked down, her thick, ebony lashes covering the green of her eyes, the straw covered floor looming before her.

Joseph's laughter was raucous. "Oh, Elisabeth, I don't mean *that* way, I mean she screams if I so much as touch her shoulder or her hair."

"Joseph, *do you think perhaps she was attacked again*, you know, no one really knows what happened except perhaps Many Hands. Truly there must be some reason for all of this, and *the child*…I just don't know, Joseph, but if there is anything at all I can do… please tell me."

He stood up from his milking and moved the small stool to the next cow. Murmuring sweet nothings to his beloved cows. He loved these cows with a passion, much like Jamie loved the horses. "It means a lot to me, Elisabeth, and believe me, I would call you, *and* I'll stick around in case she tries to hit you." He laughed his great laugh. Both of them aware he was really not kidding.

"Does she still visit Agnes?"

"Naw, doesn't come out of the house long enough to ride all that way. Have you seen her?"

"Agnes? Not for several weeks, though I thought I would visit more frequently now with Jamie gone."

He laughed. "Crazy man…don't know why, but sometimes I envy his joie de vivre." With a great guffaw, he looked up at her and winked. "I, too, can speak some French."

"Oh, Joseph, you are funny. I do feel better just seeing you, give my love to Eleanor. Bye, Wil."

With that, she was gone.

The Rusteaters

Thinking they would again be well received at the camps along the railroad, they stopped at one of the camps for the night.

The wind blustery—the cold—one would not have believed had they not experienced it. In the distance, they had seen the tents and bonfires of the workers, approached, and climbed down from their mounts and gone to enjoy a pleasant respite from their perilous traveling. Jamie and the others approached the first man they saw. Jamie extended his hand to the man and said, "Prescott, James, thought we could talk to your boss, perhaps spend the night here."

"Sven," the fella said his name was, a man large and looking grisly, informed them that it would "cost 'em a hundr'd dollars an' that black piece of horseflesh ta stay the night."

"I think not," Jamie replied. "Thought we'd simply pay our respects and move along."

"But yer here now, man, on company land an' ya gotta pay."

"Then I expect we shall just pay our respects to your boss and keep moving."

"No, now, I'm tellin' ya you pay us or ya *don't* move along." Sven strode toward the four men who stood before him.

"Mount up, fellas, we're not welcome here." Jamie mounted Danny and turned him north, with Mack, Tommy, and Micah at his side.

Even through the bitter cold, he felt the heat of the stick of dynamite as it flew past his ear, the slight flicker of light, the hissing of the wick, the explosion rocking them from their saddles. The horses, rearing, wild-eyed, whinnying in fear and confusion. Reaching for his rifle, made difficult as Danny danced on hind legs in protest, he had aimed and fired at the barbarian that had thrown the explosive.

Others of the same predilection now stood behind Sven. Jamie looked at Mack and nodded his head. Leaping from their saddles, the four men ran at the railroad workers with a fierceness Jamie had forgotten lived within him. He heard himself as he shouted orders to the three men who rode with him, "Kill them if you must!" Jamie had but a moment to assess the situation. He watched the mightiness of Mack as he held off two smaller men, scrutinized the others, as the smaller men crashed to the ground around Mack, Mack looking about for others to obliterate. Jamie looked for Tommy and Micah and could see only a dozen or so men fighting in the backlight of the bonfire.

Taken by surprise, the railroad rust-eaters stood stock-still for the brief moment it took to place a brutal uppercut on Sven's jaw. The heat of the fire, amid the stench of the men they fought, turned to the rank odor of fear. Jamie plummeted the fractious man with his fists, landing several mighty punches before the man had regained his senses and started punching back.

The weight of Sven's right landed squarely on Jamie's jaw. Blackness threatened to overtake him as he stumbled backward. Sven was a man of equal size and power to that of Jamie.

Jamie fought the blackness from the mighty blow of Sven as he stumbled to the ground; quickly he rose on his haunches, lowered his head, and with the stealth of a panther, rode the weight of his body into the chest of Sven, flames of the bonfire growing dangerously close as they both plummeted to the frozen ground. Both men rose quickly.

Jamie drew his pistols, one in each hand. "Look, fellas, we see hospitality is not your finest suit, so we'll just be moving along."

Like a wounded animal, Sven shook his head, roared, and bolted up, coming at Jamie with the fierceness of drink and the simple joy of a fight.

Strobridge *had* warned him; still, he was unprepared for the belligerence of the railroad workers. Damned jokers thought they could charge them to travel on the railroads land.

The mob of rust-eaters continued to throw lighted wicks of dynamite at them, clubs of railroad spikes raised to be used as weapons against them. All for tobacco and drink, and the spoilin' of a fight.

Hell, I don't have time for this. Thinking of traveling with broken limbs, crushed ribs—the cold. Where he was going, there would be plenty of opportunities to fight. Jamie aimed and fired. The sound of pistol fire rang through the air, the bullet meant only to pierce the flesh of the man's thigh, the moving target, however causing it to lodge in the kneecap. He heard a cry of pain as the large man fell to the ground, his hand holding his knee, the bush of his hair just inches from the flames of the bonfire.

"Now then, as I said before, we'll not be bothering you." Jamie turned to go. He heard the nearly obscure sound of *zzzzz*...

Oh, shit, the sizzle of dynamite.

The pistol he held in his left hand, still loaded and primed, his hand flying swiftly—the shot taking the end off the wick. The four of them watched as Sven proceeded to light the end of another stick of dynamite.

"Put it down, sir. Now. Or your hand will be next." He heard the click of the pistols and rifles as the Parsons brothers and Mack prepared to back him up.

Inwardly heaving a sigh of relief, he needed to reload.

The stick of dynamite rested in the dirty hands of Sven, the match hovering ever so slightly from the wick.

"I'd no' be doin' it. Meself have seen the man before ye take down a mighty grizzly."

Relief flooded Jamie as he watched Sven return the dynamite carefully to the box. They watched as the others backed away from the bonfire.

"If'n it be all the same ta the likes o' you, I'll not be wishin' ta be acceptin' of their hospitality." The laughter of Mack echoed in the blast of wind and snow.

A whistle of piercing sound echoed throughout the area, and Danny stood at Jamie's side. "Mount up, men, seems these fellas are not up to company tonight."

They had gathered their horses, the mules still tethered to them. They rode through the blizzard of wind and snow; the horses struggling through the deepening snows that held the world of the prairie in its dreadful stead.

The excitement of battle having left them less weary, although they had checked repeatedly behind them, with only minor concern. The railroad bosses were not likely to let their workers ride off into the night looking for revenge. It was a hell of a place when you had to watch your back for Indians, animals, and now men with a score to settle. He chuckled to himself at the thought of what drove men to love a fight, especially if they won. *Josiah would laugh.*

He wondered what Josiah had in mind for him. His orders only instructed him to meet General Piedmont and Senator Douglas, as well as Sherman in the Herndon House, a hotel in Omaha, on or before the first week of November 1862, bringing with him as many men as were willing. He smiled to himself at that; he had with him but three men. The right to draft men into duty not one they could readily enforce on the territories, although he knew Stephen Douglas had passed the Kansas Nebraska Act some six years before they had come over the Oregon Trail, but that act had had little effect, none of them wanting statehood as long as the issue of slavery was at hand.

Jamie felt the bite of the wind and the loneliness of its howl and turned his face, looking for Tommy and Micah, Mack. Faint shapes enshrouded in the white of winter lopped as an apparition behind him. The heat from their bodies was not enough to melt the ice and snow that whirled around them. The drifting of the snow coming in froths of ice off the hooves of their horses, the clouds of breath from the horses drifting in smoke like spumes to the mounted men. For a moment, he wondered what this country would look like in the dead of winter—as it was not yet upon them. A sobering thought to be sure.

With the Platte River to the south of them, the four riders were scarcely visible as they rode east against the mighty gusts of the prairie. The snow coming in horizontal sheets of wind that howled with temperatures of thirty below. Their faces hidden from view by hats, scarves, and collars turned up against the wind. Nothing had changed on the prairie since they had come this way on the Oregon Trail. Nothing, that is, but the weather, the extremes of the heat, Jamie could remember as being reminiscent of the stories of hell; so nothing had changed, just the story of hell. The country still desolate and unforgiving, the explicable heat now replaced by equally devastating cold. How in the hell could man live in such a hellhole?

Jamie looked at the lashes of Danny, the black Arabian he rode, the ice having joined the black lashes of those great dark eyes to spikes of crystal white.

He could make out the smatterings of the sodbusters' homes, scattered along the site of the railroad land. He had read this, seen the ads in the newspapers, but seeing it, viewing the reality of it, all he could do was wonder at the horrendous conditions that had driven men to come from all over Europe to live in this godforsaken land. He had read in the newspapers that the railroad was offering land to settlers for two dollars and fifty cents an acre, 6 percent interest, and ten years credit. The U.S. government was offering 160 acres of land with the Homestead Act, giving persons the right to claim that land if indeed they worked it for five years and built a home on it. Jamie felt a chuckle rise in his throat as he thought of the "homes" he had seen. Little more that holes dug in the ground. But then he knew the country. God bless the man with the gumption to build a house from sod and live without water, or worse yet, to dig deep into the earth and burrow like an animal and call it home. The fact that 160 acres of land located in this desolate part of the American continent could barely support a family seemed to make no difference, the Germans, Swedes, and Norwegians had gathered up some two hundred and fifty thousand acres in six months' time.

Jamie wondered if any of them would respond to the call of patriotism.

They rode as close to the railroad land as possible; it was warmer there, but more dangerous. The men—men of carnal appetites—men that would and could do this job. The thunder of dynamite only to be heard occasionally now, the wagons filled with rails, ties, and spikes, set guarded heavily next to track that had been laid. The bitterness of the weather dampening the spirited men employed by the Union Pacific Railroad.

He expected to arrive in Omaha within the next couple of days. Eager to be done with this journey.

He still felt the pain that radiated up his jaw and into his ear. Glad for the cold that seemed to diminish it to some extent. The abrasiveness of his gloves, painfully frozen to the flesh wounds of his hands.

It had been nearly a week since the run-in with the railroad workers, pushing their horses as fast as the weather permitted, yet they were still some distance from Nebraska. The snow was deep and icy, but worse than anything was the damned wind. It was steady and unrelenting, often gusting to levels of sixty or more miles an hour, the riders indistinguishable within the whiteness of the ever-deepening snows. Still, they pushed their animals hard.

Jamie reached down and patted the snow-covered black flanks of Danny, born and bred to withstand the desert heat of Arabia, now made to withstand the extremes of the North American winter. They traveled more north than east now, the sounds of blasting and the clanking of iron upon iron having long since diminished. Jamie felt his jaw, thankful that Sven had not broken it.

Men in small groups of three and four had joined them. From the north of them and the south, men had ridden toward them, asking "if indeed, they were going to join in the war against the Southern States." Each conversation bringing with it a strange feeling of sickness in the pit of his stomach. To fight against his brother...

A nation about to be divided. America, the land of opportunity, of equality...of freedom, to be divided. Certainly, there had been opportunity of negotiation, of compromise.

He and Mack brought up the rear of their band of soon-to-be soldiers, for safety's sake, and he looked through the many riders for the backs of Tommy and Micah Parsons, knowing they would head south in the next few hours, to join the Confederate Army. The Lord willing, he would not see them again, until they were all home in Montana. The thought of going against them in battle was nearly more than he could fathom.

Early this morning, he had once more turned Danny to the south, in search of the Platte River.

The many men set about him, tin cups of steaming bitter coffee. They were now some forty strong, all traveling through the dead of winter to join Lincoln in his war on the South. All having issues regarding the owning of another human being.

Jamie knew that President Lincoln had charisma, but he had been astounded at the number of men willing to leave their newly established homes—their families—to fight for the freedom of a nation.

They had all come from countries of oppression and hardships, hunger and cold. They had no intention of this, their new homeland falling within the clutches of such as that. He knew that was why Josiah would fight, remembering the loss of his wife and children, his escape from Austria.

Abraham Lincoln was their leader, both admired and trusted. They were ready and willing to follow him wherever it took them. Men that reminded Jamie of the tales of old England, of the Vikings. These men were blond and blue-eyed, thick and muscular, armed with weaponry from their own countries as well as American weapons.

This was the beginning of a new age; the people would have their say.

The American Revolution may have given America its freedom from England, but this was the heart of America that spoke now.

Freedom from slavery, freedom to protect yourself at all cost. His heart swelled with pride as he thought these words. That pride somewhat diminished by the thought that they were in fact fighting other Americans—Americans that felt they, too, had the right to act in their best interest. Quickly, he tried in vain to push those thoughts from his mind. The South, the devastation to them and their way of life. The effect it would have on the United States. Lincoln was right; it had to be stopped. Like a wound left untreated, ultimately it would be the undoing of America.

They sat now against the bluff of what he hoped was the North Platte River. By nightfall, he hoped to be sitting drinking scotch with Josiah Piedmont, perhaps even enjoying one of his fine cigars. He took up the small journal he kept and marked off the day. It had been nineteen days since he had left Elisabeth. Again he envisioned her back as she had walked into the house.

Home, *their* home.

Best not to think of that.

Omaha

The Parsons brothers, Micah and Tommy, were in turn, clenched within the strong muscular arms of Mack MacKenzie and James Martin Prescott. The two great men hugged them and beat them upon the back.

The boys would follow the Missouri, the Mississippi, and the Ohio rivers on down into Kentucky. It had been their and their families' decision that they fight "for our own folks, not the Union."

Pulling away from Jamie's bearlike hug, Tommy looked up into his eyes. "If'in I don't see y'all again, you been good ta me and my folks. I be right honored to have ya let me come on with you."

Jamie was more than a little shocked by this from Tommy. Once more patting him on the back, Jamie looked into his eyes. He saw no fear, only sadness. "I'll be seeing you again. Remember you are a *volunteer*. Go home if you want to." Laughing, he added, "Or you can come fight for Mack and me. We'd be glad to have you."

"Aye, an' I be feelin' the same, do not be worrit', lad."

Tears twinkled like diamonds in the young man's eyes, and Jamie thought his heart would break.

"Come on now, little brother, we be seein' 'em sooner than you think. We gonna whup their asses." Micah looked so much like his pa it was hard not to laugh. His sail-like ears red from the freezing wind and snow of the Nebraska plains. His slight frame and blond, sparse hair covered in snow. Micah held his hat in his hand in respect. "Now then, you big brawny fellas, lets git on with this war, see if we kin' get this little disagreement over with."

Mack and Jamie watched as they remounted their horses. "You boys remember how to get there?"

"We do, Mr. Prescott, sir."

Jamie and Mack stood and watched as they rode away, taking but one mule with them. They were fine boys, Jamie thought to himself. *God be with them.* "Shall we go in by ourselves, or do you want to catch up to the others?"

The forty or fifty men that had joined them on the trail would be heading in the same direction as they; there was an enlistment office there, and most of them were going in as volunteers for the Union Army. There had been little comment made about Micah and Tommy going to fight for the South. These men had all come here for a new way of life, and they understood loyalty and freedom.

"Meself now, I be thinkin' this be the most peace we'll be havin' fer a time."

"I think your right about that. Tell me, Mack, should we stay together, or do you want your own division?"

"I be thinkin' on thet. Seems we be gettin' the job done a wee might faster should we be splittin' up. Yer thinkin' be the same?"

"Yes, those are my thoughts as well."

Behind them, the evening sky shown of winter purples and pinks, striations of color that would prompt the coming day. The snow had stopped abruptly and the burgeoning town of Omaha sat flat and straight before them. Railroad "brutes" and the tiny "Celestials" strode the boardwalks; the town was abuzz with activity even at this hour.

Starlight twinkled within the heavens, a new moon hung over the night sky, Venus hung loyally below—ostensibly, a guardian of sorts. Jamie's thoughts ran to Elisabeth, to the nights they had spent in their sleeping bag, the one she had sewn together. They had looked up at the many constellations, each able to identify them, each in awe of their very existence. He thought of the Southern Cross on another vastly different continent and gave a great sigh of relief. The journey had been long, the trials vastly different from those he had encountered prior, but he was damn grateful to have arrived safe and sound. In the morning, he would send a message to Elisabeth. He thought of her now, the exquisite Elisabeth, for the first time, her appearance being one of a woman about to have his child.

It was late evening as they dismounted their horses in front of the Herndon Hotel. The two men looked at each other.

"I be liken the looks o' this Jamie, me boy."

"Quite impressive to say the least. Do you think they'll have hot water? I can't imagine what it would feel like to shave and bathe."

"Aye, meself, I be prayin' to the Father…" Mack chuckled. "Think they be givin' the likes o' us some fancy uniform?"

"I certainly hope so. I brought no clothing. Only weapons."

"Aye, I too. Jus' a wee might." They both laughed as they entered the hotel. Mack had brought an arsenal of weapons.

As they stepped onto the marble carpeted floors, Jamie was but for a moment taken aback. His and Elisabeth's home was but two rooms, built of logs he and his brother, Joseph, Mack, and his other friends and hired hands had hand hewn from the forested land around them. The logs daubed in mud by the women. He smiled as he thought of his laughter at Elisabeth, her lovely nose wrinkling in disgust at the stench of the mud. He thought of the fancy door and glazing for the windows he had bought for her birthday. Yes, it had been some time since he had been in a real house, let alone a fine hotel.

He looked about for Josiah, excitement racing in his mind and heart. It had been months since he had seen his good friend, his thoughts immediately going back to the hotel where they had first met. Both had been festooned in ensembles of fine woolen cloth, vests, top hats, and polished shoes. Would he ever live like that again?

They had been enlisted, issued uniforms, and summarily dismissed by the youthful captain in the hall they were using for these purposes. It had been two days since their arrival at what once was called Florence—now Omaha—and the headquarters for the Civil War involvement. Why this was, Jamie had no idea.

Returning to the hotel, Jamie was astounded to see Josiah walking toward him. The blue of the Union Army uniform, making the man look, what Elisabeth would call, *dashing*… He smiled. The sea-blue eyes of Josiah smiled back at him. His hair shot with silver, the sword tilted ever so slightly on his hip, the butt of the Colt could be seen, the brass of the buttons on his jacket and the four stars on his epaulets making it clear he was a man on a mission of import.

Josiah strode toward Jamie, grabbing Jamie's hand in both of his, his hands hardened and rough, the strength of them matched only by Jamie's own. This rugged man who had led them to the West on the Oregon Trail felt his heart lighten at the sight of James Prescott. However, he was stunned that he had forgotten what a strikingly handsome man he was. Standing well over six feet, as they could look straight into one another's eyes, heavily muscular, apparent even in the Union uniform, straight-backed. What the man needed was an insignia and some medals. He smiled, and looking into Jamie's amber eyes, he said, "I'm damn happy to see you. Damned happy. So they got you all signed up?"

"They did, and I am damn happy to see you as well!"

"And, Mack, you're in uniform, didn't know if they'd have enough cloth to make you one."

All three laughed and beat each other upon their backs, happier than all hell to see one another.

"Now, Prescott, you and Mackenzie, we'll go meet with the other's in the War Room. Sounds a might ominous, I'd like to sit an' chat—but..."

The three of them, joined by others standing within the lobby, turned to enter the War Room.

"How's my Lizzy, and your Ilene, Mack? Still pissed, are they?" He gave a resounding laugh and patted them on the backs while pushing them onward.

The *War Room* was but the ballroom of the hotel, not at all ostentatious for a ballroom, but an unlikely location for discussing the demise of the Southern States, or more accurately, the Confederacy, as Maryland had thrown her loyalties to the South. With West Virginia casting her allegiance with the Northern states, there was now a chasm within the country. As they walked in the room, Jamie was heralded by all those men he had not seen in nearly two years. Surprised by the numbers that were in attendance, the weather bad, the transportation even worse. But then, these were *patriots*. He expected nothing less from these stalwart men.

The tables were arranged in the pattern of a U, graced with snow-white linen, with table settings of fine china, silver, and crystal, all glistening in the flickering candlelight of the many chandeliers and wall sconces. You could hear the clink of crystal, amber liquid slouched within the glasses, and the air was a gray cloud of cigar smoke.

The room was a sea of indigo, the uniform of the Union Army. A shiver shot down James Prescott's spine, nothing less than he had expected. He felt Josiah's hand upon his back, and turning, he saw the raised eyebrow of Josiah. "So, Prescott, impressive?"

"In a word, yes."

"Haha," Josiah laughed. "This is the fun part. Come, I believe there are some people that would like to see you, then there are some preliminary formalities. I believe they have a couple of stars for you and Mackenzie. Then we can commence with the meeting. It is set to start at 9:00 pm, or in military terms, twenty-one hundred hours."

My God, a major general, he would have eight thousand to twenty-six thousand men under him. How in the hell?

Yet he knew his rank was determined not just by his skill but by the monies he brought and the persons he was acquainted with. He looked at Mack, knowing that would not go well. The pay would be good. He had heard he could expect well over five thousand dollars a year for the rank of major general. He and Mack had talked of this, and he knew Mack would never take on that many men. He was neither as ambitious as Jamie nor as willing to be in the limelight. Mack was a gentle giant of a man, with a heart that was befitting a man of his size. No, Jamie thought, he would be surprised should Mack assume to take on that much responsibility. He looked at Mack and saw the determination in his cerulean blue eyes.

"No. Thank thee, Mr. Wagon General, I'll no be needin' two stars, how bot, just give me one an' I be helpin' the major general here. Wha'd ya say, Jamie, me lad?"

"I would find that a very comforting position to be in, with you at my back, we will have this *little disagreement* over shortly, as Micah said."

"The Parsons boy? How the hell are they? They come with you?"

"Well, as a matter of fact, they did, but no, they are going to fight with the confederates, that is where they are from, the South."

"Of course, how are Ma and Pa? And my spunky little Lizzy? You never said how she was?"

"Well, Josiah, I am to be a father in February, so I am expected home."

"Well, I'll be damned. Well now, that *is* good news. Congratulations!"

They mingled among the high society of generals and colonels, and quite suddenly, they heard the sound of a bugle. For all the reasons war was an outrage, the patriotism and the feelings of love for America welled within the heart of Jamie; the flag was raised and the national anthem began.

He listened with interest to the speaker...

"At his inauguration on March 4, 1861, *Abraham Lincoln* stated that the U.S. Constitution was a binding contract and that the Southern states' secession had no legal basis. He said that he had no intention of ending slavery where it already existed and did not plan on invading the South. He was, however willing to use force to retain possession of federal installations in the seceded states.

"As of April 1861, the U.S. only retained control of two forts in the South: Fort Pickens at Pensacola, Florida, and Fort Sumter in Charleston, South Carolina. Shortly after South Carolina seceded, the commander of the Charleston harbor defenses, Major Robert Anderson, moved his men from Fort Moultrie to Fort Sumter, located on a sandbar in the middle of the harbor. After refusing requests from the South Carolina government to vacate the fort, Anderson and the eighty-five men of his garrison settled in for what essentially became a siege.

"In January 1861, President Buchanan attempted to resupply the fort. However, the supply ship, *Star of the West*, was driven away by guns manned by cadets from the Citadel."

Jamie looked at Josiah for affirmation of this, as he had not yet heard these facts. Josiah simply nodded his head.

The speaker continued.

"During March 1861, we have reason to believe a debate raged in the Confederate government regarding how forceful they should be in trying to take possession of Forts Sumter and Pickens. Our informants reported that Jefferson Davis, like Lincoln, did not wish to anger the border states by appearing as the aggressor. With supplies low, Lincoln informed the governor of South Carolina, Francis W. Pickens, that he intended to have the fort reprovisioned, but promised that no additional men or munitions would be sent. This news seemed to have been passed to Davis in Montgomery, Alabama, with Davis making the decision to compel the fort's surrender before Lincoln's ships arrived.

"This duty fell to Beauregard who had been given command of the siege by Davis. Ironically, now remember, General P. T. Beauregard had previously been a protégé of Anderson.

"On April 11, Beauregard sent an aide to demand the fort's surrender.

"Anderson refused. Further discussions, running long after midnight, failed to resolve the situation. At four thirty in the morning on April 12, a single mortar round burst over Fort Sumter signaling the other harbor forts to open fire. Anderson did not reply until seven o'clock in the morning, when Captain Abner Doubleday fired the first shot for the Union. After thirty-four hours of bombardment, with his ammunition almost exhausted, Anderson surrendered the fort."

Jamie and Josiah looked about the room; you could hear a pin drop. "Guess they thought ol' Lincoln started the war." Josiah whispered in his ear and leaned back in his chair. Smoke from his stogy curling up to join the gray-blue cloud that hung over the room.

The speaker resumed; "In response to the attack on Fort Sumter, Lincoln issued a call for seventy-five thousand, that's right, seventy-five thousand, ninety-day volunteers to put the rebellion down and ordered the U.S. Navy to blockade all the Southern ports. Then the Northern states readily sent troops, but those states in the upper South hesitated. Unwilling to fight fellow Southerners, the states of Virginia, Arkansas, Tennessee, and North Carolina opted to secede and joined the Confederacy. In response, the capital was moved from Montgomery, Alabama, to Richmond, Virginia.

"On April 19, 1861, the first Union troops arrived in Baltimore, Maryland, on their way to Washington. While marching from one train station to another, they were attacked by a pro-Southern mob. In the riot that ensued, twelve civilians and four soldiers were killed. To pacify the city, protect Washington, and ensure that Maryland remained in the Union, Lincoln declared martial law in the state and sent troops.

"Next, the commanding general of the U.S. Army, Winfield Scott, used the Anaconda Plan. It was designed to end the conflict as quickly and bloodlessly as possible. Scott called for the blockade of Southern ports, capture of the vital Mississippi River to split the Confederacy in two, as well as advised against a direct attack on Richmond. Thoroughly mocked by the press, most elements of the plan were implemented. It looks as though that has been effective, we shall see."

Once again, Jamie looked at Josiah. Surprised by the look of surprise on his face. So…there were things he too was not privy to. Jamie listened intently. The speaker was succinct and precise.

"As troops gathered in Washington, Lincoln appointed Irvin McDowell to organize them into the Army of Northeastern Virginia. Brigadier General McDowell was concerned about his men's inexperience, still he was forced to advance south due to growing political pressure and the impending expiration of the volunteers' enlistments. Moving with twenty-eight thousand men, McDowell planned to attack a twenty-one thousand man Confederate army under Beauregard near Manassas Junction. This was to be supported by Major General Robert Patterson who was to march against an eighty-nine hundred man Confederate force commanded by General Joseph Johnston in the western part of the state.

"McDowell moved forward and attacked Beauregard. His troops succeeded in breaking the Confederate line and forcing them to fall back on their reserves. Rallying around Stonewall Jackson's Virginia Brigade, the Confederates stopped the retreat and, with the addition of fresh troops, turned the tide of the battle, routing McDowell's army and forcing them to flee back to Washington.

"Casualties for the battle were…"

Jamie watched as the speaker referred to his notes, heard the catch in his voice as he continued, "Two thousand, eight hundred, and ninety six, nearly five hundred dead, over a thousand wounded, and I am sad to say, thirteen hundred and twelve captured, for our Union Army, and our intelligence says, nine hundred eighty two, some four hundred dead, for the Confederates, we took no prisoners."

He paused and looked about the room. "Now, gentlemen, this brings you up to date with how we have arrived at this point in a war that we neither look forward to or anticipated. However, here we are some nine months later, and I believe we are in for the long haul. President Lincoln asks that you represent your country with pride and honor whenever possible. They fired the first shot. We shall indeed fire the last."

"Major General James Martin Prescott, your orders are here in this envelope, as well as a roster of your men. Good luck."

For Mack and Jamie, *it had begun.*

Love at First Sight

Elisabeth hated this emotional turmoil that seemed to go on within her. Her heart felt heavy and she seemed engulfed in sadness... *Lord how she missed Jamie!*

The holidays loomed ahead, and all she saw was darkness. Thoughts of last Christmas played out in her mind, the Christmases of her childhood, the linen laid crisp and white on the Jupe table, sterling glistened and china sparkled, the crystal as it glittered beneath the gas lighting of the exquisite chandelier that hung high above the table, laughter and anticipation of all that were present could be heard. The Christmas tree that sat within the bay windows of the parlor. The fragrance of turkey roasting in the oven, pies set about the large wooden table that sat in the warmth of the kitchen. Mama beckoning them "Come..." Papa calling for silence, as he said the blessing.

It seemed as if her life had fractured. She looked about her and wondered at what had happened. The oak table sat within the kitchen, a room she lived in, cooked, and ate her meals in, sleeping but a few feet away. Alone, without family or friends... *or her husband.* Choices she had made had prompted this and the grief engulfed her once again. Was this how she was intended to spend her life? To what purpose did this...this *despair* promote? If someone had told her with assurance that she would be spending her days thus, would she have done it? It seemed unlikely. Yet when she thought of the loveless situation of her childhood friend in Philadelphia; Prudence, she thought, *I could not bear such as that.*

She *would* do it again, just for the time she had had with him. Indeed she must be daft. *Lord, let this feeling of remorse pass*, she prayed. Knowing it was not good for the child she carried within her.

Strange how life seemed to make its own rules as you went along. The most trivial of decisions, of emotions—changing your entire future. *Of course*, now she knew that those decisions had been made previously—without the interference of emotions. Her reaction was the testament to her acknowledgment, her understanding, indeed her acceptance. Again her reverie began.

She heard Mama's voice as she had looked up from the blessing on that Christmas not so many years gone by, and for the first time could see what a beauty her mama was. And Grandmère, in many ways, they looked similar, although Elisabeth thought Grandmère had the greater beauty, for she was peaceful, content. Her eyes sparkled within the depths of them, as if she held a secret. What must that secret be? She could read Grandmère's journal, perhaps the secret lie within.

The journal still lay in the trunk, not ten feet from her, but... but what? What if it brought only more sadness, more loneliness? More fear of the future.

She thought of the first time she had seen Jamie, and her heart trilled. As she thought of that evening, she closed her eyes and allowed herself to become immersed in past sensation. *She could hear the chamber music as it drifted up the winding staircase. Smell the fragrance of women's perfumes, of foods from the kitchen. See the glint of light that seemed to set everything it touched aglow.* The evening was early and they, the children, had been instructed to stay within their rooms, as Mama and Papa were to be entertaining dignitary that evening.

Prudence had been allowed to stay the night with her, but that was not enough; Elisabeth had desperately wished to join the party.

The women had been dressed in lavish gowns, jewels dripped from their ears and wrists, diamonds sparkled that lay upon unblemished skin next to their throats. The rustle of crinolines, silks, and satins could be heard above the soft, melodious chamber music.

She could once more smell the wafting of the cigar smoke as the men wandered to and fro from the library where Papa had escorted them to discuss business and plans for the nation's future.

She remembered now Grandmère's face as she had spied Elisabeth and Prudence as they stood on the mezzanine of the stairs, her ivory skin clear, the fine lines of old age that threatened to mar her youthful beauty, the threads of silver that shot through the ebony of her hair, hair that was piled high and elegantly upon her head and adorned with a Spanish comb set in diamonds. She remembered the twinkle in Grandmères eyes, those green, flashing eyes that looked up into Elisabeth's own. Eyes that she had inherited from Grandmère.

Papa's eyes were round and small, intelligent, beady eyes, although not without humor, simply clever and understanding. Sometimes Elisabeth thought he had looked as if he might cry, and she remembered how frightened that had made her, if Papa were indeed to cry, her entire world would have been in jeopardy.

Mama's eyes were most often harsh, and the light within them withheld, as if she, too, had a secret she kept, a secret not nearly as wonderful as that of Grandmère's.

Now within her small rough-hewn home, Grandmère's image loomed before her once again, the sounds of the music from her childhood echoed in her heart and her mind. How she had wished to join in the festivities. She had been fourteen years old and wished desperately to go downstairs.

She had watched with interest as her parents friends had filtered into the foyer, watched as Gilles had taken their cloaks, for it was early spring and the evenings were chilled. There was to be only hors d'oeuvres, no seated table, only drinks and finger foods were to be served.

She had sat with her mama and Grandmère as they prepared for the party, going over the guest list, the grocer's list, the arrangement for the flowers. She knew who had responded and those that Papa was most desirous of speaking with. She had not been privy as to what this party was about or why he wished so desperately to speak to these gentlemen, but she remembered thinking instinctively that it was concerning the political affairs of the city, perhaps that of the nation. She felt now the feelings of frustration she had felt at the time. Thwarted that no one had taken her seriously enough to answer her questions.

Letting the long-ago incident recede within her memory, she rose now from the rocking chair and pulled her burgeoning body to a full stand, her back arching in an attempt to stretch her body to its full height. She patted her stomach and felt the stirrings of the child. Lying the knitting to the side on the small stool; perhaps a cup of tea. *She was lonely.* She had had no visitors in some time and knew full well that with the weather so dastardly and the wind howling as it if it would indeed blow down the house, she would not receive them on this night.

The huge fireplace crackled with warmth and light, the candles sat now within the hurricane lamps that gave off a more adequate light. As she strode to the flatiron stove, she looked at the wall lined with ammunition and weapons.

Instinctively, she felt for the knife that she carried strapped to her inner thigh. It had become a part of her. She had learned the hard way.

She smiled at this, what in the world had she learned the easy way…to love…from Grandmère and Papa, she had learned to love.

The knife had saved her life more than once… She pushed those thoughts from her mind. Better to be sad than terrified. Although she held no concern for the attack of the Indians, not that it could not happen, but Jamie had made friends with all of the neighboring tribes. They had food this early in the season, though the weather *was dreadful*; she couldn't remember a storm this bad since they had arrived here in Montana.

She poured the tea into the china of the teacup and could hear Jamie's teasing laughter at the audacity of china in a place so rugged and wild. Tin cups hung on hooks above the stove, but very seldom did Elisabeth opt to use one. Her china was the only elegance offered here in this untamed land.

She stood now in the center of the room, looking out the windows at the snow that fell, not great lacy flakes of snow, but ice pellets that pinged when they hit the windows, streaks of them that came in torrents on the wind.

She thought of Trésor and Mercy in the barn, along with the other animals, wondering if she had secured the entrance, thinking of Charlie; he would have gone behind her and checked, making certain all of the animals were safe.

Did Mercy long for Danny as she longed for Jamie?

Smiling, she pulled her shawl closer about her shoulders and went to sit down, the faded calico of her dress floating around her ankles, her new boots, although somewhat feminine, could not compare to the white kidskin of those she had left her papa's home in. She sat down and placed the teacup and saucer on the stool and took up her knitting once more. Would she indeed have clothing enough for this child? The shoes and the child causing her to think of Eleanor. Not necessarily a better place for her mind to go.

The thought of *boots* made her laugh out loud, as she recalled Eleanor's insistence that she discard her city footwear for boots that, at the time, Elisabeth thought to be an abomination! *Thank God for Eleanor.* She imagined herself walking all the way on the Oregon Trail in her white kidskin boots. Eleanor... *Lord, help me to mend that...* She proceeded with her knitting once more, now able to do so without thinking—knit one, purl two... Thanks to Ma and Ilene. Wondering how many of these soakers this child would need. Grateful for all of the lovely things Mama and Grandmère had sent.

The steady clicking of the knitting needles, mesmerizing in the quiet. What was Jamie doing? Was he with Josiah? Was someone shooting at him? Was he thinking of her? She felt the swelling of her heart and the lump rise in her throat. *Lord, please keep him safe.*

She stood and threw another log on the fire and sat again to resume her knitting.

The cacophony of voices rose in her memories once more. She could envision her grandmère's hand, long and slender, the sparkle of diamonds played on the rings on her fingers, her nails buffed and manicured, holding the crystal of Waterford in her hand, the amber liquid catching the light as well. She recalled the comments of her mama concerning Grandmère's propensity to consume strong drink. She smiled now at the thought—of Grandmère's voice, as she had said, "Yes, dear, I shall remember." *The wink that had followed.*

In her mind, she stood once more on the lustrous flooring and grand carpets of her parents' winding stairs, waiting as Gilles opened the door to admit the guests.

She remembered now; it had been his cousin he had come with, William Hickling Prescott, however, he had seemed to know everyone there. Patting men of great importance on the back, shaking hands with others of wealth and position… She had stood as if in a trance as he had looked up at her.

His suit of clothing, impeccable, his vest, visible with the gold of a watch fob, as he handed off his overcoat to Gilles, his wide shoulders and narrow bottom revealed. He towered over Gilles, whom she thought to be a big man, Gilles being as tall as Papa. The stranger's hair was thick, black as her own; a lock of hair fell across his forehead, the sideburns long and impeccably altered at the strong jawline, his lips, full and sensuous, his eyes the color of jewelry her mama often wore—amber, she had thought, amber, he has *amber* eyes.

She remembered having placed one hand to lie upon Prudence's own. A slight "Oh!" had escaped her mouth, and Prudence had looked at her, following her gaze as her eyes had rested on the most beautiful man she had ever seen. She remembered now Grandmère's look as it flew from hers to the man that had entered the foyer. She felt again the warm glow that had seemed to light within her as this man—this mortal being first had felt her eyes upon him *and looked up at her.*

He had stood still for a long moment in time. People around him speaking to him, shaking his hand, and still he had gazed *at her.* All the while Grandmère had looked on—taking a long pull on the amber liquid in her glass, Grandmère had turned to the strikingly handsome man, extending her hand to him. Without awareness, Elisabeth had seemed to float down the stairs, the silk of her dress making a soft rustle, the cream of her bosoms turning to a sheen of pink, the onyx of her hair drifting in long soft curls about her face. She thought again of Prudence, her bosom friend, having whispered, "Elisabeth, you shall surely be in grave complaint! Come back, Elisabeth!" She had had no intent of going back, whatever the punishment.

"*Madame la, je suis plus s'il vous plaît faire votre connaissance.*" This exquisite man was speaking French to Grandmère. How would he know?

As she had stood before him, the strangest sensation had enveloped them. It seemed there was not another person in the large expanse of her papa's house.

Her grandmère had turned and watched as the handsome man bowed before Elisabeth, taken her hand, and kissed it. She could still feel the brush of his lips. The heat on her hand from the tenderness of his touch. "James Martin Prescott, mademoiselle, *je serai toujours à votre service*—I shall be forever at your service."

She smiled at the memory, "*Forever* to be sure." Sending a prayer of thanks to the heavens. *For better or worse, for richer or poorer...but not to obey.*

My, how her life had changed, realizing she would have it no other way.

Joy

*L*ord, *I give thanks that these missives bring with them only joy and peace.* She thought of the command in Proverbs: 18:21, "Death and life are but in the power of the tongue." She must not fear, there was no need. Jamie would return; her child would be born strong, healthy, and of sound mind.

Ashamed, she thought, *and beautiful.* She knew it to be sinful, but beauty was something a woman needed to survive in this world. She laughed in spite of herself. Beauty out here in the wilds of the Western territories was perhaps wasted. Sadly, her child would likely never see the likes of Paris, or Vienna, or London, perhaps not even New York City.

However, she would have never thought to be here within the majestic nature of Montana either, or to have ridden a horse, or been privy to rites of passage for a young Indian male. Or to have killed one; for a brief moment, she could feel the weight of his body…smell the bear grease that covered it. *The taste of his blood as she had sunk her teeth into his hand, his ballocks—oh, Lord! Quite disgusting!* In truth, it had not been that many months ago, perhaps…perhaps, she would think of that no more.

My, her mind did wander.

Perhaps her child would experience ever so many things. Lord, let them be pleasant experiences.

She looked at the lovely layette within the package from Grandmère and Mama and her heart swelled in gratitude. She had sensed when she had held the small clothing that which her mother had made and that made by Grandmère.

Thank you, Lord. Mama was no longer so angry with her.

She felt she owed that in part to Papa as well as to Grand-mère. Mama was wont to hold a grudge. *Ah, perhaps* that was where Samuel came by his anger. Narcissistic, Jamie had termed him, for everything was a reflection of his own desires. *She* thought it to be a lack of self-esteem. That one would consider others to judge you by what a member of your family did…*seemed…* Tsk, she truly must not dwell on that.

Should she read the letter now? She needed to rest. Should the contents upset her—she would have no rest. She smiled, rather a quandary to say the least, for should she not read them, she would lie awake all night, her imagination running havoc in her mind.

She lifted the fine parchment from the pile of infant's clothing. The writing neat and concise. Fluid. She was momentarily taken aback, she would have thought her mama's writing to be stilted and firm.

> *Dear Elisabeth,*
>
> *We, your papa and I are readying ourselves for a trip to Paris, as Jeremiah is studying at Clifton in England and Samuel has been accepted at Oxford.*
>
> *We are quite well and look forward to seeing friends and acquaintances on the Continent, as we have not been in nearly two years.*
>
> *I hope this finds you well and shall write upon our return.*
>
> *Love,*
> *Mama*

Oh dear, the letter fluttered to lie once more within the small clothing. Not *once* did she make mention of the baby to come. She would never understand her mother! Would she? Perhaps when she had children of her own… *I shall not let this upset me.*

I shall not! She did write, and she made effects for my child, I know she did.

She wished to stomp her foot she was so very angry—*hurt* was more the truth of it. She carefully folded the letter and reached for the next. Grandmère's letter.

*Ma petite fille chérie,
Mon excitation…*

The letter was in French—oh, how it filled her heart to see it so.

For the birth of your child is so near the surface of my heart, I cannot contain it. Your mama and I have made these few items of clothing. I know I have sent so many, but I cannot seem to stop sewing the small things. Your mama has knitted all the soakers and buntings, the small batiste frocks and the embroidery you know I have done.

As you will know, your mama and papa and brothers are to be gone, so I shall go to visit my sister in New York for the remainder of the winter. Your great-aunt Eva and her husband Jules have insisted and promised a plethora of activities. I have enclosed their address so that you may post letters there, as I wish to know at the moment the child is here and you are safe, perhaps Western Union would be a more expedient delivery.

What do you intend to name her? Her, I feel it shall be a girl, is that as you feel as well? As you see I have many pink roses on the tiny kits.

I will not ask of the provisions you have made for the birth, as I do not wish to be overly concerned. The birthing of a child is a natural event and you shall be fine.

The child shall be a joy to you… As with all joys, there shall be some sorrow. Mais oui, we might not know what joy was, should there be no sorrow.

What of your Jamie, what do you hear from him? Enfant, do not be fearful. Pray for him in earnest and know that all is as it should be.

I read in the papers of Lincoln, I daresay I have great admiration for the man, but one never knows. The paper reported that he said, "What constitutes the bulwark of our liberty and independence is not the guns of our war steamers or the strength of our gallant army. Our reliance is in the love of liberty, which God has planted in our bosoms. Our defense is in the preservation of the spirit which prizes liberty as the heritage of all men in all lands everywhere. Familiarize yourself with the chains of bondage and you are preparing your own limbs to wear them."

I feel certain that to be true, I see it in my own country. Most certainly in a dissimilar concept, but I must say I am quite proud that your husband has the courage of his convictions, and harbors such profound patriotism.

My darling, stay well, and above all, keep your mind on the path of right. For within the mind of man, lies his life. I laugh, this is a "proverb" of your grandmère. While in New York, I shall shop for fabric for clothing for you. Let me know should you have a preference. Or is it footwear you are in need of? Toiletries?

Avec tout l'amour dans mon cœur.

Votre,
Grandmère

Tears of joy shimmered in the firelight upon Elisabeth's face. She struggled to push the sobbing back, for it was joy she felt, not grief, although the grief of not having Grandmère here was nearly unbearable. How very kind she was. How insightful. She placed the letter within the pocket of her apron. She would give the address of Aunt Eva to Petra. She was certain Petra would be happy to send by Western Union, the message of her child's birth.

Footwear...she smiled, if only her grandmère could see her *footwear!*

Toiletries, something other than lye soap, would be divine.

Having eaten and made tea, stoking the fire, she once more sat at the table. She had saved the best for last. At least that was her intention. She read the return address, one from the "United

States Army Headquarters"—Lord! Her heart stopped. Would they...surely not in the post. *O, Lord!*

She reached for the letter opener, Grandmères' words still fresh within her heart.

It was money. A draft on the Bank of New York, made out to Mrs. James Prescott, in the amount of eighteen hundred dollars. Her heart fluttered.

What if he had been killed... Her hand shook as she quickly read the fine print on the attachment: "In lieu of three months of active service." Oh my, what a great deal of money. Quite suddenly, she remembered Jamie saying that "volunteers were required to serve only three months." She quickly reached for the last of the letters. *Oh dear me, it was from General Josiah Piedmont.* Oh, Lord, bless this!

She fought the urge to swoon—certainly she was overreacting. She tore at the letter. Quickly putting it down, she went to the small cupboard near the stove, taking the bottle from the shelving. Lifting it to her lips, she drank directly from the bottle—the whiskey hot and burning. She set it down, thought better of it and took another long drink. She sincerely wished it not be necessary, but she had not ever received correspondence from Josiah; *it more than terrified her.* With shaking hands she tore at the envelope.

> *My dearest Lizzie,*
>
> *Yes, I know, Elisabeth it is... I am laughing, as I can see the flashings of your lovely eyes...*
>
> *Your husband is en route as you are reading this and shall be there forthwith. I feel certain I see your lovely smile. I am enclosing but a mere poem from him...ah, the romanticism of the man.*
>
> *Give my regards to Mrs. Sullivan and the rest of those who abide there in St. Helena.*
>
> *We are well and on our way to victory! Tell the child "Uncle Josiah" will see her one day.*

She laughed at the man and the care with which the letter imbued within her. What a wonderful man he was, *and* his regards to Mrs. Sullivan, would not that be the most delightful occasion but for them to marry. But then Sally Susanne presently possessed a husband. Amiss, it was. Josiah and Sally would be perfect together. She could not wait to tell Sally. She giggled and quickly looked within the pages for Jamie's poem.

> *O tell her Swallow, that thy brood is flown:*
> *Say to her, I do but wanton in the South,*
> *But in the North long since my nest is made.*

The sixth verse of "O, Swallow, Tennyson"—Oh, Jamie, how I miss you.

She reached for the letter from Josiah. When had he written it? Where had Jamie begun his journey? Would he ride the train? Certainly he and Danny would not have to ride in this weather all the way to Montana!

Oh dear! Was he alone? Would Mack come home with him? None of it mattered. Soon she would see him. *Thank you, Lord, thank you!*

She ran for the calendar and her geography books. What a miraculous day!

She patted the child within her. "Your papa is coming home!"

Now she would never be able to sleep.

The Cradle

The week had been tumultuous with activity. She rose early each morning to milk, to gather eggs, each time thinking of Maggie, wondering as she did so what Maggie was doing. The buck-toothed, pigtailed little girl would be nearly fifteen years of age now. She smiled at the thought of her, yet her heart fluttered with longing. She would never again see her. Thoughts of Maggie riding Mercy and the tale of Mack's "Queen o' the littl'uns" rose in her mind. How often on the trail here had the young, happy child offered to milk that "ole' cow," or "gather them eggs," for a ride on Mercy, knowing Elisabeth hated both chores. In point of fact, Elisabeth had declared *she would never do them again once they arrived at their destination*…strange how life…

She was startled by the sound of her name.

"Miz Prescott, ma'am?" Charlie stood just inside the barn. "Sorry, ma'am, didn't mean to startle ya, jus' thought I'd be bringin' ya up ta date… Everything's fine out in the pasture. Got a couple heifer's 'bout ta give birth…" He looked at her and laughed.

Elisabeth looked at this man who had been her saving grace—this man whom Josiah had had profound faith in—this man who had chosen to stay in Montana with her and Jamie. He was tall and lean, broad of shoulder, narrow of hip, his face long and craggy with a wide smile, laughter that lay in his eyes, crinkling them at their edges. "Charlie Wardle, are you laughing at me? I do look frightful, I know."

"No, ma'am. Jus' 'bout to pop is all." He laughed at her again. "'Kin I hep ya? Thought I'd be coming ta the house ta see ya…"

"What? Is something wrong?"

"No, ma'am. Jus'…well, come on now. Give me those things there, and come on. I got somethin' ta show ya."

She looked at him; lo and behold, she thought he looked as if he was about to burst with excitement. "Yes, of course, I am nearly finished. Here, take the milk and I shall bring the eggs."

"Yes, ma'am. I done shoveled the path. Done dropped some more thet *white stuff* in the night." Chuckling, he described the events of snowfall, virtually every hour during the winter months.

"It certainly did that." She looked at him as they walked out of the barn.

Laughter filled his eyes, and he continued to smile as they walked toward the house. The flicker of firelight came from the cabin; the windows filled with a soft golden glow. Smoke rose from the stone chimney in wisps of gray against the vanilla morning sky—the cradle of the moon still visible.

"Mighty prutty mornin'."

"It is lovely. Charlie what have you been up to?"

"I'm about ta show ya, ma'am."

She had picked up his enthusiasm, and giggling, she hung onto his arm as she lumbered toward the house. "I apologize, Charlie, seems I am quite ungraceful in my present condition."

He patted her hand. "Ya jus' fine, Miz Prescott."

Charlie opened the door of her home and stood back from the entrance, his face filled with delight! The most beautiful cradle she had ever seen sat before the great fireplace. She was stunned to nearly dropping her basket full of eggs. Her hand flew to her mouth. "Oh, Charlie! Oh, Charlie, why, why, I must say I am quite overwhelmed. It is lovely! Oh, Charlie." The tears came unexpectedly, the sobs coming in great gulps. "Oh, Charlie, did you make this? It is exquisite. How did you make it so dark?"

"Acorns, blackberries, vinegar, been workin' on it some time. 'Fraid fer a while wouldn't have it done in time fer…fer…"

For a brief moment, she thought he looked quite embarrassed. She stood staring at the beautiful cradle, the rockers slowly moving back and forth as he reached down and touched it. It was quite large, reaching her waist; the wood shown in the firelight with the rich color of gold that shown through the dark of the dye. "I…I…I just don't know what to say. Why, Charlie, it is the most divine thing I have ever seen. The child will be able to sleep in there for a very long time."

"Yes, ma'am, could put two young un's in there."

"Oh, Charlie, thank you!" She reached up and hugged him, her expanded body having to hold him at arm's length.

"Ah, shucks, ain't nuthin'. Just knowed Jamie wouldn't have the time. I liked doin' it. Where ya want it? I gotta git back out there, see to the other fellas, they're good men, jus' need a boot on occasion. Ya kin call me if ya need me. I know it's gettin' close now." That said, he turned and left, pulling the door shut after him.

Her emotions so close to the surface she found she had to sit down. Tears overwhelmed her. *The waiting for Jamie, fretting over him—the fear of the birth, Lord forgive me. I am frightened at the prospect of delivering this child!*

The excitement to have a child, the fear as to if she would be a good mother, the loneliness, a strange isolation, as if it were her against the world. All the kindness from Ma, from Petra, Sally Susanne, her family. Jamie coming home, and *now Charlie*. She had so very much to be grateful for. All this emotion was quite overwhelming; she had not the most remote idea as how to deal with it. She simply hated the fearfulness, the lack of control that lay within her present state of mind.

There was naught she could do about the birthing of the child, that indeed was in the hands of the Lord, but she could put her mind to rest—if she weren't so worried about Jamie. That would indeed help, *and Eleanor*. Dear Eleanor seemed to be a constant source of concern and, yes, frustration.

One thing she could do, she would ask Charlie to take her to see Ilene; perhaps she had heard from Mack and had more information than a poem. She shook her head—*Jamie!*

She sat a little straighter and thought, *I shall go to see Eleanor, and perhaps we can mend our differences before the child comes.*

The child. Jesse? Sylvia? Sophia? And if she was wrong and this child be a boy, he would be named after Jamie.

She wiped the tears from her face and stroked the wood of the cradle; it rocked slowly, and she could feel the care with which Charlie had made it.

Yes, that was what she wished to do. She stood and waddled to the door and, opening it, shouted for Charlie. More quickly that she thought possible, he stood in front of her.

"Are ya all right?" He looked stunned, his hat in his hand, his great coat flapping in the breeze.

"Yes. Yes, of course. I do apologize…you look quite frightened." She laughed as he looked at her quite sheepishly.

"Thought I might be birthin' thet young un', plum scaret the shit otta me. Sorry, ma'am."

She giggled. "It is quite all right. I just wondered if you would take me in the wagon today to visit Mrs. MacKenzie and Eleanor? I would drive myself…you know I would…"

"No, ma'am, you won't be drivin' yurself, not now."

"As soon as your chores are done then?"

"Yes, ma'am." As he turned and walked away, she heard him mutter. "Hells bells! Women!"

Quickly, she readied herself to go calling. Scrubbing her face with sugar, a commodity that was costly, yet it was an indulgence she found necessary. She ever so generously applied the lard she had mixed with lavender for a face cream. *She sincerely hoped Grandmère would send her toiletries.* She rinsed her face and brushed out her long ebony tresses. Lord, what she would give for a proper bath, her mind wandering to the copper tub in the home of Henrietta King, just as quickly to that of Mercy. She must curry her when she returned, that and Trésor as well. Poor darlings had suffered some loneliness as well, her present condition leaving Mercy to simply pass her days in solitude, braving the cold of winter's pastures. Perhaps she thought it to be a holiday of sorts.

Her frock! What was to be done of that? Her customary trousers having long been replaced by the prairie dresses. Would she ever again be returned to her diminutive size? Her breasts now secreting a substance Petra proclaimed a natural occurrence—*dear me*. She smoothed out the dress, finding it rose near to her shins in the front, exposing her woolen stockings and her despicable footwear. Well, there was nothing to be done of that. Her present condition warranted many a forgiveness. Peering at her reflection in the mirror, she was somewhat heartened. Her skin, the same ivory clearness, her eyes alight now, the green, bold, and dazzling with the black of thick lashes that surrounded them. She smiled, pleased by her smile, wide and full, her teeth white and even.

She reached for the pearl earrings Jamie had bought her and thought better of it. Ilene certainly cared not that she had lovely earrings. Eleanor… Eleanor, however, would be miffed by the mere fact that she possessed them.

She would need to take *something* if she were to call. She made excellent bread—thanks to Ma, she would take that. She thought of her fit of despair last winter and its many causes; *one*, that she did not possess the ability to make bread. She thought of Jamie, as he petted her and in consolation had prepared food of eggs and potatoes for her. The only time she could remember he had cooked for her. She smiled. *She knew how frightened he had been.*

She heard the roll of wagon wheels as they approached the house and scurried to the door.

"Ready, ma'am?" Charlie stood waiting to help her down the steps and into the wagon. "Ya sure you want ta do this?"

"I am. I shall feel so much the better for it."

"The MacKenzie place then?"

"Yes, although…"

"You wanna go to Joseph's first?"

She made no answer. She was uncertain as which would be the better, to know of Jamie prior to visiting with the tetchy Eleanor, or to see Eleanor and get it done with and talk to the peaceful, happy Ilene afterward.

"Ma'am…?"

"I truly do not know, I must confess to having great trepidation concerning a visit with Eleanor…"

Charlie chuckled softly… "No need, Miz Prescott, ya can't be pussy footin' about the likes of such as thet. Too, don't believe she can help herself, an fer the most part, if ya can't help yourself well, ain't much anyone else can do for ya, an'…we know she don't listen. Sorry, ma'am."

Elisabeth found she felt not the least uncomfortable speaking with him concerning things that would be a private family matter at her families home in the east. After all, he had known Eleanor as long as she had; she suspected he held a far more objective viewpoint concerning her. *Perchance concerning Elisabeth herself.* She smiled. "No, Charlie, you are right, and yet I know I am often cause for concern—my enthusiasm, my…how would you refer to it, Charlie? Often, I am thoughtless, to say the least, which has never been my intention, *supercilious*, I believe Eleanor would term it. I seem to respond with intuitiveness…that is as Mrs. Sullivan terms it. I must say, I have hurt feelings, and I am grievous, concerning this…" She paused, waiting for what? A response she did not receive, for he made none.

The reins of the horses held within his gloved hands, the Western hat pulled tightly on his head, the scarf and jacket obscuring any view she might have of him.

"I would simply wish to make amends with Eleanor. She is my sister-in-law, and I, I care for Joseph…"

His eyes continued to look straight ahead. His breath visible in the freezing air. "Don't believe you'll accomplish such as that. But gowan do what ya must. She's not so forgiving, that one. I know it's not my place, but if she don't forgive a man the likes of Joseph Prescott, she'll not be forgiving the likes of someone such as yourself. She sees the kindness in you, ma'am, the joy of life, yur lack of fear. The wantin' in ya to live your life fully. Guess if ya never experienced it, ya don't see it the same way, but…"

She waited, watching the snow as it licked around the hooves of the trotting horses, their soft snorting, causing the puffs of air from their nostrils to cloud in wisps of vapor. The earth was silent. She watched as a mountain lion crouched near the grove of evergreens, a fox, as it pranced lightly across the snow. She breathed deeply of the cleanliness—the crispness of it.

"So what's it to be, Miz Prescott, myself now, I always clean the shit up first. Thet away you got a clean path, don't go trackin' it all over. Sorry 'bout the cursin'."

"Yes." She smiled and reached with her gloved hand to pat him on the leg. "So it is, Charlie, we shall see Eleanor first."

She rapped upon the door. Hearing no response, she lifted the latch and pushed it open. Eleanor sat at the table, a young Indian girl sat across from her. She was not surprised to see Eleanor clothed in Indian fashion and was most grateful to find she wore her spectacles. "Good morning, Eleanor, I thought I would call on you, see how you were fairing."

"Elisabeth…my—*you are* rather large!"

"Yes, yes, well, it is near my time. May I sit?"

"Of course." Eleanor spoke to the young Indian maid in a language Elisabeth had learned little of, remembering the week they had spent with the Indians. The young Indian girl rose and left the small cabin.

"Would you like some tea?"

"Yes, if it is no trouble, that would be quite nice."

"It is bitter cold out there, did you ride all the way here?"

"No, no." Elisabeth laughed. "I cannot even lift my leg to put my foot in the stirrups."

"I can see that. You must miss it."

"I do at that! However, I shall soon resume all those things." She smiled, looking around at the polished floors and the table. The bed that was of pine logs in the corner of the room. A small fire burned in the fireplace. A small shelf cluttered with dirty dishes the only indication of disorder. "Your home is lovely, Eleanor. How do you keep it so clean?" Eleanor smiled and turned from the making of the tea. Her body slight, she had never regained the overfed look that Elisabeth had seen upon first meeting her. The softness of the Indian garments fell from her shoulders to lay gently above the high leggings of the moccasins on her feet.

"Joseph does the cleaning, obsessive about it to my way of thinking. 'Cleanliness is next to godliness,' he says. A waste of time, what with the snow and mud he brings in."

"How is Joseph?"

"He's fine. Joseph is always fine." For a small instant, one could see a flicker of light dance in her eyes. She *did* still love Joseph! Elisabeth was grateful for that. "Tell me, Elisabeth, what brings you all the way up here in your condition?"

Well, that, indeed, was straight to the point. She thought she saw a menacing look from Eleanor, her mind reaching for some reassurances within her faith, within the words Sally Susanne had taught her. Something, anything that would endeavor to give her the strength to go on. She sat at the table, her small hands folded as if in prayer, as Eleanor set the steaming cup of tea before her. "I, clearly…" She was near stuttering. *Lord, help me.* "Eleanor…"

Eleanor's hand rose as she sat down in the chair at the opposite side of the table. "Stop, I don't wish to hear anything you have to say."

"Eleanor, why? I...I don't understand, what have I done that offends you so, if you could but tell me, I do wish to apologize."

"I *do not* need apologies, from you or anyone else for that matter. I know what you all think—even Joseph! Ma—*your precious Sally Susanne!*" Her manner and tone was indeed *vehement*. "They—*you*... all think I am *crazy*, plum *touched in the head*, as my pa would term it."

"Eleanor, I don't..."

"Yes, you do!" She now leaned across the table, her black eyes shot with anger, the spectacles making them seem much larger than they were. "You have screamed at me! You would have taken my child from me! You have embarrassed me in front of the entire wagon train. You've never given me credit for what I've done for you! *Why without me, you would be lost!* Was it not *I* that provided you with the information you so sorely needed to make this trip, *you and your fancy clothes, your uppity ways...*" She stammered and stuttered, rising from the chair so rapidly it tottered.

Elisabeth was aware that her mouth was agape, aware that Eleanor's voice never rose nor faltered, only continued in a monotone of intensity. Tears spilled from her own eyes, and she breathed deeply, seeking the strength to endure this...*this...* She said nothing, and Eleanor went on.

"You took my stove! You took away the medicine I needed to endure the death of my children!"

"I never...!"

"Shut up, Elisabeth! I am sick to death of your *holier than thou* speeches to me!" The heavy, thick braid swung mightily from the back of Eleanor's head as she spun toward the door.

"Eleanor, you musn't... *Eleanor, you must not think...*" Elisabeth found her own voice to be pleading.

"What do you know of life, Elisabeth? What of your treatment of Agnes? *She is my friend!*"

"But, Eleanor—"

Once again Eleanor turned and walked to where Elisabeth sat. Her arms folded in defiance. "Don't! Elisabeth! I have finally said what I have wished to say. Joseph, in his blindness, loves you, even *admires you.*" The words spit from her mouth. "He is James's brother, and I love him. He is all I have in this world, and he…" Quite suddenly, she stopped, midsentence, emotion other than anger now visible upon her face.

Elisabeth reached deep within her heart searching for something that would heal this relationship. *Lord, please.* She stood and reached out to lay her hand on Eleanor's, surprised Eleanor did not pull her own hand away.

"Eleanor, I…I…" she found it difficult to say the words, as they, too, she feared, would be misunderstood. "Eleanor, I love you, I care very much for both you and Joseph. Please believe that anything I did, I did because of that. I *do know* how very much you helped me, and I shall always feel tremendous grief over the children you have lost."

"Is that why you came here? To show me you are with child."

Anger now billowed within Elisabeth. She looked at the cooling tea, not wanting for Eleanor to see the frustration and near rage in her eyes. "Please, Eleanor, for the sake of our husbands—for the sake of our children…"

"I have no children, Elisabeth." Her black eyes once more seethed with fury.

"Eleanor, I care for you. We *all* care for you, can we let this go and be friends once more. *Please* what do you wish of me?"

"Nothing, Elisabeth. Nothing."

Elisabeth heard the sound of the door, a gust of wind that made the fire flicker.

"Elisabeth! I'll be damned. I am so happy to see you. What do you hear of that fella? My brother, the *general*, is it?" Joseph's voice filled with teasing laughter.

It took seconds to gather herself. "Oh, Joseph, you look wonderful! He's…he's coming home. I, Charlie—is taking me to see Ilene. I am uncertain if Mack is with him, but…"

Eleanor walked to stand beside the massive, effusive Joseph. She placed her arm around his waist, her head coming only to that of his shoulder. "She came to apologize, Joseph. What do you think of that?"

Elisabeth was thunderstruck… From the corner of her eye, she saw Charlie as he stood near the door.

"*What? Elisabeth? For what?* You have nothing to apologize for…not ever!" He pulled away from Eleanor and reached down and kissed Elisabeth on the cheek. "I surely wouldn't have known what to do without you. Eleanor would have died without your care. I couldn't have lived with that. You're a fine woman! So there will be no more talk such as that." He looked down at Eleanor and gave her a peck on the forehead. She pulled away from him. "Enough of this, ladies. So…tell me of Jamie and Mack! Ya really think he's coming home?"

The remainder of the visit transpired in laughter and questions from Joseph. Eleanor sat silently upon the hearth.

Joseph had pushed all thoughts of what Eleanor had said from her mind, but not her heart. Whatever could she do to make Eleanor understand she meant her no harm?

They rode in silence for some time—Charlie whipping at the horses with the reins. "So ya feelin' better?"

"No, you were correct. She only knows of the *horrendous things* I did do. But…"

"No need in tellin' me, I was there. Selective memory is fuel for whatever ya wish it. Sad but true 'nough."

The windows of the Mackenzie's home shown golden beneath the icicles that hung from the rafters. A very large redhaired man could be seen as he shoveled snow from the lean-to they had built upon their arrival. *Surely that would not be Duncan, why he was near a replica of his father.* The stoop was cleared of snow and ice, and before she could knock, the door swung open. The bright eyes and brilliant red hair of Ilene stood in the open entrance. "Welcome, welcome, lass! To be sure now, a verra pleasant surprise it be 'Lisobeth, ach, an ya bein' a wee bit over large ta be callin' now, near forty stones, ya be." Laughing once again. "So…'tis the man o' my life here now, then?" She reached out and hugged Elisabeth with great enthusiasm.

Elisabeth nearly cried; how could persons be so unlike one another. "Oh, Ilene. I was in hopes you knew something more than I."

"Come, sit. No, lass, me big fine man, he only be writtin' but a wee note sayin' he was comin' home…" Her blue eyes danced in excitement. "'Tis little meself read, even in the Gaelic but…'tis all I have need of. I be letting ya see the thing… It no be in ye own tongue. Air ye be waitin' on the fine Jamie as well? Come, 'Lisobeth, Charlie, you come sit. I be givin' ye ham an' beans and some fine haggis. Bread, butter, an' I've doughnuts."

Elisabeth laughed. "Ham and beans are fine, thank you, Ilene." The thoughts of haggis, causing her stomach to churn.

"You there, Charlie, call me young Duncan in, tell 'im ta come visit, an have a wee bite. I be waiting on hearin' of the barin'! Air ya waitin' on the bonny lad then?"

Ilene's face was alight with laughter as she scurried about the kitchen with apparent joy.

Elisabeth giggled. "I believe I am, Ilene, the babe and I shall wait until Jamie arrives."

"Auck, best get on with it. He'll be jus fussin' an yerself abed."

Elisabeth smiled as she tasted a bite of beans. "Oh, these are so good."

"Honey, lassie, honey. Duncan an' me we be hopin' thet the harshness o' the winter be no killin' the bees."

"Did Mack say where they were when they left?"

"No, the man be only thinkin' on getting home I be thinkin'. But I feel it, I do. They be here soon 'nough. I be sendin' the Lord ta seet they safe, do no fash yerself, lass."

"Is Duncan coming in to eat? Shall we wait?"

Ilene's laughter filled the room. "Me Duncan now, he be of a mind ta eat the whole of the ham. The wee one I birthed turned to the giant of his sire… Be sure now, 'Lisobeth, he no go hungry. Likely pleased to be speakin' with a man, thet he is."

They spoke of names for the child to come, of the folks in town and of Duncan—and of their husbands. Elisabeth had thought she would tell Ilene of Eleanor's harsh words but found within Ilene a peacefulness and acceptance that made that unnecessary.

"Best be getting on home now Miz Prescott, soon be dark."

"Yes, yes."

"Ya kin call on me should the need be, 'Lisobeth, I be of some help."

"Thank you, Ilene. Thank you."

Daylight was indeed drifting into evening as they set out for home. *My, where had the time gone? She was pleased she had come.* Her basket of breads having been replaced by Ilene's doughnuts.

"So you feel better?"

She snickered sheepishly. "Yes, I do, for I did try with Eleanor, and Joseph and Ilene are the most wonderfully content people I have ever known, besides you, of course."

"It takes all kinds don't it now. A hell'va world!" Charlie lifted her from the wagons bench and walked with her to the stoop. The snow was drifting heavily now. The whiteness—a curtain against the darkening sky.

"Got that shotgun loaded?"

She smiled. "I do. Always."

"Good. If ya need me, shoot it." He turned and was gone.

Time

Blue-gray waters lapped gently about her chest, cool and deep. Elisabeth stretched out her leg to touch the bottom; there was none to be found. She looked around her; she could see nothing but a wall at the far side, quite like an ancient aqueduct of old Roman architecture. *France.* Was she in France? She found she was alone in the vastness of the water, unable to discern any boundaries other than the one directly in front of her. Why she would be here perplexed her. She tried in vain to swim to the wall. She was not progressing; the cool waters held her captive.

She could see the faces of Eleanor and Joseph as they stood in distorted image upon the ancient wall. She struggled yet again, finding she could but tread water. "Oh my. *Aide moi!*" she called out.

Perhaps she was not in France. Once more she called out in English. "Joseph! Help me!"

Quite suddenly, she awakened. She lay in her bed. It had been but a dream.

Only darkness filtered through the curtained windows, swags she had sewn by hand. What time was it? She looked at the clock and found that the black hands lay still; she had forgotten to wind it. She looked for Jamie.

Would she never remember that he was not here? She felt the rolling ache of pain in her back and reached down within the bedding. The bedding was soaked... *Dear me, have I soiled the bed?* Anxiety rushed through her. That simply cannot be! Quickly she rose from the dastardly wetness of the bed. Her gown was soaked from the waist down. The fluid on her thighs smelled not at all of urine.

Oh, Lord! Joy and dread mingled within her. She reached and patted the bulk of the child she carried within her. *So it is you, is it? I have been waiting, fretting. You have been so still for the past few days. Were you but resting?* She smiled. Soon, soon it would be done. Jamie or no!

It had been over three weeks since the poem from Jamie, the letter from Josiah; she had heard not another thing. Remembering Ilene's voice and the sureness that *they be near*, she walked to the window and peered out. The snowflakes large and drifting in a slow waltz of gentle crystals. The drifts of snow heavy, the moonlight casting a blue ethereal image upon them. She pattered with bare feet to the next room. The embers of the fire lay with a soft orange glow within the fireplace, the iron of the flatiron stove—cold. Her heart fluttered in anticipation, in trepidation—*which*, she wasn't certain. *I must strive for calm. I must think. Lord, help me to think.* The child is coming… Another pain registered across her lower back. Not horribly painful, she could endure this. How long had it been? She saw the hourglass on the shelving of books and turned it over.

Going to the door at the side of the flatiron stove, she opened it. Knowing it would be empty. Still…Maria and Juan Alvarado had left, had claimed a parcel of 320 acres just north of them, most certainly with Elisabeth's blessings. They were a kind and considerate couple, and having stayed with her and Jamie since returning with them from the King Ranch in Texas, she was pleased they had ventured out on their own to claim land and to build a home. Jamie would *not* be pleased to find Elisabeth had been living entirely alone for these last few months. At this moment, *she* was not pleased.

For the last two days, she had swept and cleaned, polished furniture, baked bread, wrapping it within flour sacks, had set it outside to freeze, bringing it in to be stored in the cellar. She looked about her home and found the floor shown a heavenly golden color, the stove clean, the many books dusted and placed in the order of their content, then their authors.

Looking again at the fire, she surmised it to be nearing the early morning hours... *Drat.* But that she had wound the clock. The gown now stuck to her legs as she walked. *I shall clean myself and get blankets, the soft flannel ones.* She filled a large caldron with water from the pump, thinking of the wonderful facilities she had within her home. Many of the homes in St. Helena had no water inside their homes. She was indeed mindful of that. Using the chamber pot, *Lord, she wished someone would think of someway to bring the dreaded outhouse indoors.* Wrinkling her nose in disgust...there must be some way...

Another sharp pain! *Oh dear!* She ran to look at the hourglass. It had been nearly half an hour. The pain being not unlike the last, yet fear flooded her—if only for an instant. *Oh, Jamie, where are you?*

Her mind felt relatively calm, excited—yes, overjoyed! What was it Petra had said to expect? What had happened with Eleanor? Oh my, she musn't think of that. But indeed, she must be prepared for that intensity of pain. *No!* She would not have that! She had no fear. She would have no fear. Only joy lay within her.

A *mantra* seemed now to exist within the realm of her being. This was a child conceived in love, and there would be no tarnish on *her* soul. She would not bring this child into the world in fear.

Again she thought of Petra; what had she said? *The pains would come more frequent, with more intensity. To send for her.* Yes, if they were but say thirty... Oh dear, another one. They were coming more quickly now. "Yes, my little one, you are ready. Mama shall be ready shortly." She washed the slimy substance from her legs and changed into a loose-fitting, clean nightdress. Knowing that whatever help she received would be here, in this, her and Jamie's home.

She looked through the opening of the window once again;, the moon shown the same halo upon the snows... *Early morning?* She knew not. *Why had she not wound the silly clock?!*

She reached for the shotgun. She would awaken everyone—how she hated to do such as that.

The winter cold swept with a mighty finger though the lightness of her flannel gown. Her bare feet freezing instantly to the front stoop. She should have put on her footwear. With the shotgun pulled tightly to her shoulder, she squeezed the trigger. The blast shot brilliant orange, yellows, and blues, as the pellets flew toward the night sky. She heard the empty shell drop to the stoop and tried to bend to retrieve it, laughing as she did so. For it truly was an impossibility—the very reason she had not put on her footwear! It was just too damnably difficult; her girth would not allow it. She turned to reenter the house. The pain now—near unbearable. She had forgotten where the sands of hourglass had been. It now was nearly done, the sands having drifted to the base of the glass. Nearly one hour had passed.

She heard the sound of the door creak, felt the gust of cold air, and turning, she saw Charlie, hatless, coatless, he stood, his hair mussed. Closing the door, he reached and took the shawl that lay across the rocking chair. "Here, ma'am, put this around yerself. I'm guessin it's time, is it?"

"I think so, Charlie," her relief at seeing him evident in her voice.

"Well, that's good, you all right ta stay by yourself fer a minute? I'm sending Albee to fetch the doc...might take some time you know, the weather being what it is, so I'm gonna tell Swede to go fetch Miz MacKenzie. I'll be right back." He turned. "How long...ya know—the pain?"

"I...I think about twenty, perhaps thirty minutes, but they are coming closer and more intense."

"Good. Sit down, walk. I just...stay here. I'll be right back." His voice filled with a calm concern and—could it be?—*excitement.*

"Charlie." Embarrassment flooded her; she felt her face flush.

"Yes, ma'am?"

"The waters…my water broke."

He reached for the doorknob and turned it. "Miz Prescott, you sit yourself down, don't move. I'll be *right* back."

As he left, she heard the whinny of Mercy; her heart fluttered at the sound.

Mercy knew her mistress's *time* was near.

She watched the soft rocking of the cradle from the breath of the earth as the door closed and felt the tears as they rolled down her cheeks.

Jamie, where are you?

The Child

She sat in the rocker as she had been instructed—anxiety rushing through her, not unlike the river that flowed beyond the house. The room felt cold, her hands and back clammy with fear. She walked to the fireplace and lay logs upon the slowly dying embers. She went to the stove to build a fire. She would need boiling water. *Another pain.* She gripped the scarred counter that held the bowl for washing; she could see vividly each cut a heavy knife blade had made, scarred now with darkness. Reaching for the hourglass, she turned it over once again, looked at the great flatiron stove, pondered the trials of building a fire, and thought better of it.

Perhaps Charlie...

February, a winter child, what was today? The poem ran through her mind.

> Monday's child is fair of face,
> Tuesday's child is full of grace,
> Wednesday's child is full of woe,
> Thursday's child has far to go,
> Friday's child is loving and giving,
> Saturday's child must work for a living,
> But the child that's born on the Sabbath day,
> Is fair and wise and good and gay.

Oh dear, she was certain it was Wednesday, or had that been yesterday? She would not think of that... She reached for the bottle of whiskey; taking a long pull on the bottle, she felt the warmth of the liquid as it slid down her throat, felt the burning sensation as it entered her empty stomach. Should she eat something? She remembered the constant vomiting of Eleanor and thought better of it... Once again, she paced the floor, straightening the bedding in the cradle.

She heard the lumber of the wagon as it passed the back of the house. That would be Swede going to fetch Ilene; she heard the thunder of hooves as Albee left to retrieve Petra. She wished she knew what time it was. Suddenly she wanted only to weep. She had never felt so alone, and she was about to give birth. *Jamie where are you?* Lord, she did not wish for Charlie to help her give birth—how ghastly, how humiliating!

She longed for Grandmère. Her mama, the clean, orderliness of her childhood home. She wiped the tears from her eyes and blew her nose. I shall think of other things. Spring would be here soon; the daffodils would rise their trumpet like heads imbuing the air with their fragrance. *Silly woman!* That would be months from now. The snows now drifted to the house in mounds of five and six feet...insulation from the cold Jamie had said. *Jamie!* Anger filled her. *Damn you, Jamie!*

She heard the rap at the door; sniffling, she walked the five paces and opened it.

"Ma'am, thought I'd wait with you, that is, if you'd like, you really don't wanna be alone now." It was not really a question but a statement. He didn't wait for her reply but came inside. Charlie took off his hat and coat, looking at Elisabeth with the biggest smile she had yet to see on his face. She looked again and saw he had his fiddle leaning against the wall by the door.

"You brought your fiddle."

"I did. Music, well, it can soothe the soul it can."

Elisabeth paced the floor. "Charlie..."

"Yes, ma'am?"

"I, I truly thank you for your help. And and I know this is frightfully…well, quite honestly…"

"Aw, shucks, ma'am, done delivered lots of animals, an' my woman said if the time gets close an the doc ain't here to come and fetch her."

She looked at this quiet, gentle man and thought of all his care, of the cradle.

Lord, she would rather it be Joseph that delivered her child; thinking of Joseph, she thought better of it. His embarrassment would be overwhelming to him, and Eleanor…she didn't believe Eleanor to be capable. What if Ilene didn't come?

Ilene *would* come. Would she know what to do? She thought of Charlie's *woman*.

They each sat silent for a time.

"Charlie, do you love her?"

"Don't rightly think I ever been in love, ma'am, but I care for her and her child. And I think she cares fer me."

It quite suddenly occurred to Elisabeth she knew nothing of this man. "Where were you born, what of your family?" Another searing pain shot through her. She reached for the table to steady herself, perspiration forming on her brow.

"Are you scared, Miz Prescott?"

"No, not really," the mantra racing through her mind. "Right now, I am mad at James Prescott!" She laughed and Charlie chuckled. "I think that to be a proper anger, ma'am." He laughed and holding her elbow propelled her to the rocking chair.

She sighed. "Thank you, Charlie. Tell me of yourself."

"Well, we was dirt farmers"—now *he* paced the floor, pausing to lay another log on the fire, he went on—" my parents…like those folks the Davis's ya went to see. My ma an' pa…" Again, he paused, rubbing at his whiskered chin. "Well, guess they were from someplace, ya know I don't rightly know, wasn't old 'nough ta ask…had lots of brothers and one sister." Again he poked at the fire. "The Norther's blew in the winter and the sun hotter an' hell in the summer. I was 'bout twelve, I think, jus' decided one day it twern't worth all this. Took a horse and left. Worked fer a farrier in Kansas City awhile, slept in his shop. Damned hard work. Jus' thought things should be easier… Rode on up ta Ohio, wanted to see something green, ya know."

"You did this when you were twelve?" Elisabeth was aghast.

"Ten or twelve. Got a job with an Amish family. Not something they do, but then, I didn't know that. Learnt to read the Bible. They was kindly…taught me lots of things. I've great respect for those folks."

Elisabeth watched him as he sat on the hearth; she sensed he had never before told a soul of these things. It tugged at her heart to be given the compliment of his trust.

"Aw, ma'am, don't much matter…met Josiah…ya know the rest. Made this trip so many times. Each time thinkin' I'd stay… The beauty of it touched me. Still does." He watched as Elisabeth's hands clutched at the arms of the rocker, her knuckles white. Her face grimaced.

"Ya all right?"

"Yes. Yes. What time is it, Charlie, and what day of the week is this?"

"Don't rightly know the date, but it is Wednesday an'"—he reached in his pocket and pulled out his pocket watch—"Josiah give me this fer five years. Ain't that somethin'! It's 'bout 4:00 a.m., ma'am…I'd be getting up now." Elisabeth laughed. Charlie laughed. Why they were laughing, she had not the most remote idea.

"Can I help you to the bed?"

"No. I don't want to go to bed. I think, if I could do anything, I would ride like the wind on the back of Mercy…or dance. Remember the picnic, Charlie? Wasn't that grand?"

"That it was. Why, there were so many people there ya couldn't swing a cat by its tail without hittin' somebody, and you in that get up! Thought ol' Jamie would split a gut."

The small house was overfilled with persons. She could hear the laughter and the music through the curtains that separated her and Jamie's bedroom from the living area. She looked up to see Ilene's face, Ma and Sally Susanne, Petra. Once again, she dove into the depths of exhausted sleep.

The pain intense, she struggled to contain the scream that fought for release.

Images came to her of Eleanor and the laudanum. She now scoffed at the remembered instructions to Petra *not to administer such as that to her—not under any circumstances.* A foolish woman she was. *All this pain for the bite of an apple...*

She thought she could see Grandmère, and her mama, as they sat by her bedside. She felt the scream as it came from the deep recesses of her being, the rush of pain as it radiated throughout her body, the hoarseness of her throat—the dryness of her mouth. How insignificant these things were in comparison.

The pain was gone as suddenly as it had appeared. Perhaps she could focus on what was about her.

Her mantra...what had that been? She searched through her mind and found no recollection of a mantra. Ah, *she would have no fear...* Strangely enough, she had no fear, only submission to the responses of her body. Her mind unable to function—to seek wisdom. Pain—the only fact that registered, survival the only realm that stood outside *the real Elisabeth*. She could not endure to stay within this battered body that betrayed her with such intensity, with such pain.

Her nostrils filled with the pungent odor of all things despicable. Darkness once more alienating all sensation. She was so very tired. How long had it been?

She felt the touch of his hand, the fragrance of Jamie. She felt the softness of his lips upon her forehead. Felt the touch of his hand as he stroked her hair. *What a wonderful dream this was.* She felt the love of him as it expanded her heart and felt the heat of the tears as they slid down her cheeks. *Tears of joy!*

She could hear his voice whispering. "I love you, Elisabeth, I love you more than you shall ever know…my brave, brave girl."

Tell me, Praise, and tell me, Love

What you both are thinking of?

O' we think, said Love, said Praise…

She felt the brush of his lips once again. The end of the poem never heard…

Only that of her own voice as she screamed, "Jamie!"

Again, the darkness engaged her and she sought the *dream*… Again she felt the searing pain, more intense than any previous. She felt her body rise to the occasion, her eyes as they flew open, the hands of Ma Parsons and Sally Susanne as they held her back. Heard the insistent command of Petra's voice, "Push, Elisabeth, push!" She heard the renting of the fabric she held within each hand.

The squalling of an infant.

It was done.

She heard her own laughter and was astounded by the sound. Heard Petra announce, "You have a daughter! A fat, dark-haired daughter!"

"Yes, I knew that," she whispered. "Eleanor…her name is Eleanor." She felt the weight of the child in her arms and the sobs that rumbled from deep within her…

The tiny face was scrunched and red, the nose and mouth were hers, but the dark eyes that looked back at her were Jamie's.

"The child is wonderful, Elisabeth, sleep."

She kissed the forehead of the child and felt the hot tears slide from her eyes. *Thank you, Lord, thank you.*

Oblivion came, and with it, dreams of Jamie.

She awakened to the silence within the house, for an instant terror suffused her. She struggled to rise on an elbow and saw Jamie nested upon the bed.

She lay back upon the pillows and looked at the clock. *Drat, she had still not wound the silly thing.*

Jamie! She turned to see the sleeping form of her husband—dirty, filthy, his whiskers as long as that of his hair. His arm lay across her waist...*her waist. She had a waist.*

She had not been dreaming; he was here. *He had been here all the while!*

She looked about for the child, for Eleanor, *perhaps Ellie, Lena?* The cradle rocked ever so gently, the hand of Ma Parsons resting upon it.

Ma slept in the rocking chair.

Joy effused her. Never had she felt such joy. Her child looked as only an angel could. Blissfully asleep. Her hair as black as Jamie's and her own, her lashes dark and curling, her tightly closed fists pink and dimpled. She but briefly remembered Petra putting the babe to her breast.

She looked at her husband and gave thanks he was home, with her, with their child.

Lord, she was tired. She snuggled to the warmth of his chest and deeply inhaled the fragrance of Jamie, the musky, male scent of her husband.

Tears of exhaustion and joy swept through her; silently, she sent profound thanks to the Lord and forgave him of his declaration of pain.

Intuition

Jamie had left her yet again! Her and their child!

Paralytic fear gripped her! Panic infused her soul—*her very being*. Fear clutched at her heart as she searched throughout the darkness to rise to the surface of her mind, to find reality. Everywhere she looked, there was only darkness—*darkness and despair.*

Jamie was gone; she was alone. She was, once again, with his child. Alone. *Alone in this vast wilderness of foreboding blackness.* She viewed the events of her life as they were laid before her; many children stood before her. Her mind searched for Jamie; men appeared before her, men without faces. *None of them Jamie!* Terror now etched more deeply within her heart. The birthing of another child by herself frightened her beyond what she could have thought possible.

Against the smoldering darkness she saw the child, a girl—another daughter to be raised in the wild, untamed Montana. To never know society—to never experience education nor companionship.

Elisabeth's mind clamored for escape, only to find that within the dark, fiery abyss, fear now had companions. *Grief and despair.* Fear and isolation lay ubiquitously; the world around her was dark with the color of *blood*. The land enveloped her with its power—in its partnership with Mother Nature.

Elisabeth stood in the vastness of this land. Fear suffused her, overwhelming her, suffocating her. As she turned, she saw no beauty. The mountains were gone—the rivers were gone. The blue skies and wild flowers...*gone*. Her only companions were despair, grief, and darkness.

Elisabeth implored her God to come, to bring this terror to an end...and found no one. In the vastness lay only a sagacity of horror, of anguish. She searched the apparition as it exhibited its influences, searched for Jamie to rescue her.

Her brother Samuel stood before her. Now Jamie, an apparition within fog so thick she could not reach him. The many cords of wood Jamie had piled around the house were gone—the gold was gone, the cattle were without feed.

The Indian Brave she had killed rose before her. His dark soulful eyes locked for an eternity with those of her own.

She heard the sob as it came unbidden from the depths of her consciousness, from the depths of her soul. Some small part of her knew this to be a dream, yet she could not find the path from which to rise from within it. Surely, *she was dreaming!* She fought to awaken—the struggle to do so near insurmountable! She could feel the icy sweat of fear that suffused her body—could feel the flannel of her nightgown as it clung to her small frame. She could feel her hair and scalp was soaked with sweat—the bedding, wet with her own perspiration as she fought to control the raging fear within her. She sensed the emptiness of her life, the despair of fear and failure. But worse, far worse, the thought of being left with the monumental responsibility of the ranch, of the isolation of being alone the rest of her days, a feeling that left her wishing she could weep, to huddle in a corner and simply give up. *To go home to Philadelphia!* To be sheltered and protected. She and her child...and the child she carried. Jamie had left her with child once again.

She had known fear previously, certainly on the Oregon Trail, on the Goodnight Trail—on the day Jamie had left for the Civil War. But never like this, never so completely, never so blatantly— this fear that filled her with insurmountable terror. The dream, a dream so real, so intense, so much a part of her. It came in waves that she could not surmount—yet she could not awaken.

She felt the fear in her heart. There were no tears—just unmitigated panic. Trepidation of the future, a future in which she had not found Jamie. *Dante's Inferno had risen within her life, a future of anxiety and angst lay before her.* She fought for the will to awaken, to rise above this—this dream of despair—of soul death, of hell on earth.

She heard the soft breathing of her child, Eleanor, as she slept in the cradle at the side of the bed she had shared with Jamie. She could smell the wood smoke as it smoldered in the huge fireplace, relieved she was to rise from the depths.

This was not the first nor she felt, the last of these horrific nightmares. *Lord, help me!* she implored. As her hands rose to cover her face, she found it to be wet with perspiration, yet there were no tears. This fear was beyond mere mortal tears. Her hands ran through her thick, ebony mane of hair, and she fought at the urge to pull at it. Her hands felt the wetness at her scalp, her hair near matted to her head. *Breathe. Breathe.* She counseled herself. *Lord, help me rise from this, this abyss.*

She willed her mind to surface from the nightmare, a nightmare she recognized to be the third such one she had had since he had again left to fight.

Her diminutive body now sat at the edge of the great bed. Her feet dangled just above the pine flooring. The room was cold. She looked down at her sleeping child and padded barefoot to the keeping room, the water pump; she needed water, and if that did not work, whisky. She must be rid of this paralyzing fear.

Pulling a shawl about her shoulders, she sat down in the rocking chair. She thought of Grandmère's journal, this was no worse than what her grandmère had faced. The dream had substance...the realities within it solid and true. She *was* alone... with her second child in the womb. *Jamie was gone! To fight the damnable war! The supplies were diminishing; she was alone.* Tears of salt traced her face. The sobs came unwillingly. Her small body shook. A dream it might have been—or an acknowledgment of what lie deep in her subconscious—an acknowledgment of truth, her intuition heralded all of these events, imposing themselves even during her waking hours. She *feared*! God forbid; *she feared*. Her thoughts ran to Sally Susanne and her explanations of *fear*… She felt the anger as it came to reside in the place of fear—*Jamie…he had left her!* It was his fault she was alone! This…this life was not as he had promised!

The tears came more readily now, engulfing her, suffusing her. With the tears came guilt. In truth, he had promised nothing, nothing but his love for her. It was *she* that had envisioned a perfect life. The dashingly handsome man with gifts of diamonds, of horses, saddles, and guns, his land—*as far as the eye could see*, his beautiful poetry, gone. *James Martin Prescott was gone.* How was she to live without him?

Many decisions had placed them both here, here in this land of isolation and beauty.

She clutched more tightly at the shawl that covered her shoulders, watched as the fire spit flames. Was he dead? Great, heaving sobs shook her body. She could not live without Jamie. She could not bear the thought of never having his kisses, his strong arms enfolding her, caressing her.

She would not think of that now! Her bare feet tiptoed to the cupboard that held the whisky, and she looked at the alarm clock that sat upon the desk—*his desk*. Fear once more engulfed her; she heard the words of Sally Susanne. "*Fear* the last to be conquered…"

Only an hour before time to ride line.

She needed to speak to her friend, her mama, her grandmère. Would they console her? She thought of the depth of the snow outside her home, her sleeping child, the bitter cold. The need to tend to the animals, the ranch, and knew *there was no hope of talking to anyone.*

It was March 1863, the thermometer read nineteen degrees below as she had left the house this morning, leaving little Eleanor tucked in her cradle, the cradle Charlie had fashioned for her. Elisabeth sat now on Mercy. She would ride line for forty-five minutes and return to look in on her. Her heart wrenched at leaving her child, yet she must see to the cattle. The snow last night had been unrelenting and the wind had blown hard, leaving great drifts of icy snow. She knew that several of the cows were near their time. The cattle needed birthing pens. She would have to have the hired hands construct them as soon as the weather abated.

Elisabeth had struggled with the idea of bringing the baby with her, the biting cold and wind was near more than she could abide, let alone an infant.

She looked across the land and saw only white. The mountains in the distance, with their winter coats of ice and snow, the cedars and hemlocks shrouded in frostings of ermine. The darkness of deciduous trees held in an icy glaze.

Mercy snorted great puffs of white and pranced in place, anxious to get on with the duties of the day. Trésor whinnied from her paddock, the whinnying of her voice a pleading to accompany her mother. Even though daylight was approaching, it was not safe to bring the two-year-old foul out, the mountain lions where hungry and Mercy's youngster was no match for a mountain lion. Her mind ran to Eleanor's horse on the Bozeman Trail. The grizzly that had brought down that horse and the dreadful fear she had felt. Fear and shock. No, Trésor was better left in the safety of the barn. "Come, girl, our babies shall be fine and safe." She patted the neck of the big white Arabian. As she did so, she took one last look at the small log house she called home. The glimmer of light that shown from the fire in the fireplace, the wisps of smoke that rose from the chimney. *Lord, she hoped she had banked the fire well enough to sustain it until she returned.* If Jamie were to be gone much longer she would have to have someone to stay with the child, perhaps Maria?

The running of the ranch was far more than she had given thought to. But then *she had given thought to none of this*. Her mind ran to the dreadful dream of just hours ago, quickly pushing it aside.

She checked her weapons once again, pulling her hat more tightly to her head. The mound of hair beneath it tightly covered, the scarf about her nose and mouth doing little to keep the frigid wind from burning through to her face. Her great fur coat closed tightly against the elements. She thought of the lovely coat of ermine and fox that she had left her papa's house in—this *was* indeed the same coat. She felt the stiffness of the cold smile that crossed her face—at the incongruity of her life. A coat to have been worn to fine soirées, to have shown wealth and security, to have embellished her beauty and grace—her fortune, her position within society... The coat had been worn through the trek west, through the fetid, icy, mountainous terrain, had been spattered with the blood of birthing animals. It had most certainly served a purpose, and she was grateful for its warmth, somewhat saddened that it had been spared the future for which it was intended. Was this the life she had intended? She snorted...the snort an indication of loathing, disgust. *Most certainly not!*

She thought of the sophisticated and aesthetically beautiful James Martin Prescott and his silver tongue, his grand ideas and her own youth, of her naïve expectations. Her love for him—*her own adventurous spirit*. Perhaps, when all was said and done, this was exactly where she belonged.

She would ride the north perimeter of the property this morning, hoping against all odds that the cattle had cloistered themselves in the groves of alders and cottonwoods and evergreens rather than straying into the large, open expanse of the land. A newborn calf could die in the drifts of snow, unable to rise, or simply through the struggling of the birth, causing the snow to cover them, the snow filling their nostrils and freezing them, the mother unable to encourage them to rise.

"Come, girl." She looked out across the land and could see small dots of darkness. Cattle—she hoped not, but that was why she road line each morning.

She thought of the day Jamie had encouraged her to go with him and a great foreboding nostalgia rose in her. *Jamie... damn him!*

It had been weeks since he had left to return to the war, promising to return in the spring to tend to his land and to be with his wife and new daughter; she had had but one letter. Each evening she wrote to him, sitting at the table he had built surrounded by all they had accomplished and told him of her day—of the child that was theirs. Each week she would gather the letters, and placing them in an envelope, she would be certain they were posted. Posted to an address he had given her...did he receive them? She knew not.

In the distance, she could see the glimmer of light from Charlie's cabin and knew he would ride line to the south, meeting up with her at her house. Whatever would she do without him?

She looked down and across the great expanse of she and Jamie's land to the small valley, at the hovel where Agnes Corrigan lived with her child, amazed at the woman's ingenuity and resolve. A slight curl of smoke rose from the shelter that was once a mere tent of canvas. Surrounded now by stacked cords of wood, animal hides tied securely to the roof of the dwelling. Snow blanketed the area, leaving only small posts to be seen in what was in summer, a garden. A lone cow stood in a lean-to. Agnes had no horse, no wagon. Elisabeth could not remember the last time she had seen or heard of Agnes venturing into the town of St. Helena. She thought of the beautiful child Agnes had given birth to. Hair as black as night, large round eyes that shown the color of the Montana skies, lashes that surrounded them, thick and dark. Who would have thought that this child would be so lovely! A child of Agnes Corrigan and Jeff Tallman.

Joseph had said that Eleanor had told him... Agnes was with child again. Elisabeth's mind wandered to the bruising she had seen on Agnes, the missing teeth. Astounded that she, Agnes, an outspoken, demanding woman, would stand for such treatment by a man who refused to marry her, a man who lived within a cozy cabin with an Indian squaw. Lord! People…would she ever understand?

Elisabeth doubted Agnes stayed because of Jeff Tallman…but out of pride and shame. If it where her, she would have gone to Salt Lake City to be with her family. Amelia and Morgan Chandler would be happy to take Agnes and her child in.

She, herself was with child again, the eerie thought causing a flurry of mixed emotions. How did that happen? It had been her understanding that as long as she was nursing she would not conceive…another *wives' tale*.

The lopping of Mercy and the accompanying morning sickness…another of those things you simply get on with. What would Jamie say? She had not mentioned it in the letters to him, not yet. She would tell him when he returned. Certainly the war would not last much longer.

Jamie's orders had been *"to go to Tennessee, the fighting had been most prevalent there."* She shuddered at the thought. Tennessee, where Mack was. She looked to the north and could see the flickering lights of Ilene's home, of Joseph and Eleanor's home. They were perhaps a mile away; still there was little to hamper her vision on the flat plains they had homesteaded. Copses of cottonwoods, hemlocks, and spruce, all a whispery white in the last of the winter's snowfall, lay to the west of her, down by the river. Hopefully she was right in thinking winter was nearly over.

She thought of the town of St. Helena and Sally Susanne, of Caroline and her pretty chocolate children. Ben's thriving business within his general store and wondered if Ezra was wandering the mountainous terrain or perhaps sipping tea with Thomas Sullivan in California.

Elisabeth looked forward to seeing Sally Susanne. Would she share her secret with her? She felt Sally would know simply by looking at her, as would Ma. She felt Charlie knew, as she had been sick on several mornings of late. Often dismounting rapidly, running through the snows to vomit. Her secret was safe with him. He made no comment and probed no further. As he said of so very many things, "None a' my business, ma'am."

As she thought of the new child, fear welled within her. What if Jamie were killed? What if the war went on? She thought of the certainty that their men felt… "It would be over in a few short months." She thought of the tenacity of the Southerners, of the fight in them. The war was not as any of them had expected. She had read the death toll was nearing two hundred thousand men. *Men and youngsters.* It frightened her! It made her angry, and it made her sick to her stomach. War! War was all men thought of.

Thankfully, the bawling of a calf interrupted her thoughts. In the small copse of trees, she saw the newborn, the umbilical cord dangled from its belly, the mother licking at its fur.

The Hunt

Deeply rich amber eyes stared back at her from the eyes within the cherubic face of her child, Jamie's eyes. She rocked as she nursed the child. Crooning to her soft sounds of a lullaby she remembered from her childhood. The memory tugged at her heart—the soft voices of Mama and Grandmère played on her heartstrings as the words fell from her lips. *Treasured moments of a life long ago.* Of a life she would never know again.

The child gurgled and giggled. "So you are full, are you? You wee little thing," the words conjuring up Ilene Mackenzie's soft Gaelic tones. She lifted Eleanor and placed her on her shoulder, patting her soundly, waiting for the burp that inevitably followed. Bringing her down to sit upon her lap. She was a stunningly beautiful child, with hair as black as the night sky, lashes as dark and thick as that of her own, her skin a creamy white. She laughed at the good-natured child. Still amazed at the love she felt for this diminutive person. The camaraderie she felt between the two of them. They seemed to understand one another. She laughed at the preposterousness of her thoughts; the child was not yet four months old. She hugged her tightly to her breast and laughed at the giggling little child. She patty-caked with little Eleanor and told her stories of her father, of his great love for each of them, that he was a soldier in the Union Army, fighting for the solidarity of the Americans and how proud she should be of him. "He shall return very soon, my darling."

As she played with Eleanor, more urgent thoughts niggled at the back of her mind. This evening as she had gone for firewood, she had seen the markings of a bear, a *great* large bear, by the size of his paw prints. The tracks rested deep within the snow. Its weight must be massive, as the snow was deep and frozen around the perimeter of the house. Her arms laden with wood, she felt the cold of the wind that whistled through the plains, and she shivered. Dusk was falling—the skies having turned to gentle hues of lavender.

Her thoughts turned to that of Mercy and Trésor—of the cattle and herds of mustangs, to the disgusting, but life-giving, *dirty* pigs and chickens. She smiled at the incongruity of her thoughts. With all the life-endangering situations surrounding her, she found the dirt to be the most unsettling. She and the child went for weeks without bathing—the water frozen within the pipe Jamie had run from the river to the house. Placing it more than a foot beneath the ground, it still froze. The small hat tub they had purchased sat in the corner of the small bedroom awaiting the spring thaw.

A bear was not something to be taken lightly. It was early for a bear to be out of hibernation, the ground frozen solid with its winter veil of protection. The bear would be hungry.

She thought of Ilene and Duncan…of Joseph and Eleanor. Of the hired hands she had so generously let off to go to town. Of Charlie—gone for the week into St. Helena for what meager supplies they offered this late in the season. The root cellar was near empty—too, the larder as well. They had food for another month—perhaps two.

She would think of that tomorrow.

She read to little Eleanor Humpty Dumpty and from the newspaper of November last. Eleanor's fat, tiny hands clasped in utter rapture at her mother's ability to read and the lilting quality in her voice. Elisabeth felt certain they looked a fine portrait of contentment, the fire ablaze, the shiny, golden pine of the flooring.

Elisabeth, young and beautiful, sat in the rocking chair reading to her child, the log house alight with lanterns and candles.

She looked about her home as she prepared Eleanor for bed; at the small drain board, with the pump for water that came straight from the river beyond the house, the enormous flatiron stove, the pretty sash windows that reflected the candle light, their shutters had been nailed in placed for months now. The great ornate door gave credence to Jamie's efforts at providing his wife with a small measure of decorum. The memories of the King ranch rose within her, with its spectacular ornate rooms and elegant gardens…perhaps after the war.

Perhaps after the Oregon Trail…when they reached their destination…perhaps when they had staked a claim to the land… perhaps when they returned from Texas…perhaps… She felt she waited with little faith for what would come next—for the *Father's* approbation.

She looked at the flickering light reflected in the shuttered windows and was grateful they were safe. She and her child were safe. The barn was as secure as the house—Jamie had seen to that. The only animals that were truly in jeopardy would be the cattle.

Was there more than one bear? She had seen only the one set of prints. Bears were not prone to travel in packs, other than the females and their young. It was certainly too early for a mother to be out with her cubs—no, it had to be a male.

Should she go to Josephs's? Should she wait for Charlie to return?

She knew the bear had to die. It was a threat to all of them. Danger would lurk at every niche until the bear was dead. Bears didn't go away; once they discovered an easy access to food, *they did not go away.* She thought of the wolves that ran in packs, of the deer and moose and goats and of the elk. All so willing to let bygones be bygones. Not so with the bear. They lived a life of isolation.

To emerge from hibernation so early had numerous innuendos—none of them favorable to Elisabeth or her child.

She thought of all the methods of tracking animals Jamie had taught her, thought of the impressions in the snow. She had lain her hand in the paw prints, and the pad of the print was larger than that of her hand. She could envision the wisps of snow left by the fur of the animal as it had lifted its great girth from the snows, the logs that lay scattered about on the snow, logs of heavy wood that now rested randomly upon the frozen snow. This alone was reason to cause her heart to skip a beat.

She prepared her evening meal of bread and soup, a soup of carrots and potatoes in a beef broth. She looked at the mason jars filled with bear meat and her heart quivered.

She would have to kill the bear.

When was Charlie to return? In all honesty, she could not remember. Day followed endless day as she went about the duties of survival for her and her child. She thought of Agnes and wondered if she had, as Elisabeth, become accustomed to the isolation of their lives. Not only *accustomed*—but embracing the isolation. There was a certain quality of quiescent safety that lie within that isolation.

How long she had slept she had no idea, only that she was frightened—apprehensive. The welfare of her child being her primary concern, she thought of Sally Susanne—their agreement that should anything happen to Elisabeth she would care for little Eleanor. Strange, she would choose someone other than Joseph and Eleanor—they were family. Yet Eleanor—Eleanor, how unstable she seemed. How she treated Elisabeth as though Elisabeth was her enemy…had done her some great injustice, treatment none who knew of them understood nor condoned. Elisabeth had been heartbroken that Eleanor had not come to visit the child who was her namesake. Yet Elisabeth's heart understood her sister-in-law's mind; her emotions were damaged, perhaps beyond repair. Naming her child after Eleanor was her way of professing her love for her sister-in-law. Joseph and Sally Susanne—even Petra seemed to empathize with her in this. Jamie, above all others, comprehended it not at all. Why was it not an acknowledgment that Eleanor could embrace? She pushed the thought from her mind and rose from the bed, set the coffee to boiling, and nursed her child, changed her nappies, and tucked her in the cradle.

As she gathered her weapons, she thought of the many obstacles that might present themselves. Her knife was sharp—her ammunition dry. She would take two Enfield rifles, as well as her pistols. She could envision the bear—hit and lying down—and knew she would have to shoot it again through the eye. Jamie had always insisted, "*Just to be certain.*"

What if she merely wounded the animal? Would she track it? She thought of the possibility of this. No, she would not. She would have the men track it. Not many things were as dangerous as a wounded bear. She must return to her child.

This was not the first nor would it be the last animal she would be required to kill, and with so many other events in her life, she felt her back straighten. This had naught to do with the fact she was a woman. A clean, steady shot was what it took, with no more strength than to hold the long rife. Steady—to aim properly, to shoot, to kill—Jamie's voice rang in her ears.

She kissed Eleanor on the forehead, the child smelling of sleep and the warmth of having just been nursed. Elisabeth crossed herself and traced a small cross on the forehead of her daughter. "*Should I not return,*" she whispered.

Stepping off the stoop, she looked up at the early morning skies, the starlight not as bright now, the moon, a cradle of shadowy perimeters. The light of the sun a mere glimmer above the horizon, it would not be full daylight for a time yet. She needed to saddle Mercy and tend to the other animals.

Why had she let all the hired hands leave? In truth, she was weary of their presence. Swede in particular, there was something disquieting about the man.

Danny's empty stall was the first thing she viewed as she entered the barn. For a brief moment, she wished simply to fall to the floor and weep; for all that implied. *Oh God, Jamie, I miss you so… Lord, please be with me.*

The odor of the barn was alive with the smells of hay, feed, and animals and excrement, an odor not altogether disgusting to her, only offering her a sense of comfort. Although she could see her breath, the barn was somehow cozy and inviting. She looked above the rafters at the bunkhouse Jamie had built within the barn. The door was shut. She placed the lantern upon the empty barrel, tiny dust moats of straw and fodder drifted in the golden lantern light. She looked to the far corner of the barn; her eyes rested on the barrels of whisky; the southern Scotsman had nothing on James Prescott. He and Mack MacKenzie had made some fine, powerful whisky.

Trésor neighed and pranced about in her stall, the perfect white stockings of her legs as definitive as when she was born, the young horse was nearly as tall now as Mercy, an auspicious sign, for Mercy was large for an Arabian. This summer she would have to put a saddle on her back. She would be a fine horse for young Eleanor. "Mercy, my great brave girl, we are going a trek this morning of grave importance. You must be a very brave girl."

The mare nibbled at the shriveled crab apple Elisabeth placed beneath her muzzle. Elisabeth reached for the tack, the saddle heavy with silver—the initials; that of "EP" that had been carved so artfully within the black leather. For a brief moment, she thought of the strawberry field in which she had lain with Jamie in all their naked glory. It seemed now to be another lifetime.

She breathed deeply, knowing that Mercy would sense her hesitation—her fear—her trepidation. She could do this! *She felt she had no choice.*

She led the horse from the barn and secured the door, checking her weapons once again. She no longer wore but the one knife at her thigh; Mack had fashioned for her a more lethal buck knife she wore strapped at her waist.

She watched the clouds of vapor that escaped from Mercy's nostrils as the horse snorted and pranced in the depths of the snow, the Southern landscape that lay before them slightly rolling and devoid of trees, a landscape of alien quite.

Elisabeth tied the scarf more tightly about her face, pulling her customary Western hat tightly over her ebony mane of hair. She knew the bears to have a keen sense of smell, and she knew she must be ripe with human odor; the cold being her only defense against this. She looked to the Eastern mountain range of the Little Belts—their summits held a cloud like formation of snow. She watched as the sunlight seemed to dance at the horizon, the skies turning ever so slightly to the brilliant blue she had come to expect in this world of infinite beauty. The silence of the early morning was one she had learned to expect of winter. The sounds of the river hushed by the ice flow, the wind that often howled—stilled by the coming of spring. Icicles clung to the eaves of the house. She knew the shutters to be frozen in place.

She and Mercy would head north, that would be the most likely place for the bear to be. She had no definitive plan; she would rely on her instincts alone. During the hours of her sleepless night, she had determined; should she feel great fear, she would return to the house and wait upon Charlie's return.

Mounting Mercy, she again crossed herself. *Father be with me...* she prayed.

She turned the horse and picked up the grizzly's tracks at the back of the house; it was indeed going north, between Jeff Tallman's and Joseph's spread. She looked across the horizon and wondered if she should have waited until evening. Would the bear be out now? She knew they were not necessarily nocturnal, but were they early risers? She smiled as she considered the audacity of her thoughts.

The tracks led down to the river and back up toward the house. Back and forth the horse and the woman rode; she stopped momentarily to check the cattle that lay in the copse of aspens not far from Charlie's cabin. They seemed undisturbed. She wondered at that, surely if the bear was hungry, he would have killed one of the cattle. She watched as a lone fox skittered across the snowy plains, a white hare, as he glanced at her and her magnificent horse—turned and skittered to safety. These animals verily skimmed the surface of the snows, the depth of the snow likely to be three to five feet at this time of year, their light and graceful bounding leaving only a wisp of trails.

The leather of the dark Western hat shielding her eyes, she sought the plains for signs of a huge animal. She turned again from the vicinity of her home and rode northward. Small indiscriminate specks lay in the distance. Cattle, horses—they stood as if frozen in place. Standing far to the west of the stock, a lone red apparition could be seen, perhaps four, perhaps five hundred yards away.

Removing her glove, she raised her hand to the wind, it came from the northwest, a good omen. He would not be able to discern her presence. She in her white mink coat and Mercy's stark whiteness against the glint of the rising sun would make her nearly invisible to the shortsighted animal.

Was it the bear? It had to be! It's very size an indication as well as its color. Would she have a kill shot from here? She doubted it. She bent and whispered into Mercy's ear. "Come, girl, let us see how close we can get without alarming the creature. Her thoughts rested not on the dangerous endeavor, only on the mission—a mission she was committed to.

Her mind ran to the buffalo hunt of the Indians on the plains near Scotts Bluff—their stealth—their control. But there had been many of them. She was but one small woman, on a mission to protect her child and her home.

She and Mercy rode in silence—the horse instinctively aware of her mistress's distress. The footfalls of the horse near silent; they walked slowly, the clouds of her own breath could be seen, freezing the bandana to her face. The temperature perhaps ten degrees below. The sunlight bounced from the crystalline snow, leaving it to glimmer in the sun. Time stood still as she paced the horse—side to side, always in a forward motion, in an effort to not alarm the bear, if indeed it was the bear. She raised the heavy telescope she carried as she rode more closely. It was indeed a grizzly; it's reddish hair tipped with gold and gray that appeared to stand straight out from the body, giving it a distinctive appearance, unlike the black bears they had encountered on the trail west. The black bear's coats had been sleek and shone as if they had been coated in the brilliantine often used by men.

The grizzly was approaching the cattle. She watched as the mustangs neighed and rose up on their hind legs, turning to flee. The cattle stood, as if frozen in place in this vast land of snow and ice. *Stupid animals!* She was certain should she be close enough to observe, she would find their eyes wide and wild. Yet they stood.

She scrutinized the bear as he rose to stand on his hind legs. Enormous. Magnificent. She pushed the thought from her mind. Would the temptation of the cattle and his hunger make him more dangerous? Perhaps.

She dismounted and crouched in the snow. *How far was she? Perhaps two hundred yards—she would be safer mounted on Mercy. The shot would be more difficult mounted—still she would be safer.* She looked to the east; the rising sun would be in the eyes of the bear. She chastised herself. She was only putting off the inevitable. She once again mounted Mercy. *Trust in yourself. Do not think.* Jamie's words came to her as she thought of their lessons in the woods of Virginia. Her shooting lessons—the lessons with the knife. *She could do this!* The memories of the Goodnight Trail rose before her. The Indians she had shot and killed—the young Indian Brave she had slaughtered with her knife. *It is kill or be killed, Elisabeth.* These words were not just Jamie's now but hers as well.

She knew by the stance of the grizzly, he was looking at their cattle as his next meal. The grizzly had come to her home. *It was* kill or be killed.

She pulled the rifle to her shoulder and took aim. Stopping, breathing deeply, she whispered to Mercy. "Mercy, I am going to shoot. Be very, very still. Stay, stand, girl." She heard the soft neigh of response from the animal, pulled the rifle to her shoulder, and squeezed the trigger. Her mind screaming, *Forgive me, Father*, her shoulder absorbing the brutality of the shot.

The bear dropped to all fours. She looked up and saw him stand and take a great leap toward the cattle that stood frozen in fear. She was now close enough to hear their bawling voices.

The grizzly rose again.

Again, she squeezed the trigger and watched as the bullet flew past him, feeling the adrenaline as it coursed through her veins, her heart racing. A cold moisture rose on her skin. Fear, anxiety, excitement! She felt only determination as she watched the bear turn in her direction, to rise once again to his full stature.

"Oh, Lord!" She was perhaps seventy-five yards from him. Chills ran over her skin. She could feel the sweat as in trickled along her scalp; in ten-degree weather, *she was sweating*. Fear rose like bile in her stomach...

Elisabeth could feel the tension in Mercy, as the horse sensed the fear in her, the horse's eyes wide with alarm, her coat lathered, her flesh quivered in the great effort to do her mistress's bidding. Elisabeth reached for her other rifle and aimed for his head. Again, she squeezed the trigger.

Blood formed a collage of droplets against the winter white snow, dancing amidst the air in a pattern of slow motion—droplets not unlike the froth of the tumbling rapids of the river below, the crimson color slowly descending to rest on the virgin white landscape. She watched as the majestic animal shook his head, heard the mighty scream of terror, of anger, watched as he bounded ever closer to her. Felt the grief that welled in her heart, as he screamed once again...and lay down on the pristine snow.

She heard the sob—felt it—as it rose from her chest... "Oh, Lord, forgive me."

She heard the snort of Mercy. The pungent stench of blood something neither of them would ever become accustomed to. The horse pulled at the reins, backing away. Or was it Elisabeth? Her heart raced. Fear embodied her very being.

Now what? Had she killed him?

Eleanor's Visit

Eleanor took a deep breath of the crisp, cold air. The sun was shining, and it *was* a fine day. She truly hoped it was a precursor to her visit. She hated this…this feeling of trepidation that seemed always to come with seeing Elisabeth. She was only doing this for Joseph and to make him cease his incessant innuendos as to what *she should* do. She did wish to please him; well, in truth she cared not on most occasions.

She found most persons she came in contact with—to wish her to be someone other than who she was—at least *who she had become* since coming west. It was a constant battle within her mind, to rise above the doldrums that seemed to pursue her. For certain, she had changed—*even she knew that*! Everything about her had changed.

She pulled the drawstrings of the leggings more tightly about her once again—sizeable waist, smoothing the leather of the tunic she wore; the leather clothing of the Indians, soft and supple. She pulled the moccasins over her feet and up over her calves. The braid of her near black hair, thick and wide as it lay down the length of her back. Her body was once again nearly as plump as when they lived in Maine; with a diet of meat, potatoes and eggs, bread and butter, with few, if any fruits or vegetables, having contributed greatly to her girth. But then, she was always willing to eat and Joseph and Many Hands were good cooks.

Many Hands had returned to help her about the house as per Joseph's request. She could truly say, she saw no reason for the constant concern over the tidiness of the house. After all— there was but the two of them. She guessed that was all there would ever be. Thanks to her bad luck— to Providence— to the gods... she didn't know, she tried desperately *not* to care.

She dreaded the visit. About the time she felt well enough to endure the constant turmoil of life something always happened, sending her straight to the laudanum—to the bed or wishing to sit in the corner, looking for a room to hide within the barn. *Any place, anywhere,* she would not be subjected to the dreadful decisions of life.

She reached for her spectacles, and smiled into the mirror, not at her reflection, she cared very little as to her appearance, but smiled because of what Joseph would think if she were not to wear her spectacles. Her spectacles seemed to be a sign, of sorts, to Joseph, as to her well-being. *Silly, lovable Joseph.*

She would much rather visit Agnes. At least Agnes was a real person, with frailties and faults. Perhaps she would go see Agnes rather that visit Elisabeth and her child. Joseph would never know—and if he found out, what could he do. She hadn't visited anyone since Jamie was home last and that—*that baby*—had been born. Everyone had gathered at Elisabeth and Jamie's house then. It had been nice. It was nice to see everyone. Joseph had played his harmonica and Charlie had played his fiddle. Ilene and Duncan had sung. She had to admit Ilene had the most beautiful voice. She wondered how Ilene did that. Live up there all by herself—day after endless day. Probably sang and prayed and made doughnuts. "Ignorance is bliss," her ma always said. She smiled at the thought. Peacefulness is evidently given to the daft.

Thoughts of Ma Parsons came; she had lost at least two children that Eleanor was aware of and seemed to have dealt with it just fine, but then, she had lot's of children. Maybe she didn't love them as much as she loved Henry and... She would not think of that—*of Henry*—hard as she tried, she could not let it go...*and the other child—what had she done!* No wonder she felt crazy. None of those other women had any idea of what it was to lose a child. Oh, they went through all the motions of consoling, cajoling, whimpering at her, but in truth, they didn't know how *she* felt. Many Hands seemed to be the only real person in her life. Well, perhaps Joseph…

Eleanor had gone many times to visit with the Indians since the time Charlie had taken them to Little Flower's village. She felt an affinity with these kind, simple people.

She pulled the great coat of buffalo skins around her and trudged to the barn carrying a knapsack of rice pudding Joseph had made. She doubted if Elisabeth knew how to make rice pudding…after all, *Her Highness* hated chickens and milking cows.

The lanterns burned in the barn, the flicker of light could be seen through the shuttered window holes. Joseph would be in there by now, having milked his precious cows, their hired hand Wil having delivered the milk to the area nearly ten miles down the lane, where old man Jensen picked it up of a morning.

Oh! *She did not want to do this!* She had visions of the refined, elegant, and beautiful Elisabeth personified in a small child. Why Elisabeth had named the baby Eleanor—*well, that was a good one.* To make Eleanor bow down to her, no doubt! Agnes had told her that Elisabeth and Jamie had made arrangements with that—that uppity Sally Susanne to care for the child should something happen to Elisabeth, since *Mr. James Martin Prescott* had left to go fight the stupid war. The mere thought infuriated her. That certainly was an indication Elisabeth thought her to be incompetent—deranged. Not that she would want the child. Who would want someone else's child—just…well, it was unkind of her. They were the child's kinfolk. She and Joseph, and Joseph is a good man. Perhaps she had a small problem with the laudanum and the wonderful medicine the Indians had, but…but she would have seen to the child. Most of the time…

The creak of the barn door resounded, and Joseph looked up from the tack he was repairing. "Ah, you're up and looking happy I see. Where ya goin', or did you jus' miss me?" He smiled up at her. His happy, twinkling eyes—something that always warmed her heart. As long as it had nothing to do with the bed… "You see nothing of the sort, Joseph Prescott! How could I be happy to be going calling in weather such as this?"

"It's a grand day, Eleanor. The sun is shining, and the winter is 'bout over. A damn good day, I'd say. What have you there?"

"I've the rice pudding you made yesterday. I did take a little bite, but I shall take it to the child."

"You're going to visit little Eleanor then. Good for you!" He knew it was best to say nothing of Elisabeth. For the life of him, he did not comprehend her feelings for her sister-in-law, but he no longer brought that up; it just exacerbated the already strained relationship they shared. As for Elisabeth, she came to the barn many a morning, just to peek in and say hello. Try as he might to understand Eleanor's concerns over Elisabeth, his admiration for Elisabeth had grown over the years. She was intelligent, hardworking, and yes, incredibly beautiful. Jamie was a lucky man. Been him—he damn sure wouldn't left her to go fight some war three thousand miles away. Joseph rose from the bench he was working at. His size and towering height always stunning to Eleanor, after all these years—since they were six and nine, she found him to be the most wonderfully attractive man she had ever seen. She loved him. It was sad for both of them that she could not show it. It had been nearly two years since she had allowed him to touch her. Her fear of being with child, something she simply could not overcome. The gentle, kind man seemed to suffer in silence. "Let me saddle up for you. Ya think you'll be back for supper?"

"I'll be back by *dinner*. I am calling only to mollify you, Joseph Prescott." The look on his face, one of sadness, a sadness that pulled at her heart strings.

"Surely you can't mean that?"

"I do, Joseph. Sorry to say, I do, and I don't want to hear what you have to say of it."

He walked to her and, leaning down, kissed her on the forehead. "The baby is a *bonny lass* as Mack would say." Again he smiled his toothy grin. Pushing all words from his taciturn wife's lips—*from his own mind*.

The horse saddled, he helped her up and opening the barn doors, waving good-bye. "Do ya have your guns?"

"Yes, Joseph!"

"See ya, take care," he hollered after her.

She could see in the distance, for it was over two miles away, the curl of smoke that came from Jamie and Elisabeth's home. The smoke was but a faint wisp for this time of a morning. *Perhaps the goddess lay abed*, she snickered to herself. As she neared the house, barns, and the original lean-to, she was surprised by the lack of activity about the structures. Perhaps Elisabeth had moved into town…but no, Joseph said she had visited him early of a morning just a few days ago. Seemed she rode the property line like one of the hired hands each morning. *Guess when your husband leaves you, you had to do those things*. She wouldn't have, you can be sure of that—Joseph knew it as well.

Again, her mind wandered to Agnes. At least Agnes did not have all that horrible responsibility. She thought of the frail and pregnant Agnes—teeth missing…her arm had been broken last Eleanor had seen her. *I'd gut the man. I would*, she thought.

It *was* a fine day. It was most certainly cold, but the wind was light and the mountains gave off a luminous brilliance in the winter's sun. Coming upon the barn, she heard the neigh of a horse. But all was closed tightly. Not a chicken or pig could be seen. Nor a hired hand. Where were all the hired hands? She walked her horse to the back of the house. Wood aplenty was staked, some scattered here and there. She could hear the rushing waters of the river below and see in the distance the cabin Charlie had built for him and his squaw, Little Flower. Within Elisabeth's home there were no sparks, no roar from the chimney. Had the fire gone out? For a moment, she felt alarm.

Dismounting, she tied her horse to the hitching post at the front stoop and looked up at the great ornate door. Lovely as it was, it looked ridiculous surrounded by a simple log cabin. Retrieving her knapsack, she strode through crusted snow to the door. She saw the petite footprints that had left the house, she rapped on the door calling, "Elisabeth!"

She turned the knob and entered the house. The very first thing she saw across the expanse of the room was *her* stove! *Her stove!* Drat that woman. She knew full well *why* Elisabeth had it, and she didn't care. Better Joseph had left it on the Oregon Trail than to sell it to his brother, fuming once again at the weft of her and Elisabeth's lives. The house felt pleasant; it was clean and somehow sparkled. She heard the clock that chimed on the half hour, remembering Elisabeth's father had sent it to her. It was a lovely clock. There were muslin curtains at the windows and china set at the table. "Harrumph!" she uttered to herself. That woman! "Elisabeth... Elisabeth, are you here?" She knew there to be a bedroom and a library—*a library for god's sake.* In this vast wasteland, *they had a library*! As well, a closet, *for Miss Elisabeth's finery*!

"Elisabeth!" Still no answer. Perhaps she had gone to town...

She heard a tiny gurgling noise and turned; it was coming from the bedroom. Closing the door behind her, she tiptoed through to the bedroom. Next to the bed was the exquisite cradle Charlie had made for Elisabeth's child, and in it lay one of the most beautiful babies she had seen. Equally as pretty as Agnes's child. Turning, she took her coat off and placing the pudding on the table she returned to the bedroom. "Oh my, what have we here. Why, aren't you the loveliest little thing." Jamie Prescott's eyes looked back at her, but the face was that of Elisabeth. Arms and legs fat and swinging, the soakers could be seen; a butterfly was embroidered on them. The tiny batiste dress filled with intricate handwork.

The child giggled and cooed. "Hi, Eleanor, I am your aunt Eleanor. May I hold you?" She reached in and lifted the child from the cradle, her concern for where Elisabeth was—had vanished. Her heart filled with delight, her eyes filled with tears. Grief spilled throughout her as she held the small child tightly to her. Emotions that had lain dormant for years surfaced and coursed through her as she held this child.

Willing herself to muster a miniscule amount of composure, she walked to the rocking chair with the child. "My, my, you are such a tiny little one and where is your mother? Is she feeding the chickens or milking the cows at this late hour of the morning? The child looked up at her and giggled, her fat little hand reached out to Eleanor's face, her finger's splayed and each perfect tiny fingernail shown.

"Wait till I tell Joseph, you are wonderful, and you are *Eleanor*! My Eleanor, aren't you?" She crooned to the child. "Where *is* your mother?" She heard the clock chime again and found she was surprised to see she had been here half an hour. "We had best go see where your ma is."

She returned the child to its cradle and donned her coat. She was a bit surprised to find she was truly concerned for Elisabeth's welfare. She had seen Elisabeth with all the children who had traveled with them on the Oregon Trail, never was she given to neglect, quite the contrary. She thought of the day Elisabeth had ridden them each on the back of Mercy and the story Mack had told of the Queen of the Fairies that rode a fine white horse.

Peeking back around the bedroom door she whispered, "Auntie is going to look for the Queen of the Fairies, but I shall be right back." The child giggled and squealed in delight.

Exiting the door, she thought she heard hoof beats. Her gut clenched. So…now I shall be obliged to be kind—as surely that will be Elisabeth.

The hoof beats thundered down from the far north pasture, coming straight between the house and the barn. Perhaps she had been mistaken, certainly that would not be Elisabeth. She shaded her eyes from the glare of the sun on the snow—looking more closely she could see the faint outline of a white horse against the winter white of the snows. But who—it looked like a very small man on the horse a *pissy sort of a man*—as Joseph would say. As they came nearer she could see what appeared to be the cape of a bear, slung across the pommel of the saddle. On the horses back—a raw-bloodied hindquarter of...*what in the world?* She walked out to get a better look as the horse ran straight to her. "Good heavens Elisabeth, is that you?" Eleanor called to the rider.

Reining the horse to a rapid stop Elisabeth leapt from the horse. "Eleanor! Why, Eleanor what a wonderful surprise. Oh, I am *so pleased* you have come!"

As Elisabeth ran towards her, all Eleanor could see was *blood! Blood*—as it had spattered, had dotted Elisabeth's face. A great smudge of blood rose along her forehead and beneath her nose...her hands covered in the rich crimson color, which was darkening even as Eleanor stared at it. "Elisabeth, are you hurt?" True concern evident in Eleanor's voice.

The petite Elisabeth only laughed. "Oh, dear Eleanor! I would hug you, but I daresay I am, as you see quite unsanitary."

"Are you hurt Elisabeth? Shall I go for Joseph? Why are you laughing?"

"No, no I am quite well! Eleanor! I just killed a bear! A grizzly! Can you believe it! I..."

"You what?"

"I killed a grizzly bear. Truly, I was unsure he was a grizzly—but I knew he was quite large by his tracks! He was coming around the house, and I was scared—for little Eleanor and myself." She laughed again, taking several steps towards Eleanor. Charlie's gone, the other hired hands are gone, and..." Elisabeth suddenly stopped her explanation.

Eleanor stood looking at her in horror. *"You what?"* All the while backing away from Elisabeth. Eleanor was mortified. She was beyond words. She ran to her horse—mounting it she kicked its side's until it ran like the devil himself. Her mind centered on but one thought—*The perfect little woman—can hunt and kill a grizzly!*

Elisabeth stood watching the distraught Eleanor and her horse high tail it across the snow-covered expanse of Montana. She was stunned, stunned beyond belief—*now, what had she done to upset Eleanor?* Immediately her thoughts ran to her child… what if…surely not…Eleanor would not take her child…but Eleanor—Eleanor…one never knew *what* she might do. She ran into the house, caring not of the blood and guts that covered her.

The child lay in the cradle sleeping. A knapsack set upon the table. "Oh, thank you, Lord! Mama shall return shortly. Sleep, baby, sleep."

She had two more hours before the child would need to be fed. She could not think of Eleanor now—not now. Drat the woman. Why did everything happen this way between her and Eleanor?

She grabbed a great pot and returned outside to fill it with snow. She would sit it on the hearth; by the time she returned, it would be melted and she could take a bath in the hat-box tub. Thinking of the ridiculous invention and substitution for a bath, she laughed.

Perhaps she was a bit overwrought, perhaps a bit frenetic…but then, *she had just killed a grizzly*, certainly enough to cause anyone to be distraught. Nor did she have time to be concerned about she and Eleanor and her apparent…what *did* Eleanor think? She had no time for that.

She had devised a plan to skin the bear and get the meat back before the wolves and coyotes got to it, and she immediately returned to Mercy. She took the meat and hide into the safety of the barn, grabbed some rope, pondered the sled…the bear was far too heavy for her to move, and she had found she didn't have enough strength to dissect it—perhaps a saw? Back out into the wilderness she rode. She would cut it up tomorrow. Between the excitement, fear and exhilaration she was quite exhausted. If she had to leave some of the meat out there—so be it.

Eleanor's horse flew like the wind over the crusted icy snow. The snow was some three feet deep and the speed with which she rode, the hooves of the horse made little indentation. Eleanor had no tears—only frustration. Anger! Unmitigated anger! Her thoughts moved through her mind as swiftly as the horse's hooves flew over the ground. *Why was she so upset? It was that woman!*

She thought of her now...the great bustle, the cocky little hat, the stunning green eyes with lashes as thick as—as... The white kid boots, as she had climbed into the carriage from the home of her father. A veritable *mansion* in the wealthiest area of Philadelphia...her constant chatter! Her infatuation with the *god to all women*—and some men—*James Martin Prescott*! The trek west...she and Joseph had planned this for years. She had maps, lists of supplies to procure, a new life for them. Elisabeth had brought nothing! *Nothing* but books and fine clothing. Costumes for morning—costumes for evening soirees! Not a blanket, not...

She thought of the general store. Elisabeth's hesitation at the throngs of unkempt women and children, of Eleanor's constant encouragement—that she should have sensible shoes. Elisabeth's disgust, as she had indeed given in to the purchase of them. It was she—she and Joseph who had planned this, this new life, this adventure. Elisabeth had come only for Jamie—besotted with the man. Eleanor had thought perhaps, even hoped, Elisabeth would fail. Fail to be up for the challenge. A spoiled, pampered, unwed sixteen-year-old, who was willing to give up riches and position for the likes of James Prescott!

She, Eleanor, would be the one to succeed, to make the crossing—for the love of Joseph and their new life together. It was *she* who was capable! They had planned this! She and Joseph had planned this...

She slowed the horse and stopped, realizing she was weeping. The tears, cold upon her hot cheeks. She could barely see through the fog that covered her spectacles. Taking them off, she wiped her face with her scarf, and she wept.

She had been wrong. *She* had failed... Elisabeth had risen to each and every occasion, most often with joy. It was Elisabeth who had sat with her day after endless day, throughout the horrendous rocking of the wagon—the incessant, sweltering heat, the wind, the rain. It was Elisabeth who had gotten her through the birth of Henry, her *Joseph Henry!* She hated her.

It was *she*, Eleanor who had failed; she who could not meet the demands of the journey. *She* who could not give birth to a living child; she, who was so distraught and weak she had pulled the child from her womb and...and looking at it with disgust, had shoved it beneath the bed. *She hadn't killed it—not really. Did she?* She couldn't remember.

Her whole body shuddered with grief. She knew Joseph wouldn't want her if he knew...did he know...did everyone know...

And now, Elisabeth, left all alone, had the strength and fortitude to kill a bear. *A grizzly bear!* An animal given so much credence by the Indian, that they wore its claws about their necks in homage to the Great Spirit!

She wanted to run—to find sanctuary, to find peace! But where would that be? She could go to Joseph.

Joseph deserved better. Would she go home to Maine? Her heart leapt in her chest. The thought of the trip back across America, frightened her beyond belief. *The Indians...* She felt safe there.

She sat upon the horse, and for the first time in years she sobbed, unrelenting, earth-shattering sobs of grief, of fear, of hopelessness. She needed laudanum—hashish—something to stop this pain.

Joseph stood outside the barn, a milk pail in each hand. Across the horizon to the southeast, he could see Eleanor's horse, a mere shadow on the land of white, moving as if the devil his self was chasing it. The hemlock trees to the west the only other sight before him. He stood and watched. The horse and rider now stood stalk still in the distance. He turned and took the milk into the cooler. Hoping it did not freeze before he could skim the cream from the top. *Ole' Gertrude gave good milk.* He smiled.

Turning back to look, the horse still stood. Perhaps it was young Duncan. Or one of Elisabeth's hands. But then, she had said she had let them go on the "grub line." Lots of hired hands went from home to home during the winter months, with nothing they could find for work…still Elisabeth had kept them on for a great long time.

He hadn't expected Eleanor back so soon; he watched and waited. The horse stood still against the landscape. Was something wrong? She had seemed fine this morning when she had left, but with Eleanor… He thought of her nature of late; actually since the last child was born…dead. His heart skipped a beat. If only he had been here and not bringing cattle up from the King ranch… Quickly he placed his emotions in that little box within his heart.

Still the horse stood. He turned and went to get his horse.

As he rode more closely, he could see it was indeed Eleanor. He watched as she turned her horse from him. She knew it was *him* and was turning from him. Christ, Lord Almighty—what the hell had happened now? There were a few moments he had wished to shake her, a very few for the most part. He simply wished he could assume her pain. She was the love of his life; it was his duty to protect her, to keep her safe. But how did one keep safe, what lived in the mind of another. She would not speak of it, not even to him.

He could feel her love for him, yet he could dare not touch her in intimacy. A damned difficult situation… Her horse was walking from him now, not running. "Eleanor, honey, Eleanor, wait up!" She turned the horse as he came nearer.

"Eleanor, honey, why ya cryin'?"

"It's nothing, Joseph, it's nothing."

She dismounted and stood in the snow, her spectacles falling from her hands.

"Did ya see the baby?"

"Yes, Joseph. I held her," she whispered.

So that was why she was upset. "I'm sorry, honey, was she not what you expected?"

Eleanor turned to him and, from her diminutive height of five-foot-three, looked up at the giant man who was her husband. The father of her dead children. "Yes, Joseph, she is a wonderful child. More wonderful than I had anticipated, and she liked me."

"Ya held her then and had a good visit." He reached and picked up her spectacles.

"Why ya back so soon?"

"Joseph, I find I am once more unwell."

"Ah jeez, Eleanor! Come." He held out his arms and she collapsed against his chest. Her body shook with what he thought to be tears. "Shush, shush, you can tell me, Eleanor. It's all right, honey…"

She pulled back and looked at him through black, small, round eyes; fire lay beneath their depths. Anger seethed from her as she pounded on his chest.

"Eleanor, honey"—shock shown on his face.

"*She—that woman! She* —Elisabeth—*she* killed a bear—a grizzly bear!"

"Really! Elisabeth? When? Is…" He grabbed at the words that threatened to fall from his mouth, now was not a good time to ask as to Elisabeth's well-being. "How do you know that? Tell me what happened."

"This morning she wasn't there when I arrived and…and I went in the house, the house was empty, the baby was just lying in cradle. I picked her up and I held the child, Eleanor. She likes me, Joseph, she liked me, I could tell. Some time passed and I placed little Eleanor back in her cradle and went out to see if I could find… And then—then Elisabeth came riding in from up north at a *gallop*. She had the hide of a grizzly draped across her horse. She and the horse were just covered—*covered in blood*. She was so happy to see me she nearly flew from that horse of hers, was gonna hug me with that blood all over her! I just left, Joseph! How dare she!"

"I don't understand…" He truly did not understand his wife's anger—why, he'd be near bustin' his buttons!

"Can't you see? *She*—*Elisabeth Prescott*—can do anything! I hate her! I hate her!"

"Oh, Eleanor, honey, come here. You're fine. It's okay if you hate her." His understanding of the relationship between the two women—was…well, *he didn't understand.* He thought he should go, go see if he could help Elisabeth. My God, Jamie was off fighting the damned war—the hired hands gone. Where was Charlie? Best not to say a thing of his thoughts to his distraught wife. "Come, Eleanor, git back up on your horse or better yet, ride with me. Let's go home."

She once again dropped her head to his chest and now sobbed as if her heart would break. "I'm so sorry, Joseph…for everything…I am so sorry."

"Shush, come with me, you've nothing to be sorry for." He lifted her to his horse.

He could sense her distance—the loss of intimacy between them. She sat behind the saddle on the horse they shared, and he could sense her oncoming distance, her retreat from his world—*their* world. Sadness enveloped him as he thought of the days, often weeks when she said not a word to him. Dreading now the looming absence—days of isolation, days of foreboding gloom, of emotional turmoil for Eleanor, an Eleanor he could not seem to reach, not to provide help to her or to give her solace. It wasn't simply Elisabeth that brought *it* on; there were many and various circumstances, none of them he seemed to be prepared for—the birth of a new calf, the dreary days of a long winter, the list seemed endless, and he was weary of the ordeal. In the past, he had spouted chapter and verse of the bible to her, seeming only to further anger her. He wanted to fix all of this for her, to hold her in his arms and tell her—tell her *what*. What more was there he could tell her.

She smiled when her told her he loved her, often saying *Thank you*—was that enough for him? *A greedy man you are, Joseph—that you can't be content with the woman you love simply being here.* He chastised himself. Yet they were once a team, a real man and wife! If she was going to descend into the depths of depression on this day, well, perhaps he should really have a sit down chat with her before she closed herself off.

He felt the wind on his face; he could feel the moisture in the air. The temperature was dropping; he could feel it, it was going to snow again. *So much for his fine day.*

Elisabeth once more surfaced within his mind. If she was alone…out trying to salvage the meat, the carcass of a bear, he needed to help her. Someone needed to help her, and she was his brother's wife. The visions brought on by a small, pregnant woman, shooting, killing and butchering a bear—the dangers that image brought to surface in his mind were insurmountable! Packs of hungry wolves, fox, everything and everyone out there was hungry. The winter had been long and a hard one…ole man Jensen said it was *one of the hardest he'd seen*—he'd lived here all his life. Yeah, he needed to see if Elisabeth needed help. He wondered if Eleanor had seen that Elisabeth was once more with child. He hadn't had the heart to tell her; in truth, he had only heard from Charlie. —'*thought Miz. Prescott was in the family way…been sick of a mornin', only sayin' it ta you, Joseph. Don' really know.*'

"I don't like it here, Joseph." The words spilled from her lips as she stood outside the house. He looked down at her in utter shock. "Eleanor, what are you saying…this is what we planned for, since we were children, *this* is what we planned for!" He couldn't believe his ears! "Gowan' in the house, I'll be right there."

He sighed as he put their horses up and took care of the tack and saddles. Once again, a huge sigh came over him, and he wiped his hands over his face, up through his hair. "Lord, if you could just help me…I've no idea what to say anymore." He trudged through the snow to the house. The wind now blowing, the snow coming in horizontal waves of ice. His ma always said if "ya got blue sky enough fer Dutchman's pants, it'd be a fine day." This morning, there'd been enough blue sky fer the Dutchman's pants…

Opening the door, he found the house much like it was every day. Eleanor sat in the chair, still clothed in her coat and bonnet. Her shoes still wet with snow. No lantern light, no candlelight, no fire in the hearth. Without Many Hands, this was frequently a daily occurrence. And yet she had seemed so well this morning, in fact for nearly two months.

He thought of the laudanum he had hidden, of the weather, of Petra, the hashish from the Indians…oh, he knew of the hashish. Perhaps it was that time of month—how the hell would he know… He simply could not bear the thought of his wife being crazy…depressed—whatever the hell they were calling it nowadays. His patience was near as thin as a man's could get… He knew he would do near anything for this woman he loved… but he seemed to have run out of options. He ran his large hands down his face and through his dark hair, feeling the weight of the world on his huge shoulders. "Honey, let me make you some tea and build up the fire. I'll help you with yur boots."

"Don't you touch me, Joseph Prescott."

He stood shocked. Her porcelain skin was flushed, her small round eyes, a steely black. *His wife was pissed.* What the hell!

"Eleanor."

"Don't' *Eleano*r me… I can tell, Joseph, I can tell what you are about to say, and I don't wish to hear it. Do you understand!"

"I, I…Eleanor…"

"Oh, I know all the fine little quotes from the Bible you are ready to spout at me. About predestination about—about…what is the one you tell me? Well, I don't care about your God! I don't believe there is a God, Joseph! I don't! This—this life we live is not of your God! What has happened is of the devil! Diablo, Joseph, Diablo!"

"Eleanor, honey, that is not true, lots of bad things happen to people, life is hard and you're just making it…" He was stopped mid-sentence; her screams pierced his heart, to lay forever there to fester…

"Stop! Stop now! You've no idea—you will not believe what I have told you. But it is true, Joseph! I did that abominable thing… Go, Joseph. I know you want to go. Go to your precious Elisabeth. Help her. There is nothing you or anyone can do for me. Go now!"

Most Bizarre—AKASA

From the heavens and the snowy skies of Montana, the Sentinels—*Akasa, they were called*—the subtle, super sensuous, spiritual essence that pervades all space around the earth, looked down from the firmament to the planet that had been assigned them. They had been here for millennia; they were not guardians nor were they to interfere but only to observe, as God in his infinite wisdom had given *free will* to the inhabitants of this glorious sphere. They had watched in awe as the great waters of the oceans had appeared—observed as the crusted surface had given life to the abundance of flora and fauna.

The scene was not one of silence, but of vibrant, hushed activity. They could hear the symphonic songs of the earth planet—could feel and hear the beat of her heart. They could view the vastness of the land, the mountains, and the deserts.

This great expanse of the blue planet called *Earth* revolved purposefully through the heavens. At this moment, they viewed the great forests of trees that held winter coats of shimmering white, as they hovered over the land called North America.

The Observers looked more closely, their vision one of scrutiny and acclaim, of profound gratitude.

This was a landmass of few humans, a new rich land of abundance. The Rocky Mountains shown dusky hues of purples within their great crevasses—crevasses and gorges formed during their enormous struggle for preeminence, for domination. These rugged, majestic mountains appeared to the north and west, so heavily laden with snow from the Akasa's point of observation, as to be but a ripple on the surface of terra firma.

To the east revealed a myriad of smaller mountain ranges, each with its own value—each with its own scars that defined their efforts to rise above the vastness of the land. The land that lay amid these mountains was a world cloaked in white.

There were small streams and rivers that numbered many, all meandered listlessly in their frozen state. The great Missouri River executed its supremacy as it thundered through the ice flows and the boulders, foraging all, to claim what was to be its domain—as few powers reined sovereign over the mighty river. Its origins had begun in the northernmost Rocky Mountain range. As the snows had melted and the watershed from the gorges of the great mountainous terrain descended, this river in particular, had grown to be the fourth of God's great rivers, and it rushed with fervor through the land to the south and to the east.

The *Akasa* or *Observers* had been drawn here by the *beings of light*—these were the *Guardian's*—with one that shown more brightly than all others…was the woman to be taken *Home*?

The landmass between the majesty of the mountains was speckled with small homes, barns and lean-tos. The Christ light from within the homes varied in intensity, always something the *Akasa* found perplexing, they would indeed require that light should they wish to return to God.

Across fields of white—through the haze of yet a dusting of new snow, they could look from the heavens and see a large smattering of crimson that lay surrounding the lifeless carcass of the greatest of the *Ursus arctos horribilis*—the grizzly.

Small dots of white, black, and gray, hunched low and encircled at a distance the crimson setting—unseen, unnoticed by the young, diminutive woman that crouched at the carcass of the grizzly. These small dots were wolves—wolves that possessed a cunning unlike most animals and a ferocious and ravenous need for food. The pack followed their leader with a military precision and dedication. Their leader moved with stealth few humans could fathom, nor execute. Across the crusted snow they slithered on their bellies. Signals sent to the rest of the pack by their mighty leader—surreptitious and mysterious to mere man. Their motive, nothing more than food. Not to maim or kill but to eat.

The defining dissimilarity in the human desire of the woman and the wolves, formed but a thin fine line. All were creatures of the Almighty. None being diminished in His eye, for He had given dominion to humans over the animals.

From the heavens, the Akasa viewed this as an interesting turn of events.

They observed the *Guardians, the beings of light,* their fears for the young woman, for she was greatly outnumbered. The Akasa watched as the *light beings* danced beside the kneeling woman, dismayed at her inability to perceive them. *Unusual for this soul.* The Observers—the Akasa—viewed the *beings of light* that surrounded the woman, her *guardian angels.* Her attention lay elsewhere.

The alpha male of the wolves had crawled on his belly to lay but some hundred yards from her now, perhaps twenty-five wolves lithely closing the circle they had created around her and the carcass of the grizzly.

From the small home far to the northeast, small specks appeared against the white of the snow, the snow now coming from the skies in great lacey flakes of crystals that blanketed these specks, making them indiscernible.

To the far southwest, a lone horse and buckboard traveled up an incline towards the house and barn.

From the heavens, the *Observers, the Akasa* watched but for a moment longer; *is it predestined?* Endowed with no emotions, only interest in the vivid scene below. Each of them, the Akasa and the humans were each given free will, an opportunity to execute that free will had presented itself and they had all seized the moment.

Beauty and order reigned.

Elisabeth's fingers were numb with the cold, her eyes watered, and her nose dripped unceasingly. *She had made a grave error.* Her heart pounded within her chest, her breathing—halted and inconsistent with the fear that coursed through her. She had been foolish and, yes, arrogant—to put her child in danger as well herself and her unborn child.

The reins of Mercy were tied to her wrist. The horse skittered continuously in unease. The snow now coming in large, lacy flakes—to cover the carcass—to further add to the freezing temperature. Soon they would turn to small icy balls, as the skies had turned heavy and she sensed the temperature had dropped.

How long had she been out here? The fire in the house must certainly have gone out. *Her child—*

This act of aggression—this, this act of what had been defense…had turned.

Her knife had dulled. The saw took great skill to use, skill she did not possess. The great bear was warm to the touch. His eyes open and staring up at her, eyes filled with accusation. She could not find within her the *will* to do this.

Perhaps three feet about them, lay blood soaked snow…her clothing was covered in the blood and guts of the bear. She was cold, her teeth chattered, her jaw clenched tightly against the urge to vomit. Her mink coat tied to the back of Mercy to protect it from the spattering of blood and guts. She knew she should finish gutting the bear. But found not the strength within her to do so. The odors of blood and urine, of feces—all repugnant to her senses. The animals' bodily fluids had exited the body—all of these smells ripe and warm.

She crawled from where the bear lay…and vomited. *She had made a vital mistake.* Perhaps she could kill a bear, but she could not butcher him. She thought of the many braves that hunted together and saw the wisdom in this. She considered the further danger of wolves, of foxes that would come to claim the carcass and the meat of the bear should she leave it here.

She had to return to her daughter. What *had* she been thinking? Was that why Eleanor had run off?

She should have gone to Joseph, even young Duncan, or Jeff Tallman. Jeff had not left Agnes to deal with such as this… rapidly she closed her mind to thoughts of Jamie; it would serve no purpose.

She had eaten nothing this morning, intent on removing the threat of the bear. Her stomach was empty—the vomit was but bile that rose from her stomach.

Mercy pranced willy-nilly, pulling at the tether of the reins at her wrist. She would have to abandon this…this foolish endeavor. She stood, pulling at the reins of Mercy. She was cold and near exhausted, the exhilaration and the labor of skinning the bear having taken its toll on her body.

For the very first time, she felt the stirrings of the child she carried, to have it take place here, under these circumstances, an auspicious sign. "Close your eyes, my child," she whispered.

She crawled back to the bloodied scene and retrieved her knives and her saw, removing the rope from the bear's neck. These things were not easily replaced. She would go home and stoke the fire, wash herself, and tend to her child. The snow falling now was not in soft, fluttering flakes of lace, but pelting round pieces of ice.

She stood and pulled again at the reins; she looked at Mercy to bid her come, her eyes were wide and white—her great body quivered. "Mercy?"

Elisabeth turned and looked across the expanse of the land. Shades of black dotted the snow in a semi-circular fashion about her, for the first time she heard the low, guttural sounds from the wolves. *Holy Mary, mother of Jesus!* She felt the hair rise on her neck and arms—felt the pounding of her heart, the shortness of her breath… "Forgive me, Lord," she uttered, backing slowly to stand next to the ever faithful Mercy.

Charlie slapped the reins that led to the bracings on the horse. The buckboard was laden with supplies and the snows were deep and rapidly becoming ever deeper. The incline to the main house—Miz Prescott's house—at the top of the knoll, made for a long hard pull on the beast. He smiled, thinking, *It was a fine place she had picked for a home.* His and Little Flowers was down closer to the river, amongst the trees. He liked it fine. It was quiet and peaceful.

He had procured beans, some lentils, onions, and flour and a small bag of rice. That should keep 'em fed until the snows let up. Should be happenin' soon to his way of thinkin', but the damn stuff was fallin' now and getting heavier by the minute.

He thought of Miz Prescott's face when she got the letters… There was a whole parcel of 'em and a couple he thought fer sure where from Jamie. Yessiree' the little lady'd be happy. He thought of Jamie—a fine man. Damn sure didn't think this war would last this long. But he figured no one had. He could'a tol' them though—the Southerners were not gonna give up that easily, they were a resilient bunch. He should know, he was from down way of the Carolinas. The newspaper was full of what had happened in Columbia. Looked to him like his people jus' might win. He chuckled to himself.

He'd talked to Ben an' Pa Parsons…read all the damn papers and had called on Miz Sullivan. Caroline and Tobias was gonna have another kid—made three now. Miz Prescott, she'd be happy. Again, he slapped the horse with the reins, anxious to get on home.

Pulling up front of the house, he climbed from the wagon and went to the stoop, opening the door, he called, "Miz Prescott gotta bunch a letters fer ya."

He was surprised to find the house empty. The fire had gone out and the child was whimpering from the bedroom. *What the hell...* "Miz Prescott?" He knew it was not the most descent thing to do, but he tiptoed into the bedroom. The pretty little thing lay in the cradle fussin' to beat the band. "Miz Prescott!" He called again, alarm now present in his voice.

He piled the wood from the hearth upon the dying embers of the fire and looked in on the child again. "Where's yur ma?" On the stoop he saw the footprints, a small boot and an Indian moccasin—*that ain't good.* Alarm clenched at his gut. He leapt from the porch and ran to the side of the house. Maybe she had gone to replenish the wood. But in his gut, he had a funny feelin' an' it t'were't good...

Blood lay deep in the snow, horses' hooves that tore up the ground aplenty. More blood wherever he walked. Further and further he walked, seeing only more tracks of a horse or perhaps several, the ground so tore up it was hard ta figure. But one thing was fer sure—blood trailed everywhere. *Shit!* He couldn't remember the last time he'd be scarit, but he damn sure was now.

It took him perhaps ten minutes to retrieve his weapons and his horse—saddle it and set out following the tracks of the horse. *If it was Indians had taken her, he'd have ta go back, take the kid to Little Flower, then he'd look for Elisabeth.*

The snow was falling heavy now, making it difficult to find the tracks of the horses—difficult to see through the damned white stuff.

Joseph pulled his hat down more tightly, pulled the collar of his greatcoat up about his neck. The terrain a drape of white, he couldn't see a thing.

He had gone into the barn and told Wil, "Come with me. Jamie's wife just killed a bear an' that can't be good."

Wil's horse kept time with Joseph's Roan, Gracie, as they trotted quickly over the landscape. Joseph knew the land well now. Glad it was his, beyond grateful to have his own spread. They had well over four thousand head of cattle between he and Jamie. Not countin' Mack's. Then there were all Jamie's mustangs, an' some he was sure were part Arabian—that black stallion of Jamie's was a randy horse. He and Wil picked up their speed. "Where we goin'?"

"Eleanor said she killed it north of her house. 'Must be 'bout halfway, shouldn't take us mor'n half an hour—which is too damn long if she's in trouble."

"Why the hell did she kill a bear? Wee snippet of a girl like that." Wil was near shouting to be heard.

"Ah, ya know Elisabeth. Got a temper that one. Seems the bear been hangin' 'round the house. 'Don't know much, jus' what Eleanor said." Joseph thought of Eleanor, she would be pissed if she found out where he had gone, and taken Wil to boot, leaving her all alone. But well... He figured she was gonna be pissed fer a number of days anyhow, might jus' get on with his life. On the other hand he might jus' come home and find her right where he had left her, still wearin' her coat n' bonnet, sittin' in the dark...

"Ya think she's all right?"

"Nope...I don't. Got a bad feelin' in my gut." Joseph felt fear for this woman, his brother's wife, a fear he had come to know intimately with his own wife. He hated this feeling.

"Where's Charlie and the others?"

"Ah, ya know...the other's went on the grub line—goin' from ranch to house fer work until the snow lets up. Elisabeth kept 'em on a long time though, even without workin'. Charlie, he went to town a couple days ago, told Elisabeth he'd be gone a few days, a week maybe."

The snow was blinding, the wind had picked up and was coming off the face of the Rockies...cold and biting. They pushed their horses on. Wil turned to say something to him but Joseph couldn't hear him. Joseph's mind clamoring for what they would find. With the snow, wind and cold making it a treacherous situation for her to be out in, let alone to be trying to butcher a bear in this. He thought of the wolves that howled at night—often during the day. *What the hell was she thinkin'?*

For a brief moment, his heart fluttered in fear, Eleanor said the baby was alone...he knew Elisabeth. He knew her heart. She would never leave her child if she weren't scared out of her breeches. Scared people did rash things, an' Elisabeth was one of those people who had instantaneous response. He thought of the Oregon Trail, of little Paddy and the fire. She had not given a thought to her own safety, just gone in and slapped the fire from the kid, then plunged into the river with him. And Jamie...*Hail Mary, full of grace...Christ...*

He spurred the roan harder. Wondering what he would find—if he found her.

Letters

Elisabeth knew it was not good practice, yet again she had nursed small Eleanor and lay her in the bed beside her. The child slept the better and so did she.

She looked at the clock on the bedside table—its hands ticktocking away, the hour said two. She was fully awake now and rose from the bed. Perhaps tea would calm her. She had still not recovered from the attack of the wolves or for that matter—the killing of the bear! *Lord, have mercy, what a foolish woman I can be.* Yet it did seem the right thing to do at the time. She stoked the fire and put the teakettle on, her thoughts running back to the scolding she had received from both Charlie *and* Joseph. They were right. She knew that she owed her life to these men. She thanked the Lord for that.

She remembered nothing of those last moments—only trying desperately to mount Mercy...Mercy had reared her head, pulling the reins from Elisabeth's hands. The mare's ears laid tightly back against her head, her eyes wide and her teeth showing yellow. The blur of black and white fur—mouths wide, with sharp, jagged teeth bared, as the wolf had leapt through the air.

Elisabeth had heard the crack of a rifle shot and thought hers had gone off by accident, as she held only a skinning knife in her hand. *Her bloody hand.*

The teakettle whistled and she poured the boiling water over the tea ball. Perhaps a small bit of whisky would be of help. Her hand shook as she reached for the bottle, the exhaustion of the last week finally having caught up with her.

Thank you Lord, that the snows still lay heavy on the land. I still have time to rest. Her mind wandered again to Ilene. Joseph had sent his hired man Wil, back for Ilene. Elisabeth had awakened to the lilting Gaelic sounds of Ilene… "'Lisobeth. Kin' ye hear me, lass? 'Lisobeth ye mus' wake now…the babe she needs a feedin'… iffnin' ya kin't wake fer the likes o' meself, wake for the wee one…'Lisobeth. Ye be a bloody mess—*Ciamar a tha sibh* —a bloody mess. Come stan' up, lass…"

She smiled now, remembering the disgust in the voice of Ilene.

"Wha' in the Lord's world would ya be doin', lassie. Behavin' as you be big as me Duncan ya be."

"I am so sorry." Those being the only words she remembered uttering…over and over, as Ilene pushed the whisky to her lips.

Ilene had lit the fire in the great flatiron stove, waiting while the water boiled…waiting to eradicate the traces of Elisabeth's hunt—her foolishness.

"Mercy?" she asked.

"Aye, lass, the mare she be fine. Be thinkin' them men would havin' ta be hobblin' the *failbhe*…she wished to folla' ya into the house…she did. Thet big ole horse. Guess they be more of them *sèitheach* then Joseph and Charlie ever see'd here. But lass, I be thinkin' ya got their ire up, ya did.

Elisabeth sat down at the table with her tea, thinking of the time Ilene had spent with her. Three days she had stayed. Elisabeth had no way in which to thank her. Duncan had arrived late of an evening to fetch his ma. With Ilene's kisses upon the cheek of Elisabeth—giving last orders. "Member the babe…me bonny lass…no doin' thet'll leave her with no a ma now."

Elisabeth had not seen Charlie but once, as well Joseph. They had each stopped by to inquire of her health…and left. With Charlie staunch in his admonishment to "stay in the house." He had summoned one of the hands back… He would ride line of a morning. "It is what Jamie would want. You know it well Miz Prescott." They were still angry with her.

Pulling a shawl around her nightgown, she went outside. The cold night air brushed tenderly at her face and hands. The sky covered the earth in the blue black of ebony, stars twinkled their messages to one another, the cradle of the moon hung as if carved of Carrera marble above the glimmer of Venus. The moon shed its luminous light upon the frosty white cover of snow upon the ground. Tiny twigs of bushes poking through; soon now, soon, the land would awaken and life would abound. Was Jamie looking at this moon? She felt she could sense his presence…silly, she knew—and yet…

She heard the cry of a wolf and felt her body quiver. Inexplicably, it caused her little fear. They had always been there; the sounds of the wolves howling in the depths of the wild land. It was a sound she had grown accustomed to, an echo of the vitality that existed here, here in this place she had learned to love.

The table lain strewn with the letters Charlie had brought from St. Helena. So many letters, she had been overwhelmed with joy and loneliness—weeping the whole of the day. A day Ilene had been there, causing Ilene yet more concern.

Why must they all come at once—it was overwhelming. The longing for Jamie, the fear. Waiting to see if he was alive and well. The ever constant wait to hear from her family, then to be plummeted by missals of joy and triumph—of illness and death and desolation… It was a great deal to abide.

Thinking better of adding the whisky to her tea, she tipped the bottle to her lips. She felt the rush of the hot sting of the liquid as it rushed down her throat and settled into her stomach.

She sat the Havilland china cup and saucer upon the table and reached for the letters, knowing they would provide both grief and solace. Emotions she acknowledged as part and parcel of her existence. *Lord, give me strength.* She had read them a dozen times over the course of the last days, sharing them with Ilene as Ilene had shared hers from Mack. Smiling, she thought of Ilene's tenderness when she had read the letter from Mack to her... "I not be sayin' ta ya no' o' the words." She had smiled a serene smile as she had placed the letters next to her breast.

Elisabeth took a sip of tea and reached for the missive from Mama. "Lord, thank you," she murmured to herself.

February ~ 1863

Dear Elisabeth~

We received the missives you posted November of 1862~ as well~ those brought by your husband Mr. Prescott. Your Mr. Prescott visited briefly en route to his posting, extolling enthusiastically the virtues of your daughter and yourself. I found him to be quite charming despite his obvious lack of scruples.

Elisabeth~ I see that you have called the child Eleanor Juliet and yet in one letter your spelling is 'Juliet', in another 'Juliette' please do make up your mind. As we are anxious to hear more concerning our granddaughter and great granddaughter~I write this at your grand-mère's behest, as she is unwell and has been confined to her bed. Do not alarm yourself~ she has but what the physician describes as 'consumption' ~ more than likely caused by the frigid winter. The remainder of us, as yet, have not succumbed.

I do hope you have found the button with the larger shank, as it will be a deterrent ~ might I say ~ of further inconveniences, although it shall not be needed where as you are without your husband.

Your papa talks of joining in the war efforts and Samuel has joined with the Union, leaving but Jeremiah to fret and stew, saying he will go as well. It shall certainly be over before either your younger brother or your father can engage in the effort against those who threaten the democracy of the Union.

I remain,
Mama

Elisabeth's hand smoothed the pages of her mama's words. Words that left Elisabeth missing her more than she had thought possible…words that implied Mama *would forgive* her. Perhaps she would never forget—yet she would forgive her. She sent a silent prayer that Papa and Jeremiah would be spared. Samuel… she wished him no harm. Her heart ached at the thought of him, of his lack of affection in regard to her. She folded Mama's letter and placed it carefully in the envelope and reached for Papa's letter. Thinking as she did so of the bond that held them tightly, Papa was forgiving and accepting. Did her brother's feel that as well? He had given each of them a place in his heart; it had been given freely, without restraint. Elisabeth could envision Papa now, tall and impeccable in his dress; kind and laughing eyes of green, speckled with brown, bushy brows. Mama had married a man not unlike *her mama*. This revelation one that made Elisabeth chuckle. Oh, how she missed him.

My Dearest Elisabeth, as Well, my Granddaughter Eleanor~

I must say it is with supreme honour I address small Eleanor, it however makes me older than I feel.

I hope you are well and Joseph Prescott and Mr. Charlie Wardle are looking after you. From what your James imparts to me you do indeed need looking after! Not from incompetence certainly~ but displaced bravery.

I have spoken with your James, a fine young man. It was most thoughtful of him to pay us a visit. I feel I shall have to forgive the young man for loving you, as I am of the same mind.

I daresay he has furthered my feeling of patriotism and the need for some persons of competence and sound of mind to join in the efforts; as it is said one of the officers, a fellow by the name

Joshua Chamberlain, sighted George Washington in the hills not far from here.

My young Samuel, your brother, has joined in the fight. Against our wishes, but with my blessings, I believe he is to be a young lieutenant, however with his determination and acumen I feel he shall be a fine leader, although quite unforgiving.

Young Jeremiah continues to badger his mama and I to take up the cause. I strictly forbid it ~as I strictly forbade you to marry. Your papa is so very powerful is he not?

Mama has been ill (your grand-mère, not your mama) for quite some time, appears to be on the rise now. I am certain she has not informed you, as she would not wish to cause you concern.

The crocus' are pondering the spring and the daffodils shall be up soon. How does your garden fare and what of your Mercy and her young Trésor? I smile as I think of my granddaughter mounted upon the young Trésor.

The devastation continues to unravel the country~ most disturbing.

I send you my love and young Eleanor as well. We look forward to your missives with her growth and the well being of all of you out there in the wilderness. It does cause me great consternation Elisabeth.

With the Greatest of Love for each of You~

Your Papa

William Bunyan

Papa was correct...Samuel would make a fine officer...for *whomever* was willing to pay him the most. She smiled at the thought—perhaps the Confederate Army would offer him a post that was more lucrative... Papa was also precise in assuming Samuel would give his men no quarter.

Certainly Papa would not join.

She thought of the image of Jamie and her mama. *Thank you, Jamie, that you cared enough for me to visit my family.* She had known all along that Mama would love him, should she but give him an opportunity.

Strange—Jamie had said nothing of seeing George Washington's ghost, but there were so very many men that had joined in the fight, the numbers he wrote of astonished her.

She reached for the missal from Grandmère. Lord, how she wished she were here with her. She felt the hot sting of tears and swallowed hard, all this was simply not good for the child she carried. And she truly should go back to her bed.

Ma très chère Elisabeth chérie et ~

Oh cher c'est vraiment merveilleux —Oh dear it is so wonderful to say those words. I would give anything to hold the child~ Eleanor. Your dashingly handsome husband (I must say, he is far more handsome since he was last here) has extolled the beauty of the child to us with such love and warmth that I believe I can actually visualize her. His description in such great detail, he proclaims that she looks as a great beauty, just as her mother, with blue eyes… do you think they will change? They often do you know. I can not express my joy at my great~ grand daughter. Although Jamie was as explicit as one could be.

I do hope the birth was one of exceptional ease… did you find the button? Your husband was so very thrilled to have arrived in a timely fashion for the birth and extols your bravery and your exceptional skill at mothering his child. I, for one knew you would be an exemplary parent.

Even though you have written of your great adventures I found it was simply exhilarating to hear first hand of your adventures and your bravery, although I felt that much was held forth in an effort not to overly concern my person. How I would love to hear those words from you in this very room.

I believe you may rest your concerns as to the acceptance of Mr. James Prescott by your parents. He has charmed even your mama. I thought your papa would not let him go.

Tell me of the child. Will you baptize her in the Methodist church there? Please darling… it would serve to give your grandmother much peace. Do you miss the church? I feel you must.

Tell me of the clothing, is it suitable or are the things in the layette yet too small? How much does she weigh now? Why... she must be near four months old...and by the time you receive this! Oh my dear, how I would love to touch you and your child, to see you with my very own eyes.

I do apologize for being maudlin. I suppose you're papa or your mama informed you I have been unwell. I thank the Lord I am on the mend, up and gaining more energy each day.

The social season will be in full swing soon and I must make appointments with the seamstress. I am so looking forward to it. Such a long dreary winter!

Your mama and I shall visit your friend Mrs. Sullivan's mum in the next few weeks. 'Mum' a very Irish form of speech.

I sew assiduously at small clothing and knit for the winter to come once again. I await quite impatiently for the bloom of the apple trees and the lovely scent of the hyacinths.

Whatever happened to the young French woman you met on the westward trail? How is your sister-in-law faring?

James assures me Joseph and Mr. Wardle are looking after you. I dearly pray that is so. Perhaps, shall this war continue you should come home my darling! I miss you terribly. Again I am being maudlin...I laugh.

I am quite certain your papa informed you of Samuel and his call to duty. As for Jeremiah~ I pray he is more obedient than you my darling.

Your Jamie tells me you receive the missive's all at one time. How do you know which to read first? I daresay, I am much relieved you shall not notice that I did not write for several weeks.

I must end this as much as I wish to just write and write.

Please darling, care for yourself and your child, my little Eleanor... I can not express my love for you.

Pour toujours
Votre grand-mère

Elisabeth placed the fine stationery next to her bosoms and felt the tears well in her eyes. Perhaps she *should* go home...

April 1863

Ma chérie, Elisabeth et mon Eleanor peu merveilleuse~

Only the angels in heaven would comprehend my longing for you. My soul is torn by my wish to be a patriot and my great desire to be at your side.

I so very much wish to be there to celebrate your day of birth (you shall soon be as old as your husband my darling. I chuckle.) and to celebrate the day we wed. I contemplate now quite lascivious thoughts that we could thus engage in to do so.

Please my darling, always hold in your heart the essence of my soul, for it resides with you. You alone are the blessing in my life. Know— that to be truth— forever hold the knowledge within your heart.

Tell me of our child Eleanor, and of your days. Have the snows melted? What of Trésor and Mercy and our many friends there? In my minds eye, I see the wonder of nature that is ours to care for and my heart leaps with joy and a great sense of peace.

I find it to be a strange sensation to sit in your childhood home writing this letter to you. I think of the first time my eyes beheld the beauty of you and wonder that you have given me the gift of becoming my wife. Of the great adventures we have encountered together, in but brief moments in our lives.

Your family has been most accommodating. I must say I suffered some qualms at the reception I would receive. Your papa and I have quite a great deal in common— an outstanding gentleman! Your mama seems to have somewhat forgiven me... at best, it is what I would wish. Jeremiah is a young rascal, filled with joy and the exuberance for war... I am most certain you wish not to hear of that. But the young man makes me smile, as he is very much like yourself, Elisabeth. I must admit to being pleased Samuel has not been in residence, as I would have to throttle him for his treatment of you, my wife. Grand-mère— what dare I say? She fills me with her light and her love, all for the love and caring of you, my darling.

Tell me of our daughter, I daresay I cannot fathom what she is capable of at this young age, although, your mama and Grand-mère try desperately to convey childhood growth to me.

> I shall leave your families' home early of a morning on the morrow. I am somewhat heartened by the fact that Lincoln has established a new commander in charge and that I am acquainted with him. As well, Josiah holds him in high regard. It is rumored that the south is venturing to the north, wishing to stave off the terrible devastation to its southern lands. Personally I believe it would serve us well should we employ the tactics of the Arabs and dispense with the organization of Napoleonic war. If it is indeed to end— we must be more aggressive, as our opponents are admirable, to be certain. I must say in closing that the obscenity of the war has had a chilling effect on my very soul, as I feel certain, it has on all who serve. I am reminded of a poem I read in a wonderful book in you fathers' library;
>
>> From an infinite source midst realms of light,
>> An offspring from nature, my soul stood its flight,
>> To gain amid matter, with its trials and its pain,
>> The knowledge to carry it homeward again.
>
> It is difficult at best to refrain from the continuation of this correspondence as I would but wish to see the image of your face in my arms, to feel the silky caress of your flesh against my own. Should it be forgiven a man to weep, I would do so.
> Throughout eternity, with the depths of my soul I love you, my Elisabeth.
>
> Your Husband,
> James Martin Prescott

The tears now came in droves of sobbing…her heart filled with the longing for her Jaime. She must stop this! She must! She looked across the table at the flicker of candlelight, the wax having pooled about the candleholder. Swiftly she moved the letters from the melting wax.

There was a letter from Prudence, a lovely letter extolling the virtues of her husband and exclaiming her joy at Elisabeth's child Eleanor. Soon, she too, hoped she and Edward would be parents—as she had given up the button.

There were two more from Papa and one from Jeremiah... He had joined the war effort and would leave the first of June. Her heart had lurched; he was but a child! *Lord, let it be done before then.*

The table held yet the most precious of all, those from Jamie... letters of love and of joy, of fear and of desolation...one such letter she had read to Charlie and to Joseph...as she had been saddened to the very depths of her soul by its contents.

How she longed for him. She placed her head on her folded arms on the table and wept.

Tomorrow will be a better day...

Gettysburg

July 5, 1863

Elisabeth, Elisabeth, My Love~

As I write this my hand yet trembles.

What has transpired here is— is —I wonder at the manner of my soul having witnessed this— or is it my soul that has brought me thus, into this foul region I have foolishly come. It seems without air, without light.

After nearly three days of fighting the atmosphere has the darkness of the blackest of nights. Souls wander hopelessly and helplessly in body and in the ghostly apparitions' of my mind and profound guilt. There is no peace, no calm, nor rest. Nor quiet of mind or heart. The smoke of gunfire and the odor of sulfur and blood permeate the air. Cries of pain and fear plummet my hearing… they cry for their mothers and to God— to the Lord Jesus— and yet again their mother's. We men in our lust for power and privilege have brought to this earth… Hell!

If it were I, I would call for you Elisabeth, my beloved wife… as you are the first I think of a morning and the last of a night. Never shall I forget the gift of you~ 'He' has bestowed upon me; never shall I fail to show Him gratitude.

They have established makeshift surgeries and the screams of the men whose limbs are being sawed off make Petra Gilky look as the angel of God, as she cared for the sick and the wounded on the Oregon Trail. To my left is a growing pile of limbs, as they discard them and move on to yet another. It is surely an abomination of desolation. Woe is the soul of those of us that have partaken in such as this.

As I write to you of this, I am filled with the guilt of doing thus... yet I find it to be essential to tell you, and you alone of the sorrow that lies within my heart, for I know you know the purity of my soul.

This has been a battle like none other I have seen. The dead lay piled upon each other— the numbers so vast as to make an evaluation as to their actual death unfathomable. Thousands upon thousands lay with limbs in most inappropriate positions. Blood scourges the earth of this once verdant place called Gettysburg. Burial of these poor souls and notification to their families— something that shall most assuredly never transpire.

The land is open farmland here, with many fences—some parallel and some oblique to our line of battle. These were formidable obstacles for the Confederates. They could not stop under fire and dismantle the fences— that was out of the question. I watched as they clambered over the top. I am certain that seemed but an age of suspense, for it was not as if there was a leaping over— it was rather an insensible tumbling to the grounds. At that particular time their units appeared to fall apart, leaving gaps within their units that I was certain would bring us victory—for my men filled those gaps—opening fire on the enemy—yet these men— these indomitable southern men— rallied 'round. Cries of mortal agony could be heard above the roar and rumble of the guns. The dead and wounded now piled so high as to make the fences invisible to the eye.

The two armies impinged upon one another with the force of two great rivers. I can not foresee they shall ever form one in harmony.

It has been Fredericksburg all over again, yet worse, far worse! To have survived——leaves me with a guilt so extraordinarily profound, I find perchance I shall not recover. And yet, and yet I wish to lay before God and Give Thanks that indeed I am alive, unscathed of body.

I thought I spied Tommy and Micah Parsons...with the grey coats...yet... I can not be certain. I have searched for Mack—all to no avail. Josiah is presently with Seward. At least he is safe.

This battle leaves the battle of Thompson's Station in Tennessee that I wrote you of last... to be mere child's play.

The Confederates retreated, I am not yet certain as to why... did we win this battle? If so, the cost was far more than any of us would wish to pay. It has been but a senseless waste of life. For the life of me I can not now remember why we fight thus. For honor—there lies none here. For the right to instruct others— how to live their lives? Cruelty, the thirst for power, for triumph? I can not say...

My heart lies heavy at this hour. I wish only to hold you in my arms and crush you to my chest, to see the blue open skies of our home... to see our child.

Elisabeth, Gettysburg was a simple, small town with farms and a railroad junction, a college and a seminary. We knew the Confederates were in the area...we had heard that Lee had rode through Hagerstown, Maryland on his way to Chambersburg, Pennsylvania, we heard all the northern ladies surrounded him, when one of the northern girls waving a Union flag at the column of men as they rode through and called out "Oh, I wish he was ours!" Others of the ladies calling for locks of his hair. I must assume him to be quite handsome.

They; the Confederate army, arrived in Gettysburg wishing to plunder our provisions—to resupply their army, looking for caps, food and shoes, as the Union army has most recently supplied the men with right and left shoes. (I can not tell you of the significance of this) It is now most obvious they were unaware of the presence of the Union army nearby. We had heard disturbances of the atmosphere— as if someone was beating a rug, far over the horizon...and yet each town we had passed through had appeared to be delighted to see us. Persons out along the roads, waving and offering us milk and water. I think we looked quite illustrious with flags unfurled, mounted on our fine steads. A vision of blue conqueror's— how very wrong I was.

> I ask that you forgive me for these despicable words that shall haunt you as well, yet I feel I must divulge them to you or lose my senses.
>
> Please rest assured that I am well of body and with this letter I shall find the courage to go forth.
>
> I ask of you that you may recall the day I found you huddled in the bed with the nasty cap and my clothing…breakfast, a fire and some whisky was all you required to stave off the effects of despair.
>
> You, my darling, are all of those things to me and I shall rally 'round.
>
> Perhaps it shall be done. This war! Perchance I shall once again ride the range of open land and gaze at the beauty of nature, with you at my side—always with you at my side.
>
> My love for you Dear Elisabeth, Remains Ineffable.
>
> Your Husband~
> James Martin Prescott

Elisabeth placed the pages upon the ground next to her. She sat now on the small hillock just above the bubbling sounds of the Missouri River. Small Eleanor sat beside her—Ellie; she had begun calling the child. The breeze from the north—soft against her face as she reached to wipe her eyes. Her heart as heavy as her body. She felt the unborn child move within her and patted her stomach, watching as Ellie crawled across the clover, all the while placing everything in her mouth to be tasted and savored.

Her heart swelled with love for this small person, her skin the sun-browned ivory of Elisabeth's own, her head a mass of tousled black curls that matched the beauty of both her mother and her father, her eyes were decidedly Jamie's amber—and like his, would turn dark if she was angered or in distress. Her temperament very much more Jamie's than that of Elisabeth, for that—Elisabeth was grateful. To have a child that had temper tantrums was not something she wished for. She smiled at the thought of her own disagreeable side.

She knew Jamie to be physically strong; she also knew his mind and soul to be as sound as his body. He had an inner clarity that few persons were gifted, with the exception of Mack—Ian Mackenzie.

But this, this lay on her own soul, perchance as heavy as it lay on his.

This being perhaps the hundredth time she had read this letter in the last week, since it had arrived. With each reading, his soul seemed to rise before her in a vision of the most glorious of blue... she must ask Sally Susanne what, if anything, that meant.

Jamie, her strong, handsome, poetic Jamie. She could hear the stories he had told of his fight with the French against the Arabs. Hear his words as he defined the negotiations—the money offered him to fight *for* the Arabs. A mercenary! A man contented to fight a war for the adventure of it. A sense within him, a masculine inclination, she surmised.

This letter—these words—bode not well. He appeared broken—if not *broken*—deeply, deeply troubled. To write this to her... She thought of the Battle of Thompson's Station in Tennessee, that she had shared with Joseph and Charlie... of Jamie's enthusiasm, of the lack of discordance within his words. Was thought and caution beyond men's virility in this war? Was it not possible to sit down and talk of this... Certainly it had ceased to be a war of *honor and division*! Now it was of *treason and shoes*—how preposterous.

She reached for the last of his letters that had come last week...

My Darling~

This shall be brief, as we are again in a small skirmish— so to speak. I am very much the better. Having found Mack and learned from a Confederate comrade of mine that Tommy and Micah are well—as well, sharing my despondency with you.

Thank you darling, for your courage and your love. Knowing you are there is all the encouragement I shall ever need. All of this—and a small amount of rest have greatly restored my emotional stability!

Dare I say, I would not have thought it possible to have felt as I did —or to have disposed of those feelings.

We were triumphant in the battle at Gettysburg— if one does not consider the tremendous loss of life and limb. It is estimated fifty thousand men and boys succumbed on the battlefield in those three horrific days. Twenty-eight thousand Confederate and thirty-three thousand Union. The very thought of those days continue to cause me great distress.

For every one soldier that died there are two that succumb to disease…I think of your dear friend, Sally Susanne as I write the word dis-ease… And of Petra—the surgeons here use not anesthetic, as they think it does more harm than good, believing it to cause gangrene. I believe that many of the men died of infection. I think of Petra as she sutured Toms face and of the care in which she took to use abundant alcohol, both then and with the cholera. They are using strychnine; arsenic, calomel, opium and a great deal of whiskey, during the amputations, as well, the treatment for illness. The illness is great, most prolific is dysentery; the unsanitary conditions truly could not be greater.

The desertion rate of the men is said to be some two hundred a day…I shall not desert! However, my enlistment shall be up at the end of the month, I find the patriotism that lies in my heart is not sufficient to stay such a great distance from you my darling and I shall be home as fast as Danny can get me there. Mack is coming with me, as well, Josiah! Is it probable for you to make lodging arrangements for him in St. Helena?

It is not within me to say how long we shall stay. Truly my dear, I can not say how long… perhaps these men need but for me to leave— to end all of this. And I shall be home for all time.

Un peu de temps mon amour j'ai doit te tenir dans mes bras une fois encore une fois.

Pour toujours,
Your Jamie

Thank you, Lord! A stifled sob rose from the depths of her soul…

The Waiting

The brilliant gold orb of the sun rose in the east against a cerulean blue sky, foretelling another magnificent day of sunshine. The fields that had been planted the fall previous were verdant with hay and alfalfa, the tops waving in the gentle breeze with signs of small tassels. The fragrance of honeysuckle, moved from the nearby woods, wafted through the air. Cattle dotted the pastures, sturdy and sound cattle they had brought from the King ranch in Texas. Mustangs grazed beside Mercy and her filly in the lower pasture. *Jamie will be pleased*; Elisabeth knew he would.

The fences had all been repaired; the new cattle had all been branded…with JEP as well a miniature *fleur-de-lis*, to distinguish them from Joseph and Eleanor's cattle. Elisabeth felt certain there was no need, as Joseph most likely knew each of his cows and had given them each names. Joseph had fewer head of beef cattle. He had milk cows, black and white milk cows he called Holsteins; yet said they were *but plain, old dairy cows*.

Each morning, he or Wil stopped at her house and left her milk and cream. She had been so thrilled not to have to milk those cows; she had wished to give him *her* milk cows.

"Gowan', Elisabeth…let Charlie's Little Flower use them. She'll be happy for the milk and one day you may need them. I got lots a cows."

If she had returned from "riding line" when he came, he would stop in for bread and coffee. This morning, he sat in the rocker, teasing Ellie and bouncing her on his knee. "So ya think he'll come today?"

"Oh, Joseph! I wish I knew! It has been more than two weeks since his enlistment was up... and I've heard nothing. I would wish to go to town to see if a letter awaits...yet I am afraid to go and miss him."

"Ah, Elisabeth! I think he'll wait for ya, should ya not be home." He laughed a great guffaw.

"Joseph! You know what I mean."

"I do." He laughed once again. "How am I going to know when he's home? Ya gonna come get me?"

She giggled. "Maybe the next day...but you could bring the milk and see if he is here, or Wil can tell you. Should we have a big party? You think he would like that?"

"I don't know, keep thinkin' of the letter about Gettysburg. Makes me damn near sick to my stomach. And Jamie—he ain't one to be squeamish! Musta been the worst thing he'd ever experienced, and with all the things he's done—just hard to fathom, isn't it? Makes me glad I didn't go...although I do feel somewhat unpatriotic."

"Joseph! Someone has to stay home. What would we women out here on these ranches do without you? Why think of the dozens of times I have needed you! And you couldn't leave Eleanor...how is she?"

Strangely enough—they seldom spoke of her, perhaps once a week. It seemed disturbing and somewhat embarrassing for Joseph, and Elisabeth found there was little she could say that was of any encouragement.

"Ah...I don't know...better perhaps. She went to the Indians yesterday with Many Hands...had her spectacles on when she left. She'll be happy when she comes home. Most generally is."

"What does she do there?"

"I have to admit, I don't know. Only that she comes home much more peaceful. Speaking of peaceful—how is Ilene?" They both chuckled.

"Would it not be wonderful should we all be a serene as Ilene? I think she is fine. Excited to see *her bonny great Scotsman*, she says. Her eyes absolutely dance when she speaks of him. *The Lords gift ta her,* she said to me."

"Wait until Mack sees Duncan. Why the boy might be taller than his pa, an' he's done a fine job with the ranch…couldn't do better myself." Joseph watched as Elisabeth set out making coffee. Her leather pants soft and worn—her feet clad in moccasins, the cowboy boots she wore to ride, sat by the door. A strand of coal black hair hung down over her stunning features as she ground the coffee beans. The tumultuous mass of ebony had been tied atop her head and the strands of it hung along her long neck. Joseph did not feel lust for his brother's wife…but deep admiration. This beautiful woman had given up privilege, power and wealth to be his brother's wife. At the age of sixteen, they had taken her with them on the Oregon Trail. Her with white kid boots with tiny little heels on them, a dress with a bustle and a great lot of petticoats! He knew! He could barely squeeze in the carriage for the lot of them…a great fur coat of white… He and Eleanor had laughed at the audacity of it all. Why—they figured ta send her home from Pottstown…or perhaps Jamie would marry her…but he damn sure wouldn't get her to Montana. How wrong they had been! He doubted she had any idea what a remarkable woman she was. Oh, he knew it was in part because she loved his brother heart and soul, but that would have not been enough to warrant what she had endured. Even in her leather pants she was the most feminine woman he had ever known, probably ever would know. Nope—love was not enough, look at he and Eleanor…all their lives they had talked of this and…no sense in even thinkin' of that, his thoughts abruptly ending with Elisabeth's voice.

"Joseph, do you think he'll stay home?"

He could hear the plea in her voice, and it damn near broke his heart. "Does he know…ya know, does he know yer in the family way?"

"Yes, I wrote him in April…when I was certain…Lord, I did not expect this. Truly *I am* pleased and after the third month of being ill it has been fine…with the exception of the *bear hunt*…" They both laughed, although Elisabeth's laughter held some disbelief.

"I still can't believe ya did that, Elisabeth. Would you do it again?"

"Oh, I believe I would have killed the bear…most truly. I trust now, having had that experience, I would leave it out there." Her laughter held *some* humiliation.

"Mmmm, the coffee tastes good. When is the child to come?"

"As best, Petra can determine, late October. That is a blessing—to have children in the winter. The summer is so very busy for me." Elisabeth's mind ventured back to the time she had spent with Sally Susanne after the incident. Ilene having left, she found she was not up to her regular chores and Charlie had demanded she go into town and stay with Sally—*or he was gonna use the telegraph and send fer Jamie…make up yer mind Miz Prescott…* she smiled as she thought of his concern. She was a very blessed woman in many ways. *Now if her husband would but come home!* "Joseph, where do you think they are?" Her voice held caution. *Did she want him to answer that?*

"Mack, Jamie, and Josiah? I got a feeling they're close…maybe stopped in Helena first…set up Josiah…what ya think? He and Mrs. Sullivan?" Joseph chuckled and placed Ellie upon the floor.

"Oh, Joseph, wouldn't that be wonderful! I am hoping that is why he came… Do you think that possible?"

Joseph chuckled. "Elisabeth, you are a hopeless romantic! She is married to Tom."

"Well, yes. I believe she is, although once again I have not seen her for well over two months. I dearly wish I could travel to St. Helena more frequently… I daresay it is somewhat difficult with Ellie and my, *my condition*." Her body was once again burgeoning with child. "However, I must confess, having spent two weeks as her guest... and that was wonderful even though I was unwell. Oh, Joseph—please I implore you, do not divulge a word to anyone... as it is...it is..."

"Elisabeth, who would I tell?"

"Eleanor. You may well tell Eleanor..." She was cut off mid-sentence.

"Elisabeth, it is not like that between us anymore—not since the last child...died."

"Oh, Joseph, I am so very sorry for all of your grief. It has been desperately difficult for you and Eleanor. Do you wish you had not made the trip west? It *has* been near an unbearable struggle for all of us, and indeed, for most, their lives simply go on as before, for the most part I cannot see there to have been improvement. Yet I must say, *for you and Eleanor*...I daresay, it breaks my heart. It is most disheartening."

He watched her face as her words meandered on. "What's done is done, Elisabeth. Ain't no undoin' it...could be worse, look at Agnes Corrigan. I would say she has suffered as much as any, and it don't look like that situation will ever improve. And think of where *she* came from. So now—tell me of Sally."

She looked at Joseph and smiled—the smile of conspirators. She giggled and looked at him through dark lashes, her green eyes flashing. "You know, Joseph, you *do know* how much I cherish our time... you have been a good friend to me...a *brother!*"

"I hope so, Elisabeth, I feel somewhat responsible...told Jamie I'd look out for you. Now tell me the news about Sally Susanne."

"Truly, I know but what she imparted to me, as I do not believe she has made up her mind... Since her return from San Francisco—I daresay that has been over a year—*Mr. Thomas Pickett Sullivan* is—shall we say *very demanding* in that she should return and live with him there. However I...she, she talked of divorce. *Joseph, do you believe it! A divorce!*"

"Is that so?" Joseph had never been so shocked. He knew no one that had been divorced.

"Oh, I know, Joseph, it was most unsettling for me as well, however, it does happen. Think of Henry VIII, he divorced his wife of twenty years, Catherine of Aragon—in pursuit of a male child. I must say, if Sally Susanne can abide the tongues of others...oh, dear me...I truly do not know what I would do. It is simply not right that she—such a beautiful and kind woman, to live out her life alone. As well, she is so intelligent and spiritual Joseph. Gathering from what she has gleaned, it seems she has not the right to make that decision. *Only Thomas can divorce her*! I daresay, I think that to be unjust!"

"But he was a king, and that was the sixteenth century, wasn't it?"

"Yes, and after three hundred years look how little we have progressed! Woman still do not have the right to vote—or get a divorce! It is simply not fair, Joseph!"

Joseph looked into the flashing eyes of his sister-in-law and laughed! *She damn sure could get fired up. Bet Jamie missed that!* "A divorce! I'll be damned. And Josiah? I thought perhaps she had a...well a, what do you society folks call it...a *liaison* with Ben Parsons."

Elisabeth laughed out loud. "Joseph Prescott...*Ben?* I do not think that is so. I believe he is courting the jeweler's daughter."

"Really, I didn't know that. It's a good thing ol' Jeff Tallman wouldn't marry Agnes, heh?"

"*That* is an entirely different subject—*why* I would have killed him long ago had he treated me as badly as he has treated her and their child!"

The clock chimed seven and Joseph started. "I gotta git going, Elisabeth."

"I hate to have you leave...tell me again Jamie is safe. Please, Joseph."

"He's safe! The three of them together could—well, I believe they could put an end to this war! They're fine Elisabeth." He reached out and hugged her, always shocked that she was such a pint-sized woman, his great height towering over her. "Take care today. Charlie gonna look in on you?"

Elisabeth laughed. "Like a mother hen…I shall be fine—go, off with you."

"'Let me know when my big brother gets here, will ya?" He laughed again.

Rising to his full height, it was hard to believe anyone could be as big as he. Giant Joseph, with his engaging smile of bucked teeth and soulful gentle eyes. "I'll bring the milk in the morning… see if he's home yet."

"Pray he is safe, Joseph."

"Ah, Elisabeth, he's safe. No doubt be here in a couple days and yeah, let's have a picnic. The weather's good an' it'll be good ta see everyone again. Gonna have it here or in town?"

Her sense of excitement rose as she walked with him to the door. "In town. More people will come. Joseph, I cannot wait!"

"Me neither."

Holding Ellie, she watched as he climbed in the wagon he delivered the milk in; the wagon he had brought over the Oregon Trail now resembled that of a buckboard.

Setting about her tasks for the day—her mind all the wile envisioning the time she had spent with Sally Susanne, the discussions of women's rights, Sally's flourishing business, as well the meditations, the breathing exercise Sally had shown her. They did help.

Home

Elisabeth finished currying Mercy and Trésor and sent them out into the pasture with an apple from the cellar and a hug. It was with great yearning she awaited the apple trees to ripen. They had been sent to her by Papa and did not bear fruit for the first two years; when she advised him of this, he had told her *to beat the trunk of them with a stick.* Imagine, yet this spring they blossomed in a cloud of glorious pink.

During her ride to check the stock this morning, she had been grateful to have found nothing that warranted her attention. Walking from the barn, a gnawing sense of anticipation lay within her very being. She was not certain it was *fear for Jamie*—as they would have to brave the Bozeman Trail, she shuddered at the thought. Perhaps it was but excitement in knowing that Jamie would soon appear… She could feel the nearness of him, of that she was certain.

On the nights she could not sleep, she rose from bed and lighting a candle, she followed the instructions that Sally Susanne had imparted during her stay this spring. She practiced the *Hermetic* method of relaxation. Most often—just as Sally had said it would—she assumed a most tranquil state, often this state of being, of utter silence, and yet communion, transported her to a place in her mind, or was it the *ether of the universe,* she knew not with any precision; it made not a wit of difference to her, for she could see Jamie, could make Jamie feel her presence, she could look in on Grandmère and Papa, even Prudence. She often found that after this experience, she felt somewhat blue, she missed all of them terribly. She hated to admit it, yet without Jamie here, she desperately wished to take up her old life. She longed to have a home not unlike that of Prudence. With gas lighting and servants and more than anything, she wished for running water and a carriage, a carriage would be wonderful. To be in the city for the social season, to have fittings for new clothing for herself and for her daughter, to travel to Paris and to other wonderful cities. She wished to attend the symphony and the ballet, to go to the library, to wander along the *Avenue* with her child in an exquisite pram. She could envision placing her jewels on, with her hair done in the latest of fashions. To have a bath, to have luxurious accommodations to rest, to perform her ablutions. Yes, it often caused her great melancholy, for she could envision their lives as if she were there in body, not only in spirit. Like all things—the ability to join with another—carried with it, a great burden, as well as joy.

Sally Susanne was to teach her of auras, the very next opportunity. Elisabeth could not imagine what that would entail. When she had inquired of the origin of Sally's education in these subjects her only reply was "my sister, Katherine."

Elisabeth knew Sally Susanne had taught herself to read and write and to do arithmetic. She knew her mother to be illiterate, speaking very little English.

Elisabeth found Sally Susanne to be one of the kindest, most clever women she had ever known, and she prayed for her each time she prayed, which was often the entirety of the day and into the night.

Was Josiah coming to court Sally Susanne? Elisabeth thought perhaps Jamie or Josiah would know of divorce laws.

She took a deep breath and gathered her thoughts to the here and now.

The fragrance of the fields filled her senses and looking to the west; the sun glistened on the blue-white snow of the mountains. The river could be heard, as it ran in great swaths of white water over the massive boulders. The fish were prolific this year, and leapt from the river jubilantly, as if they too, had endured a difficult winter and were excited to escape.

She had taken Ellie down to the river last evening after supper, and they had bathed in the small area of swirling water that formed a pool at the rivers edge. The perfumes of summer whispered on the breeze that sailed leisurely over the fields of alfalfa and wheat, near ready now for harvest.

She removed the Western cowboy hat from her head and unfastened the leather cord that held her hair, the shining black mass floating around her exquisite features and lay to rest upon her back. She had often thought of cutting it and smiled, thinking of Geraldine's hair, cropped so close to her head. Given her daily attire—*that* would certainly stir wagging tongues, for she wore men's trousers more often than not. Today however, she was going to wear one of the two housedresses she owned. *Today* and each day until Jamie arrived, she and Ellie would be dressed to receive guests, with ribbons in their hair.

She looked at her sun-browned skin and wondered at what Mama would say… It *was* quite unladylike, or as Grandmère would say, *causerait*. Mama would never understand her life…so remotely different from that of her own.

She walked to the garden; it, too, was prolific this year, with the temperatures often rising to ninety-five or more during the day and plummeting to the mid fifties at night, she thanked the Lord for that, as they could sleep. The tomatoes were as large as a man's fist, cucumbers she would pickle, yet they were so very tasty, with tiny little seeds. The corn was beginning to tassel. The lettuce and green onions stood sturdy and straight. Her garden was nearly as wonderful as Catherine's at Fort Laramie, and that was saying quite a lot. She had had Charlie place something he called *chicken wire* around the garden, what a tremendous difference! Even the wily little jackrabbits could not enter, for he had buried the wire deep in the soil.

It had been nearly five years since they had had attended the *Luncheon* given by Catherine at Fort Laramie and the time had flown by. A trifling amount of that time had been spent in despair to be certain; the greatest had been spent gloriously. And she praised the Lord for that. Just to live with Jamie, to be his wife, and give birth to his children, to live in this beautiful, bountiful land, she felt rich with its peacefulness. In the world around her she felt the hand of God in each and everything, in the sound of bird song, in the bellow of the elk, moose and deer, the howl of the wolves in the moonlit night had become the concerto of her world.

The picnic had been planned for the first weekend in September, here at the ranch, with all involved determining they could make soap and candles while visiting. She had made breads of the zucchini that was so prolific…hearth bread's and loafs of white bread. She had butter churned in the cooler and strawberries.

Would he care about eating…bathing? She smiled. She thought of the evening they had bathed in the pool at the river edge—of that icy winter that he had built a huge bonfire and they had plunged in naked and lustful.

She patted her stomach… Would he find her exciting? It seemed she had been *with child* for years, in truth it was nearly two years. *Lord, let him stay home! Please, Lord, hear my prayer…* Removing her boots, she tiptoed into the house. The clock chimed six. It was wonderful to have the entire day left. With the early rise of the sun giving her more time in a day to spend with her child, to work and to read.

She had started Grandmère's journal. She could not help but consider, if in fact she was reliving her *great-grandmothers* life, perhaps in a different land, at a different time. Her mind had wandered over the many similarities of content… Did we perhaps visit our unresolved issues on our descendants… Were there, as Sally Susanne so adamantly contested, soul groups that meandered throughout the ages in an attempt to gain full spiritual maturity… it seemed incomprehensible to her at the time and yet…

She looked in on the sleeping face of her daughter. Thank you, Lord! Never would she have understood her capacity to love this child as much as she did. She would give her life for this little child of hers and Jamie's. For the first time, she acknowledged she would give up Jamie, for this child. And she loved Jamie more than life itself.

Where was he?

Elisabeth had risen before dawn and had dressed herself and Ellie; she had a profound premonition that *this* would be the day. She had brushed her hair until it shone, pulled it tightly in a bun, and thought she looked far to stern. She then braided it, pulling it up over her head as she had seen Ilene do; that was simply not *her*. Again she brushed it and let it fall about her back and shoulders, placing a yellow ribbon within it to hold it back. She pinched her cheeks and bit her lips and was transported back it time. A time when she was but fourteen and had first spied James Martin Prescott. Quite suddenly, she stopped and reviewed her reflection in the mirror. She was a beauty, if she did say so herself, even given her present state. The same spirit of Elisabeth Parthena Bunyan looked back at her, and yet, my, how her life experiences had surrounded that spirit. She had found she could control her temper tantrums, as they were useless, should no one pay them heed. Her life here and now; was governed by the land, by her circumstances. She was *a pioneer woman*…not so unlike Mrs. Davis of the sod house. She felt the momentary grief that came with that knowledge, remembering the day she had prayed to the Lord, *Do not let this be my life, Lord.*

Indeed, her circumstances were far more benevolent than that of Mrs. Davis…and yet. She shook herself and crossed herself in obeisance to the Lord God. The last five years had changed her life—yet her spirit remained constant. For reasons she could not fathom, she was grateful.

The pounding of horses' hooves could be heard in the quiet of the early morning. Elisabeth could feel them through the pine flooring of the house. She gathered Ellie in her arms and ran to the front stoop. She felt her heart as the pounding of it increased…felt the tears well in her eyes… *Oh, thank you Lord… Thank you.*

As they neared, she could see them clearly. Jamie, Mack, and Josiah shown full beards, faces browned, and eyes sparkling. With Western hats and great coats of canvas. They *had* come on the Bozeman Trail! She shuddered.

Jamie's hair was cropped just above his shoulders, floating in the air as he spurred Danny faster. Mack's hair was the color of fire, long and bouncing as he rode. She could see the hair of Josiah was much shorter. The breadth of each man's shoulders left her somewhat in awe, with a sword and a Bandolier slung across each of their broad chests. She wondered if anyone had ever perceived such strikingly, handsome men. Her husband, with his fine, high cheekbones, his firm jawline discernable, even though his beard was full.

She placed Ellie on the stoop, kissing the ebony of her curls and whispered, "Papa's home."

She ran from the house as swiftly as her legs and bare feet would allow.

Elisabeth watched as Jamie leapt from Danny's back and ran to her, swooping her in his arms! The eyes that beheld her were near the color of the deepest brown of the earth.

Placing her once again on terra firma, his hands came to rest upon her face. "My God, Elisabeth! My God, I have missed you so!" The tears streamed from her eyes as she looked into the darkness of her husband's own, eyes that flooded with tears, the depth of his emotions shook his body.

"Oh, Jamie…oh, Jamie…" The emotions she had held so tightly could no longer be contained and her whole being quaked with them. "Oh, Jamie…Jamie…"

"I am here, Elisabeth. I am here." Her tears spilled upon his hands, and he crushed her to his chest. She felt his head rise to the heavens. His body trembled with emotion. "Oh my God, Elisabeth…"

She felt the arms of Josiah as he embraced the two of them. He said nothing, but when she looked into his eyes, she could see the overwhelming feelings that lay there.

She had forever been shocked by their resemblance to one another. Josiah looked enough like Jamie to be his brother. The slight gray that appeared to be sprinkled through his hair and beard gave him a very distinguished look. His azure blue eyes twinkled, with the exception of this moment—flooded with tears as they were; they were the same shape as Jamie's, near almond, yet Josiah's squinted, surrounded by lashes as thick and black as she and Jamie's—and little Eleanor's.

Suddenly Mack was at their side "Oh, Mack!" He bent down and picked her up. "Ye wee bonny lass! Got a babe in the oven do ye now?" She giggled. "Yes. It seems each time he leaves, this husband of mine leaves me with a gift."

"It be a gift, ya kin' be sure now."

"Come. Come, I have water and tea, whisky…"

"No, no, I be goin' ta see me own love now. I'll no be visitin' with the likes o' you two." He hugged her tightly and placed a tentative kiss on her forehead.

Mack was a legendary looking fellow, his beard of fire, his hair with its fiery curl. His chest of barrel like proportions, with his ruddy skin and the clear, sky blue of his gentle eyes.

"She is waiting for you, Mack. It's been longer for her than for me."

"Aye an' I be staying home with me family now. Seen enough o' the killin' ta last me me life."

Her heart thudded in her chest. Would Jamie stay as well? Lord, let it be true... She looked up at him. His eyes were on Mack... "Take care, Mack. I shall see you in a couple of days."

"Is thet' so now, lad...best ye be makin' it a week. Ay've some things I been meanin' to do now." He laughed his great laugh, winked his clear blue eyes, and spurred his horse to the northeast.

"Josiah, come, come in."

"First let me get a good look at you, Lizzy." He looked at her, his eyes twinkled at his address of her... *Lizzy*, a name only Josiah would dare to use. "I'll be damned, but you're a sight for sore eyes. Are you feelin' well?"

"I have *never* been better! Never!" She turned to Josiah and gave him a resounding hug. "Are you well?" Concern evident in her voice.

"I am, Lizzy. Your Jamie here had the brunt of it...while I sat in Seward's office planning strategy. I'll never forgive myself."

"Yes! You will! Damn it, Josiah, I do not wish to hear such as that... None of us could know." Jamie said adamantly.

She looked up at these men. Men, whom had been mired in the factions of war—a war that, from Jamie's letters, had left them all with a burden they were not likely to forget... Did she have the strength and courage to care for them with a spirit that would heal them? She sincerely prayed she did.

"Come, you big handsome men. I've bread, butter, eggs, porridge? What do you please? *As well*, I have the most beautiful person I should like for you to meet."

The emotion was overwhelming as Jamie stooped to pick up little Eleanor.

"Oh..." His speech halted as the sobs of emotion rose from his chest. He buried his face in the curls of the child and openly wept.

Elisabeth stood beside him and rested her head on his arm. Josiah wiped his eyes and turning, walked away.

The Gathering

Jamie's first thought upon awaking was alarm—where was he? Was there to be a battle today? He lay not on the ground, nor on an army issue cot in a tent, but lay upon the softness of a warm, dry bed. He inhaled deeply—no acrid smell of gunpowder or blood, only the sweet scent of Elisabeth. He felt his nerves calm and snuggled more closely to Elisabeth, inhaling the sweet fragrance of her—was it violets, or was it honeysuckle? Her body was warm and smelling of sleep. He nestled the nape of her neck with his face and placed feathery fine kisses there. His arm encircled her body, as it lay curled within that of his own, his hair falling to mingle within hers. He felt the slight movement of the child as it lay in her womb and felt the tears form within his eyes. *God, I love this woman. Elisabeth, you are the reason I live. You are the reason I take a breath each day.* He uttered not a word for fear of disturbing her sleep.

Today was the day of the picnic. Perhaps all the neighboring ranchers and most of the townspeople would attend. Although he had been home for nearly a month he had spent every spare moment with Elisabeth and Ellie. He and Elisabeth rode line each morning and came home to find their daughter fast asleep, waiting on her mother to feed and change her.

He had tended to the land and the animals and built a fine bed of pine for Ellie, as she would soon be usurped from the cradle Charlie had made for her. His plans to build on to the house were still lying on his desk in the library; hopefully, he would get to that before the harvest, the air fairly bristled with the ripeness of the fields. He was in awe of the changes that they had made since their arrival some five years previous. More than that, he was in awe of his *wife*. His society born, petulant, Elisabeth Parthena Bunyan Prescott! He thought of her bravery, to stay here by herself, with an infant, to endure the harshness of the land and the weather. To endure the circumstances that Charlie had told him of—the snakes in the chicken house, the harsh winter, *the bear!* Although, when he thought of their trek west on the Oregon Trail he found no surprise in her bravery. Foolhardy perhaps. His mind ran to small Paddy, Lawrence O'Quinn's nephew. That, too, without thought for her safety, had been foolhardy, yet she had saved the child's life.

It was she who was the reason he existed.

He brushed his lips across that of Elisabeth's ebony tresses, and raising his head, his gaze fell on the cradle next to the bed; he looked into the eyes of a smiling Ellie, her tiny, bright white teeth shown in the early morning light. He wondered how long she had been awake?

"Papa," she whispered, as if she knew her mother needed rest. He felt his chest tighten and swallowed hard to push back the tears of joy that threatened to erupt. She, not unlike her mother, chattered endlessly, yet the only words he had found discernable within her vocabulary were *mama, papa,* and *no*. He smiled with the delight that flooded his heart as he quietly crept from the bed and pulling his denim pants on, stooped to the cradle and swooped up the tiny image of Elisabeth—with his eyes. A most startling combination.

Ellie giggled and patted his face with her small pudgy hands. Her fingers long and tapered like those of her mothers. Joy and peace effused him as he struggled with the blankets and nappies he would need to care for his daughter, should he wish to let Elisabeth sleep.

Elisabeth and Jamie sat on the front stoop of the house. Jamie had made coffee for them, and the morning was glorious. She could see for miles over the plains, the rutted wagon trail that ran up the small knoll to their house and barns, the Cottonwoods and evergreens that stood as sentinels along the trail, the vastness of the land the eye could see never failed to amaze her. She breathed deeply of the clean, clear air. Monuments of mountains rose to the east and to the west, the snow that perpetually cloaked them gave them a purple hue that glistened in the early morning rays of the sun, with the leaves of the cottonwood trees whistling their mournful sound on the sweet summers breeze. The smell of honeysuckle wafted through the yard, as if Elisabeth had set scented candles about. The sound of the river played its symphonic melody as a backdrop to the birdsong and the wings of eagles flew valiantly against the clear blue sky. Here existed a vibrancy to the world around them, a song that resounded from the earth itself. She heard the tinkle of laughter that came from her daughter and looked into the eyes of her husband. She felt the expanse of her heart as it filled with the thrill and love she felt for this moment in time. This man—this bold, strong man, held his child with a gentleness rarely found in man. Yet she had found there to be nothing so gentle as strength, nothing so strong as gentleness. How did this man she knew so intimately, loved so deeply, *go to war,* how did he rationalize the killing and the devastation he had described to her? She reached out and touched his face. If her life were to end today, it had been worth it. All she had experienced, all suffering, all hardships, for this man and this child, for this tranquility—this moment of peace, it had been worth it. *Thank you, Lord.*

Elisabeth smoothed her apron down over the rolling of the child that lay within her and thought of the aprons of the women on the Oregon Trail. Aprons that were so very soiled they looked as the red earth they had traveled over. Lye soap and a washboard seemed the answer to clean, white clothes. She remembered Caroline's dismay at having to teach her how to wash clothing in the Ohio River. 'You'se musta been a fine lady." She smiled at the memory. That had been an extraordinary era of camaraderie.

The flour sack fabric of the prairie dress she wore was the color of cinnamon, sprinkled with tiny yellow roses. Her feet were bare and much to Jamie's dismay—her ankles were on display. She cared not at all, it was far too hot to wear footwear and she loved the feeling of the earth beneath her feet.

Ellie rose from the ground on which she had been set and took tentative footsteps toward Agnes's little girl. Ellie's small pudgy hands were outstretched and her squeals of delight at having someone to play with, evident in the peals of her laughter. Agnes's child clung to her mother's leg and screamed fearfully, Agnes swatting at the child with her free hand. Caroline and Tobias' children ran towards Ellie and were more than pleased to play with her. The soft color of milk chocolate children, children Ellie was enchanted with, as Tobias and Caroline lived directly behind Sally Susanne's shop.

Agnes and Eleanor stood over a very large kettle, from which rose steam in vapid drifts of white. The melting tallow of the butchered animals gave off the most undesirable odor imaginable, though not surprising, as they had all been saving the animal fat throughout the year. Life was a long battle of providing and doing. Even though today was a celebration of Jamie and Mack's return, all the women present would be making soap and candles today. The men would haul wood for the fires and lug the heavy barrels of ash and tallow.

With memories of the Oregon Trail present in her mind she looked at Agnes. Why, *she was an old woman. With child*, yet she looked an old woman. Elisabeth searched her memory for what age Agnes would be and could not remember, perhaps thirty and five... Her thin scraggly hair was near white. She was missing more teeth than on the last visit Elisabeth had made to her. Agnes was gaunt and thin beyond what one would think to be healthy. Her hands were gnarled—from hard work Elisabeth was certain. Not that all the women did not work hard, her own hands were not the hands of the *lady* that had left Papa's house. Yet she knew that Agnes had nearly constructed a house for her and her child with those hands—that she gardened and stored her own food, even chopping her own wood. From what Elisabeth had *heard*, the only thing Jeff Tallman did provide her was meat, children, *and beatings.*

Elisabeth thought it despicable! There ought to be a law against such abuse!

Yet they had all in turn, offered support and the opportunity for Agnes to take her child and go to her sister Amelia Chandler's in Salt Lake City. Her continuous response being "Mr. Tallman says my place is here with him." As Ma said, "What in tarnation is thet woman thinkin'!" Elisabeth wholeheartedly agreed.

Eleanor stood close to Agnes and they spoke ever so softly; there was a furtive confidence between the two of them. Eleanor was regaled in her costume of the last few years, that of an *Indian squaw.* Today, Elisabeth was relieved to see she had her spectacles on, with her long black braid that hung the length of her back, she certainly looked as much an Indian as did Charlie's, Little Flower.

Elisabeth was well aware they each disliked her, often vilifying her. It greatly distressed her, as she cared for each of these women. She had no understanding of them—that was indeed truth, though she may well comprehend their reasoning to a small degree. Each one of them having determined that she thought she was of better social standing than they.

She thought of the trip on the Oregon Trail, of her marriage, her demeanor, the gift of Mercy and of the saddle with the lovely engraving of her initials and the sterling accouterments, given her by Jamie. As well as the diamond ring, which given the circumstances of her life, she rarely wore. She thought of Jamie's outward signs of devotion to her, and yet, here in Montana, as on the Oregon Trail... She was in near the same circumstances as they. Perhaps her home was larger and more comfortable, the land Jamie had amassed being far more vast—*and* there was Ellie and the child she carried; for Eleanor, *that* alone would provide *a thorn in her side*. In truth, Eleanor had Joseph! No man could be more devoted! *None.* Joseph was more devoted to Eleanor than her own James Martin Prescott was to her. Joseph Henry Prescott was the epitome of a good husband. *He* had not left Eleanor alone and trudged off to *war*. He was accepting of her emotional frailties, he was kind and gentle. He loved Eleanor beyond—beyond what? Elisabeth perhaps would never grasp the circumstances of their relationship as Joseph indicated. Not that Joseph ever complained! He truly did not. However, inadvertently he, each morning conveyed minuet tidbits of information that gave Elisabeth a window into his relationship with his wife.

Elisabeth felt that with courage, Eleanor *could* have a child, a nice home. She chose not, she would not let Joseph near her for fear of once more conceiving; she *could not live* through the death of *another child*. Elisabeth could comprehend that, truly, yet Eleanor showed no indication that she cared a wit for the thoughts and needs of Joseph he, too, had lost those children, and with them his wife's sanity.

Elisabeth knew Joseph to be the primary caretaker of the land, the animals, and the house. That, with the infrequent help of Many Hands, he cleaned and cooked. How often had Joseph told her, "Eleanor has gone with Many Hands to be with the Indians."

—∞∞—

Elisabeth returned to the house for salads and casseroles. Every family had brought their favorite dish, a potluck, they called it.

Each dish looked to be quite delectable. Yet again her thoughts ran to Agnes. What had she ever done to her...yet she must admit to telling her she *thought her choice of men was quite unsatisfactory— that she would not abide by such treatment of her person as that of Jeff Tallman.* Apparently her sentiments were unwelcome. Truly, Elisabeth could not understand; after all, *he kept an Indian squaw* in better circumstances than he did Agnes and her lovely child. *They* continued to live in a tent! She knew it to be none of her business yet she found it appalling.

She and Prudence, her most bosom friend during her childhood, had advised each other without hesitation! She remembered now, Prudence's qualms concerning her involvement with the handsome James Prescott. To a very great extent, Prudence had been correct. Elisabeth's life had changed eternally. She would never have the luxurious life once offered her by her social standing. Yet she, too, had changed. An imposed change perhaps—yet she had been resilient enough to adapt to her circumstances. She no longer was the same person that had left Papa's home... Although, deep within her—*that Elisabeth* would always reside.

She took a deep breath and continued placing food on the large picnic tables Jamie and Charlie had built upon the decision to have the gathering here at their home, rather than in town. She felt Jamie's hand rest on her shoulder and the kiss he placed on her neck, beneath the fall of her hair. *Thank you, Lord—he is home!* Mack was home! And Josiah was here for a visit! *Was he but visiting? Lord, she hoped not.* Her thoughts interrupted by Jamie's voice, the mere sound of it sending shivers throughout her body. *Lord let him be home for all time.*

"Do you want us to put the meat on the table? Do we possess a pan or plate large enough..."

She smiled and kissed the hand that rested on her shoulder. "We do not, kind sir... We shall but serve it from the fire-pit." She shuddered at the thought...the inelegance of it all—of the barbaric world they resided in. They were forced to make soap and candles rather than simply enjoying a picnic. She could hear the sounds of sickles being sharpened and of rope being braided. The harvest would be coming soon and the women would be making mounds of food and drink—as the men threshed the fields. All of them, preparing for the long, harsh winter that loomed in their future.

Returning to the house yet again for more food, for there was indeed an abundance of it, she thought again of Agnes and Eleanor, with Samuel joining in her small party of self-pity. All this *self-pity*—and she knew it to be just that, as she had no control over the thoughts of others—brought to mind Samuel. A truly grievous condition of her heart. *Lord, forgive me*, and on such a pleasant day! *Samuel had shunned her, abolished her from his life*—just as the Quakers of Pennsylvania castigated those that disabused their ways and their laws. *Most effective*, she thought. It truly broke ones heart and spirit, to be forsaken by someone you thought would love and accept you all the days of your life. A silly thought, she supposed. As Sally Susanne said, "We choose our families to work out past paucities." *How in the world could you solve your differences should you never to speak to them again?*

Perhaps that was the lesson—to abolish them from your hearts, your mind, to send them away forever. And what precisely could he state that she had done to deserve such as this...this despicable thing he had rendered upon her... She had done what she did out of love... What had *he*, Samuel, done out of love? She considered what had driven him to exact such punishment upon her—that *she had sullied the name of the family...brought impropriety into the folds of his family name?* Perhaps, it was his very insipid nature that caused him to look at her actions thus. For *he* would never have the courage, the heart, or the fortitude to stand before the world and say; *this is what I believe, this is what I wish for my life*! Quite suddenly it occurred to her—in actuality—*he had done just that!*

It wasn't something done by most. To have made such a statement did indeed demand extraordinary courage. Elisabeth had never thought of it in those terms prior. She smiled, trying in vain to push all thoughts other than happiness from her mind. Yet as she went about the setting of the tables and waiting for the multitudes of persons to arrive—persons who would acknowledge her presence, unlike Eleanor and Agnes, persons *who cared for her*. Her mind continued its self-involvement with those who appeared to hold her in contempt. It was simply unfathomable to her that *her brother* would wish to sever his relationship with someone whom he had shared so very much of his life. Was it truly out of her admitted folly, or was it jealousy, or that through her acts of insolence she had taken center stage in his family's life? Samuel would never forgive her for that. He was fawned over by their mother, indeed, doted on. Not to be aligned with familial accolades would indeed align the doer of such a deed with implacable harm. For the first time she sensed a window into the incitement behind Samuels anger. He *had* struggled infinitely under the tutelage of the instructors at the military school in which Papa had wished—*demanded*—that he attend. His scores had been exemplary, but then, that had been an expectation. Meanwhile, she had *dallied* her way through Miss Pricilla's finishing school, with Papa continuing to laud her accomplishments.

It had been nearly six years and still, she found it to be a crushing sensation to her heart. She wished Samuel no ill will—the deed was done. She would never trust him—nor should he chose to have a family, she would not endeavor to insert herself into his life, for as he had so vehemently stated, "She was dead to him." The thought of those words pierced her heart, for she had loved her brother unconditionally. Thinking perhaps she understood, came some acceptance, however she found there to be no lessening of the pain inflicted. *With time does come a form of wisdom! Thank you, Lord!*

She heard the rumble from the wagons, the pounding of hoof beats. Running to meet them, she waved and hollered. Jamie close at her back. Joseph right behind him. Their friends clamoring from their wagons, leaping off their horses. Mack and Ilene, with Duncan, arriving from the north. Why, this was better than the Fourth of July picnic! She was so excited she could but contain herself, quickly determining—*it was not necessary to do so*. This was to be a celebration that she would always remember. Suddenly she was swooped from the ground. "Hi, Lizzy! Why, you're just as pretty as I remember you!"

"Oh, Josiah! You just saw me last month. Where have you been?"

"Well," he placed her gently upon the ground, and winked. The blue of his eyes the most incredible color of the sea, and they veritably danced in delight. "I been a wee might busy, if you get my drift." She smiled and winked back at him. "Have you now...?" They were accomplices, the two of them. She dearly prayed they had the same conspiracy in mind. She could scarcely wait to talk to Sally Susanne!

Ma was squeezing her and laughing, then pulling her head back to see her better. "Land a Goshen girl, I don't think I done seen you in a coons age. My, you be 'bout ta pop! Ya feelin' good? Got yer man here. Make ya feel lots better now don't it?" She laughed a big belly laugh and ran to grab Jaime about the waist. "Lord are you a sight fer sore eyes. Did ya see my boys?"

Pa tentatively reached for Elisabeth's hand. "Howdy, Miz Prescott..."

"Pa, please call me Elisabeth." She reached out and hugged him, his body feeling more frail than the last time she had done so. His sail like ears more prominent, the fine wisps of hair on his head, fewer than before, yet the twinkle in his eyes had not diminished. "Oh, Pa, you and Ma both look grand! I could not be more delighted to see you!"

"Got dressed up fer yer party, thet I did." She looked at him and laughed. For he wore the only clothing she had ever seen him in. Trousers than hung from his slight frame—the top to his long johns and suspenders. Still, she laughed, "Pa, you look quite elegant." He blushed ever so slightly, looking away from her, seeking Jamie.

Sally Susanne hugged her profusely. "Oh my, Elisabeth," viewing her burgeoning body, "whenever are you going to have this child? Where is my little Ellie?" Yet again her arms where around Elisabeth, whispering in her ear. "I have missed you. I am so happy for *both of us*!" Sally's sky-blue eyes appeared to dance with mischief, telling Elisabeth all she wished to know—at least for the moment.

"She is going to give birth in a few weeks, from the looks of things." Petra's soft, tinkling laughter and no-nonsense voice interceded. "Come give me a hug. Are you feeling well?" The diminutive doctor, being no larger than Elisabeth herself.

"I am! Oh, Petra, I am so very happy you are here, everyone looks so wonderful!" Elisabeth looked at her friends. Sally's red gold curls cascaded down her back, with the loveliest of blue ribbons holding it in place. Petra's golden hair was pulled into a bun at the nape of her neck, with golden tendrils escaping. "And Ezra?" No sooner than the words where out of her mouth, she spied the beautiful man coming towards her. His long thin frame, the bounce of his shoulder length nutmeg hair, his startling smile, never would she become accustomed to his feminine beauty nor the fact that he was such a skilled, intelligent person. *Asexual*, Jamie had called him. That had been years ago, yet Ezra appeared unchanged through time. "Oh, Ezra, I was afraid you would be off on another adventure!"

"And miss this? I, I don't think so, Miss. Elisabeth." He stretched out his hand in welcome.

She seemed always to forget how very shy he was. "Ezra, give me a hug!"

"Ah yes… yes…Miss.…. Miss. Elisabeth." She looked at him, and, laughing, said, "Why, Ezra, you're blushing."

"Am I? I am…" His pearl white smile glimmered briefly as he looked at the ground.

The children, Ezra and Petra's brothers' children, Spencer and Emma, scampered across the grass in search of Duncan. The physically smaller children stood next to the massive proportions of Duncan Mackenzie, an anomaly, considering they were of near the same age. In pursuit of the older children, the Parsons children ran after them, all in search of food and cold tea.

Looking from the children she found Harold Baumgartner stood before her. "May I say, you look quite exquisite, Mrs. Prescott." His blond good looks not lost on her. "Thank you, Mr. Baumgartner, Jamie and I are pleased you could come. Come, we have some home brew and whisky." No sooner than the words were out of her mouth, for she wished to remind *Mr. Baumgartner* she was indeed a *married* woman, his manner never apparent that he was aware of this fact… She was swept from her feet! Yet again, she floated through the air. This time in the arms of Mack Mackenzie! "Ye wee bit of a thing! Lassie, when do ye be thinkin' the babe be?"

Elisabeth squeezed his great thick neck, her arms holding on for dear life. The fiery color of his hair and beard—his ruddy complexion, made his twinkling blue eyes more vivid than ever.

"Ya be puttin' the lass down ya big brute… Kin ya see she be in no sort to be swingin' in the air about us?" Ilene was laughing as much as Elisabeth herself. "Mack, me love, be puttin' the lassie down." Mack deposited her gently to the ground. Ilene was waiting to hug her, her own red hair shown against the green of the grass. The twinkle of her cerulean blue eyes something that Elisabeth equated with Ilene—*peace*. Tranquility lie within these two persons she had grown to love.

Looking up, her eyes beheld Jamie, her Jamie. Lord, she loved this man. As she neared him, she could see the love in his eyes.

"You, my dear, look quite bewitching!" He placed his arm around her shoulders, and she leaned her head to fall on his great strong chest. His voice was husky, filled with emotion. "Are you happy, Mrs. Prescott?"

"I am, Mr. Prescott. I am."

Looking at the mass of friends that had come, come for Jamie and for her. All thoughts of self-pity dissolved within her mind and she sighed. She whispered against her husband's chest, "Thank you, Lord. Thank you." She felt the tender, gentle tug of his arm around her and tilted her face up to his. Lowering his head, he placed the softest of kisses upon her lips.

Men

Jamie, along with the other men left the company of the women and had gathered about the dying embers of the fire. The splashing of liquid into tin cups could be heard—whether it be ale, tea, or whisky. The fragrance of tobacco hung about them. The men sat on benches with their elbows and backs braced against the table, talking, watching, listening—many lounging within the softness of the grasses.

The tools had all been sharpened, the barrels emptied of tallow and ash and taken down to the river and washed clean. Twilight would soon descend upon them and this day would be done. An extraordinary day it had been! Friends, family—Jamie was effused with a sense of contentment he hadn't felt for some time, at least not in the company of men, men that were waging war, or far more disturbing, dealing with its subsequent effects. Lying on the earth, his long legs outstretched, he leaned on one elbow surveying all that lay before him, a blade of sour grass in his mouth. Across the land—*his land*—he marveled at the gentle waving of the grain, standing tall and golden in the late afternoon sunlight. The cerulean blue of the sky held great puffs of snowy cotton that floated in serene content. There would be no rain, for these where not the clouds that forecast rain, and the sour grass he held in his mouth was near devoid of moisture. A good omen! For it to rain *now* would destroy his crops.

A sense of achievement embraced him. He had accomplished what he had traveled across the continent for. Now what? He smiled. *Now what?* He seemed to be in constant quest—for *what? That* he had never determined. He knew he was derelict in his communications with the cattle buyers; that would need to be addressed, and soon. Too, was the diminishing supply of gold, certainly they had a sufficient amount to get them through the next couple of years, and yet...

"A copper for your thoughts brother?" Joseph's voice interrupted his reverie.

"Nothing, nothing at all. Just...*peace.*"

"I'm happy to hear that... I've...we've all been worried about you. You, Josiah, and Mack—the Parsons brothers."

Jamie looked up at his brother. "I'm fine, Joseph, at this moment we are all fine. Well, perhaps Tommy and Micah are not... Lord only knows what is transpiring at this moment...this war is...a subject that is most difficult and disturbing to speak of. It is most certainly unlike anything I have yet to experience."

Joseph looked at the three men that had returned from the war. Privately, he and Jamie had spoken of the war—the battles, the hardships. Joseph had expressed his guilt and concern for all Jamie had been through. He knew Jamie would not want those conversations to be made public, yet he found it difficult not to once again utter those words of remorse. Joseph also knew, he would *not go*, there was Eleanor to think of, there was the land, hell there was Jamie's land that needed his help, as well, there was Jamie's growing family. It was his way of lending a hand in the war effort. Someone had to *stay the home front.* "Will any of you go back? Jamie, *will you?*"

"I don't know, Joseph, right now the thoughts of war are distant and incongruously horrific. What do you say, Mack?"

"Aye, Jamie, me boy. I be thinkin' I done served me new country fine. I be no ready ta die." The big Scotsmen squatted down beside them "An' you—an-cor?"

"As yet...I cannot say." He himself was surprised by his answer...it had not occurred to him that perhaps he would return.

"And you, Josiah, you be of a mind to fight on? Seems they be no end in them—the mighty men o' the Confederate."

"I must say, I've not had the time nor the inclination to answer that. It has certainly not gone the way the Union would have it—or as expected, time will tell. At this moment I wish it to be but a nightmare, one I have awakened from." Josiah stood and returned to the table where he poured a generous amount of whisky into his cup.

Jeff Tallman was standing as tall and obstinate as he would ever rise—all five-foot-six-inches of him. His black eyes darting from one to the other. "Tell us what happened out there. Why the hell haven't ya pushed the fuckin' bastards back where they came from? Hells fire, you been at this fer nearly three years now. Ya ain't got any decent men, or you don't have a decent strategy, which is it?"

Jamie, Josiah, and Mack looked at each other in turn, each gravitating to the table that held the whisky and ale...

Tallman looked at each of the men. "I mean *we wanna know*! Don't you other fellas?"

Not one among those men gathered made any attempt at response.

Jamie's back was to Jeff. He felt his spine stiffen, his fists and jaw clench, felt the hair on the back of his neck bristle. He wanted desperately to *shut the little fucker up*. He took a long pull directly from the bottle of whisky, set the bottle back down on the table, took a deep breath and turned. He was fully aware that Mack and Josiah had not turned around. They stood with their backs to Jeff. Jamie looked at them and saw the glint of steel in Josiah's eyes, the muscles hardened in Mack's face. There were many reasons to throttle this little prick, but today was not going to be spoiled by anyone. *Least of all, Jeff Tallman.*

Jamie looked down into the coal black, blazing eyes of this little man. "Jeff, I would be more than happy to say those were the reasons—however, it is in *fact* quite the contrary. We *both* the

Union and the Confederates have excellent men and excellent strategies—*that is* the conundrum. Oh, and by that, I mean *the problem.*"

Tallman seemed unperturbed by Jamie's slight at his intelligence—*in truth* it was difficult to insult Jeff. "So what the hell's the problem, what're they doin' north of the Mason Dixon line?"

Joseph stood up from the ground and looked at Jeff. "Ya know, Jeff, I think these men have proven their strength and their integrity, don't you? If ya think about the Oregon Trail—hell, the Indian attack comin' home from the King Ranch, why, you'd be dead if it weren't for…"

From his prone position on the earth Ezra Gilky rose on one elbow, his long legs stretched out, his slender body more apparent in this particular position, his torso looking even less impressive than usual, his speech, halting—yet articulate beyond measure. "Mr. Prescott…sir, er…Jamie, indeed Mack, or Josiah—what… what…might I ask…do you think is the real basis for this war? Is it indeed to do with the issue of slavery? In California, and might I add, from what I read in the newspapers, it is the wealthiest men in the North—the industrialist—I believe they are calling them, the railroad men, those men involved in mining and…and communications…*money*. Yes. Yes…it seems money is very much a controlling attitude, an *avarice*… I believe that is the word I am searching for…that, well, I think—I believe that to be…"

"Spit it out, kid!" Jeff Tallman said.

Josiah scowled and walked to stand ever so close to Jeff. He liked Jeff Tallman no better here than he had on the Trail. Ezra Gilky had proven his worth many times over. He was a skilled marksmen and hunter. His appearance was of perpetual youth; in point of fact, he was older than Jeff Tallman. Ezra held a plethora of knowledge stored within his remarkably effeminate beauty. Whereas, Jeff Tallman was the epitome of self-righteous brutishness! "Tallman! Let the *man* speak! Ezra, I for one am interested in what you've got to say. Seems nothing we have done or said has made a wit of difference, only served to have more men die than the Hundred Years War."

"We all want to hear what you have to say, Ezra, hell's fire I wouldn't know half of what I know about things if you hadn't told us on the trail comin' here!" Joseph stood up, and looked down into the eyes of Jeff Tallman. "I think that *is* true, don't you, Tallman?"

Ezra, too, was now on his feet. His ever present self-confidence evidenced in his manner. "Gentlemen, please," he chuckled. "Yes…yes, I do have opinions. I've been thinking, what indeed would happen should you simply cease to fight? Is…is that possible? It is well, it is a fact—those men who propose the fight and negotiate the treaties are in an office…while…while men that have been, shall we say, *subjugated*, die and fight…is it true? That…well…I have read and heard of deplorable—some rather *bad*…actually *inhuman* conditions exist for the men that fight. That there is no pay and…and no shoes. What do you think of those new shoes? A miraculous invention wouldn't you say?" The men all chuckled, the tension having lessened greatly.

More men had now joined those gathered about the fire, Pa and Ben Parsons, Harold Baumgartner, Ben Moore, Tobias, Charlie Wardle, and many of the hired hands had assembled.

Jamie, too, felt the extreme anger leave his body. At least with Ezra there was never malice nor taunting, only the curiosity of intelligence. He turned and went to fill his cup, bringing back with him the bottle, freshening those that stood in wait, as Ezra was known both for his knowledge and his ability to be—shall we say, *quite long winded*—though never dull.

Jamie thought of all the information Ezra had departed to them of an evening on the long trek west. His intellect and his interest seemed to be unlimited.

Josiah laughed. "I like the shoes fine! A splendid invention, can't for the life of me figure why no one thought of it before."

The men laughed at this, even though many of them hadn't the slightest idea of what he spoke, as the *new* right and left shoe had not made its way to the untamed territory. "I for one am interested in any opinion that would shed new light on the condition of our country. Go ahead, Ezra."

"You're certain you want me to continue, you know—I can be silent for long periods of time…but…" He chuckled. All of them knew he traveled the country on foot, for months at a time—alone, no doubt thinking. They, too, laughed.

"Go on, Gilky." Josiah sat back down on the ground.

"I…I think, as I said, there is a swelling avarice with the… well…in the civilized areas of the—*this* country. Much more so than…than on the Continents that are older and more established. A swelling of individualism and…and much more liberal attitudes that will, *I think*, they will lead to a lack of appreciation, as well as a lack of cultural and well…spiritual knowledge. I believe, as do others, those attributes to be what is necessary for man's evolvement."

"Where're you going with this? What does it have to do with the war? The war has nothing what so ever to do with us, out here in Montana" Harold Baumgartner interjected.

"Oh! *I believe it does*," Ezra stated with great conviction.

"Ezra, I think you have a fine point. It seems it has had a profound effect upon Texas and California. Should we lose, the railroads will not connect the countries, much of the North's industry shall be lost." Josiah was again on his feet, pacing.

"I, too, believe it will, I think the Southerners are greatly underestimated." Jamie's thoughts running to the battle of Gettysburg, as well the many other battles they had fought. The underhanded use of the black man, by the Union…"

Was it underhanded? He thought it to have been a coup, yet the terms were none the better. "The Union government had certainly used the Negro as much as the Southerners. They had given the Negro freedom—*freedom should he survive* —after having fought for two years. *A mule—a carrot and a stick, nothing more.* Manipulation, pure and simple." Jamie went on, "I myself hold a great admiration for Thoreau and he said, *the price of anything, is the amount of life you exchange it for*—I have watched more men die for this country than for the French Foreign Legion and for the Arabs…and I…quite frankly, I am concerned as to the unfathomable destruction of land and resources *and the immense loss of life.*" Jamie took a long drink of the whisky and wondered where his perfect day had gone.

"Yes…yes! You see, that is it! I too greatly admire Henry Thoreau. He…he also said, *that government is best which governs least.*"

"He was a poet! What the hell does he know of government?" Harold was just as excited as the rest of them. The mayor of St. Helena was indeed insulted. "Why the hell doesn't the North just leave the South to govern itself? That was the original plan, wasn't it? Hell, what the hell difference does it make to the North?"

Jamie looked up at him from the grass upon which he again sat. "Harold, if we take money out of the equation, it is because men like *Tobias here* are being held against their will, perhaps not in all cases, but in many. *That* is inhumane." He looked at Ezra, dismissing Harold Baumgartner; he didn't much care for him, or the way he looked at Elisabeth. "Ezra, yes, Thoreau was a poet. Thank God, for us! He was as well, a philosopher of great standing, as well, a naturalist. Personally I would rather have a poet tell me of the world than a journalist. A poet speaks from his heart, of things felt within the soul, a journalist but points to obvious facts. I believe Ezra here to have much in common with Thoreau." Jamie looked at Ezra.

"Why, thank you, Mr. Prescott. It is indeed an honor for you to say such as that. I do remember how adroit your knowledge is of poets and…and journalists as well. I believe I remember Tom telling me you and Joseph are a relation of William Hickling Prescott, that is correct?"

"Yes, William Hickling Prescott was our cousin, dead now, but indeed a fine journalist, although his writings are quite lyrical in nature. He was indeed commissioned by the president to write of Spain and other foreign countries." Jamie and Joseph looked to each other in acknowledgment. "How the hell *is* Thomas Pickett Sullivan?" Jamie asked, relieved to have the subject of the war finished.

They all waited for Ezra to respond, speculating as to what he would say. None that had been with them on the Oregon Trail could discern *what indeed* their relationship consisted of. Ezra smiled and chuckled, "I believe he is greatly contributing to the avarice I was previously describing."

"What the hell does that mean?" Jeff asked.

Ezra looked at Jeff with a great deal of *gracious* questioning—given the circumstances. He shrugged his narrow shoulders, pushing the thick wave of his hair from his face and smiled, his full lips and perfect teeth not lost on the males present, which stood and sat, listening to him. "I haven't been to San Francisco for some time, don't misunderstand, I *do* find it to be quite exciting. The atmosphere, the city—the Pacific Ocean…it…it…I find it to be trying after a time. All that hustle and bustle, the overt concentration on position, propriety and…and…wealth. I prefer the natural settings of Mother Nature. I find the city to be somewhat unsettling in large doses. Er…I believe Thoreau also said, *It is an interesting question how far men would retain their relative rank if they were divested of their clothes.*" Once again he chuckled. "Tom…Tom, he seems quite invested there."

"So you don't think he's coming back here?" Josiah's voice was near a whisper, his eyes playing at the blades of grass that were immersed in the setting of the sun.

Jamie watched Josiah, each waiting for Ezra's response. Jamie looked up at Ezra. Ezra, when not wandering the earth, lived with his sister Petra, in St. Helena. He was most certainly no fool, and would know of any involvement Josiah had with Sally

Susanne. At this moment in time, what he said would have profound consequences on the life of his dear friend, Josiah.

Ezra stood, swiftly contemplating the question, and the implications of the answer he provided. His thoughts running helter-skelter through his mind. What would these very machismo men say—indeed what would they think, should he tell them of his thoughts, of what he suspected to be true? His mind suddenly formed an image of the beauty, intelligence, the rarity of spiritualism within the form of Tom's wife Sally Susanne Sullivan. "You know, I don't rightly know the answer to that. Thomas is, as I said, most invested in his life there…however, I've not been there for…for…in truth, since I went with my sister and Mrs. Sullivan—quite some time ago."

Jamie watched Josiah, and he could visibly see the tension leave his body. A fine man was Ezra Gilky, a wise man!

Mack was pouring whiskey; Charlie's fiddle was resounding through the air. They had had enough talk of war to last a lifetime, and Josiah, well, Jamie would wait and see what Josiah did concerning Sally Susanne.

"Come, ya big brutes, hep an' ole Scotsman with the floor fer a schottische now, will ye?"

Josiah and Sally Susanne

Josiah shot his cuffs and looked into the cheval mirror that stood in the corner of the room. He had let the room for but a month, staying in the saloon had been so damnably noisy, quite disconcerting; it had now been *three* months.

The window was raised and he could smell the cold in the air, feel the briskness off it as it wafted through the room. The leaves of the trees had begun their descent to lay a carpet of gold on the ground, and in the waning of the evening light, the stark blackness of the trees stood in silhouette against the sky. He had to admit; autumn here had been a damn fine show, nothing like the east, but with vibrant shades of gold and smattering's of red and bronze.

He had stayed overlong, his intensions had been but perhaps a month or two, however events here were nonstop. First, there had been the harvest with James Prescott and of course Joseph and Mack. He'd never done such physical labor in his life! He had to hand it to those men. They had all worked their arses off.

Had it all worked out, they did; with Jamie's land providing the bulk of feed for all three of them, in payment for work both done and work expected. They had made a fine party of the whole ordeal, all the woman cooking and then there were the great bonfires at night, with the singing dancing, reminded him of the Oregon Trail. Yep, he had to admit, they had carved out a damn fine life for themselves.

Then there was the new kid of Lizzie and Jamie. Prettiest damn thing he'd seen. As pretty as her sister Ellie, he figured she was gonna be a feisty one, like her mother. Another girl—they had named her Justine. Damn fine man; Prescott, if he was disappointed that the child was not a boy he gave no indication. He smiled, his azure blue eyes sparkling, crinkling at the corners. Elisabeth; when he thought of Elisabeth, it had always made him feel like smiling. She was a pistol, that one. When he had asked her what she was going to do next, her reply was *she was going to retrieve her eighteen-inch waist*. She looked fine to his way of thinking…made a fine mother an' didn't seem to have much trouble birthing the babes.

He liked it fine, visiting the Prescott's… It made him feel like he was home…when all of a sudden, those feelings would be replaced with nostalgia and sadness, grief for what he had lost would abruptly encompass him, leaving him with nothing to do but say his farewells.

The same was true in most of the households here; even Sally Susanne had Caroline and Tobias's children running in and out. Small voices hollerin', "Miz Sally, Miz Sally where youse at? Miz Sally?"

Sally Susanne Sullivan… Images of her rose in him—images of infinite beauty, a beauty that transcended the physical, within her lie a serenity he had seldom found in anyone. A kindness of heart that was not intrusive. He found that he held great affection for Mrs. Sullivan.

They were to attend the St. Helena symphony this evening. Last week it had been the dance at the Grange. He had to admit he was astonished at the myriad numbers of entertainment available here in this new land.

He'd see where *this relationship* went. Didn't have much hope—yet it would be fine should she be considerate of his offer. He smiled, the crow's feet about his eyes many and deep. His face clean-shaven, the silver in his dark hair sparkled. Perhaps this was *not to be*. One hell of a lot of obstacles stood in the way.

He had his own concerns—more than those of the ones that concerned her. Did he want this life? Did he want this woman? He had never loved anyone but Lisle…doubted he ever would, yet was man born to live and die alone? She was nothing like his Lisle, other than her great beauty. Perhaps that was good. She was ambitious; she was determined. She was self-sufficient. If she needed a man, it was not for the obvious reasons. Companionship? Perhaps, yet Mrs. Sullivan seemed fine with the championship of the Lord. He could damned well understand that. He himself felt that way—just didn't need that isolation to draw on it, or did he? He certainly thrived on isolation.

The constant activity of government office had given him nothing but damnable headaches. Near everyone had their own agenda…didn't much surprise him. Man was a selfish sort. He'd seen it in Austria—in Washington and on the Trail. Takin' all those trips west with folks had taught him one hell'va lot. Wouldn't do it again, but he was not sorry to have done it. He looked into the mirror again, the blue of his shirt brought out the dazzle of his eyes. The black lashes thick, his features chiseled. Baring his teeth he again grinned at the white evenness of them…a damned fine specimen you are Josiah Leon Alexander Piedmont! *A damned fine specimen*—if I do say so myself!

Briefly the image of James Martin Prescott leapt into his mind—*remarkable* how very much their resemblance was, could be brothers, but for the eyes, Jamie had the eyes of a cat, a *great* cat, yet somehow soulful.

He reached for the derringer and placed it in his boot, the elaborately engraved Colt model 1851 revolvers holstered on each hip, their ivory handles visible. He felt a might overdressed to be packin' heat, he had no desire to appear innocuous, yet he noticed the Prescott's and MacKenzie were never without their firearms.

This *was* the Wild West. Again he looked into the mirror, a bit overdressed for St. Helena...but he figured Mrs. Sullivan would be as well.

Hells fire; if nothing came of *this*—well, to hell with it.

He could envision Lisle as she stood in the room with him, gazing upon him in admiration. For a brief moment, his heart fluttered... *What do ya think, love? Should I proceed...should I return to the front?* He swallowed hard, looking at the space her apparition presented itself. In point of fact, he was no different than Sally Susanne... His Lisle and their children were among the Lord. Yet they remained as his constant companions—part of what he found attractive in Sally Susanne... She seemed to accept this, this strange preoccupation with the dead. But then, she had had her sister die...had watched as her mother grieved all these years, and had *the gift*. Did he have the gift as well? He had the great gift of sight—*of Lisle*—and often that of his children... He thanked the Father for that. He had learned to trust in the Lord. To trust in his own intuition...damned easy ta do if you thought about it. The only rational thing ta do—to his way of thinkin'. If ya had a feelin' something wasn't right—well, it damn well wasn't! Best to look around you and see what was brewin'.

They were two damned different women; he knew that. Lisle was more like Prescott's Lizzie...feisty temperament, yet Lisle had that same quietness in her soul that Sally possessed... hell's fire, he didn't know what the hell he was doing here. He had come with Jamie...needed some peace, some quiet.

He ran his hand through his hair. The friggin' war...hell, if he'd stayed in Austria and fought like his father had wanted him too. Stayed in the house, shut the friggin' door to the outside world, had had some damned patience—he'd have *his family* still. He sighed, no sense in thinkin' about what he *should* have done. *It was done! It was over!* He took a deep breath, strode to the armoire and opened the bottle of whisky, tilting it to his lips he drank straight from the bottle. A decent man, a refined man would use the glass that sat on the side table. He grinned. *A refined man.* He was certain his father was turning in his grave. *Vater betreffen nicht selbst...* Father, do not concern yourself...I am still your son. His native tongue...playing with the words that rushed from his heart.

His mind suddenly filled with the battle at Gettysburg and he damned near puked.

He had no idea of what all this was leading too. *How Sally Susanne Sullivan felt.* Would she leave here?

He needed more activity than this. He needed to serve the country, even should it be in his best bib and tucker. He had had enough of the *Wild West* and he had no desire to travel to the land of milk and honey. No, Washington, New York, or Philadelphia suited him fine. There lay language and culture, a *genuine* symphony. Would she leave here? Again the apparition of Lisle was before him... The children formed a blurry vision beside her. *What should he do?* Was he to remain single the remainder of his life? He found that did not concern him...for there *she* stood... the love of his life... the dark haired woman, Lisle, who had loved and trusted him, admired him... She was ever present, ever loving, accepting...

And yet...he remembered the whiteness of Sally Susanne's long, lean legs as they had encircled his body, the tangled mass of red gold curls that had lay upon the pillow, the slickness of her body, he felt now, again, the tiny bite marks of her white teeth as they had brushed his great shoulders. He had bedded her. He felt his manhood rise in anticipation of doing just that—once again.

Sally Susanne Sullivan's porcelain beauty reflected back to her through the looking glass she held. She rarely did such as this, survey her features within the looking glass, yet she must admit that she could now see what others perceived as exquisite, uncompromising beauty. Her skin was flawless, her hair a radiant red gold…the curls that she had always considered unruly, now giving her the appearance of angelic perfection—of a natural beauty that came from her soul. She herself was certain that indeed, was where it found its origin—for that was truly where she lived, within the presence of the unseen.

Her eyes were the blue of the Montana sky and the features of her face where fine and patrician. Her hands were narrow and her fingers long and tapered. She looked at them each and everyday as she sewed assiduously for the peoples of St. Helena. She was tall and held her head and back straight and elegant, her waist a mere eighteen inches—as was fashionable. She smiled to herself, in truth she, herself, dictated the fashion here in this distant territory of the West.

The deep blue of the velvet costume she wore was bedecked with an intricate and elegant lace jabot and cuffs. Would he find her attractive? Did she care? She thought of this… She cared enough to inquire of the laws concerning divorce. A divorce from Thomas was not something she could obtain here in Montana, or anywhere else in this world of America; however, parts of Canada had adopted English laws that would grant her a divorce. It would mean traveling through Crow territory to arrive in Canada, but…

Would he ask her, what would she say to him? She breathed deeply and raised her head to the heavens, *Father, help me.*

Would I do a disservice to this man? Is love all that matters, is admiration enough, is *trust* enough? There was Mum to think of, there was the war that was so very close, close enough to threaten her mum, she who had suffered so very much—had endured such poverty and loss. Would her mum survive this war? Was it her duty to be at her mother's side? She could accomplish that should she go with Josiah Piedmont…yet she would give up everything she had worked and strived for. *To be a wife.* The restraints of being some man's wife seemed oppressive to her sensibilities. She thought of Elisabeth and Jamie. Elisabeth seemed not at all oppressed by Jamie—and he was as near to being a carbon copy of Josiah as she had yet to see. Elisabeth...dear Elisabeth, how she wished she had her spirit... She nearly laughed out loud. That would mean she would be capable of killing a bear! She smiled. She *could* kill a bear...but *would* she? She thought of Ellie and the new baby Justine—Jesse, they called her. She smiled. Elisabeth took to mothering as if it was a natural extension of herself. Sally did not feel the need for children; it was difficult for other's to understand. She felt *complete*. *Whole*. Would Josiah wish to have a family again?

Thomas seemed to appear before her; his very presence permeated with self-importance and condemnation...*a man's property...his property*. How long could she stave him off? She smiled at Thomas Pickett Sullivan's frustration with her...*his anger—with her lack of obeisance to his, her husbands' demands*. If she thought of going anywhere perhaps it should be thoughts of San Francisco. He *was* her husband and had provided for her most uncommonly, for both herself and Mum. The mere thought gave her a sensation of revulsion. The man she had married was shallow and fearful, inconsiderate and demanding, and she believed, *queer*. Although he was decidedly cautious in his actions, she had discovered very intimate truths relating to these perversions in his life. She had no desire to be party to his indiscriminate actions, or to be a *front* for his ambitions. She tried desperately not to judge him, for she knew *we each had our own path to follow*; still, she had no desire to be a participant in that life style, to take part in the *grand charade* of his life.

She reached up and pulled at the tightly coiled tendrils of hair that hung about her face and neck and placed the pearl earbobs on her earlobes. She was near ready and felt excited and eager to see Josiah.

She thought of the strength of Josiah's body as he had thrust at her; was it love he had felt, or lust? She, too, had felt that lust, that burning desire to be one with him, to join him in his ardor.

Surprisingly, she felt that same impulse as it rose in her now. What would life be—with Josiah? She would be near her mum, live in a proper city...her thoughts suddenly interrupted...

"Miz Sally? Miz Sally, where youse at?"

"I'm in my room, Caroline. Are you all right?" Caroline entered the room in a wash of excitement, her body once more huge with child. Her pretty caramel face sparkled with satisfaction and happiness. Her hands held up in awe of Sally Susanne. "Lordy, Miz Sally, youse be a pitcher, you be! Lan', youse a beauty! The wagon massa' he be a lucky man! Youse gonna say yes ta thit man?"

"Caroline, I have no idea as to what you are speaking of! *Are you all right, is it time?*" She smiled, her blue eyes dancing, as she turned to look at Caroline. It *was* nearing her time. "Have you sent Tobias for Petra?"

"No, ma'am, Tobias say no sense in getting yur tail in a knot fer the birthin'— seems he kin't hang his toursers wif out I bein' knocked up! Says we gonna have a passel o' chillun'! Oh, my, Miz Sally youse sure a sight! I's kin't wait ta see the Massa's face." Caroline giggled, covering her mouth with her hands.

Sally looked at her and laughed. "Oh, Caroline, you are delightful! Remember *Mr.* Sullivan? I do believe I am already married."

"We knows it! We knows it..." Caroline rushed into the arms of Sally Susanne. "Youse kin't leaves me...youse kin't Miz Sally...I done know wha' ta do wif out youse." The immutably dramatic Caroline clung to Sally Susanne as Sally embraced her, her tiny body robust with child, her nappy hair held the faint odor of onions. "Hush. Hush, sweet Caroline. I've yet to go anywhere. Hush now."

She heard the knock at the door. "Run on now, let Mr. Josiah in. Tell him I am nearly ready."

"Y's 'em. He be sooo heppy ta see ya. Oh's youse so beeu ti ful!" As was always with Caroline. She was once more instantaneously joyous.

Agnes

The howling of the wind off the mountains caused the ceiling of the tent to ripple—the strips of bark she had woven together and placed as a covering over the top of the canvas, now the only roof that existed. *He* had said he would build them a house. When was that? Perhaps it would be best for her to take the girl and go to the lean-to. He had left *that* for her.

An infinite number of decision and difficulties wandered aimlessly through her mind, she was so exhausted that the thoughts congealed together like a web of indiscernible mass, with each and every thought, Agnes became more disoriented and confused as *what to do*. Perhaps she would but continue to sit here—painful as it was. There were few bones in her body that had not been broken; most having not been set by anyone save herself. The bitter cold, causing more pain than she had experienced on previous winters.

They would die here this winter. Surely her and the children would die here should she not do something.

A sod roof would have been better—more substantial, but she had no idea of what would support it…and too proud to ask for help. *Pride goeth before the fall.* She remembered those words. If she could but remember more of the Bible, the words of Joseph Smith, remember the words of the angel—*Moroni*.

The small, open fire flickered, providing little heat. Still she sat before it—Indian fashion. Her entire body shuddered. The girl, now nearly five years old sat beside her beneath the bear cape *he* had provided. She could feel the child as she too trembled, her small fingers blue from cold, her dark hair matted and filled with lice. She could feel the cold of her unborn child, her body so very thin and frail, the outline of the babe could be seen. How *would* she give birth in this weather, in this state of health. She stretched out her hands before the fire; they were gnarled and broken, the bones of her body prominent from lack of nourishment.

The rifle stood in the corner of the tent, ice glazed the metal, snow mounded around its stock—without ammunition; it was useless. There were small drifts of snow near the edges of the entire tent, the snow having blown inside between the rents of the aged fabric.

She was not as strong now, not as when they had first arrived. She had been forced to use the wood she had stacked about the perimeter of the tent and had not the strength to replenish it. The food stores were near gone from the hole she had dug in the ground, a cellar of sorts. She had a few potatoes and even fewer heads of cabbage. She had trudged through snow, ice and wind to the rivers edge for water… she couldn't remember how many days ago. She knew she would not go again. It was simply too strenuous. They had had cabbage soup for days. Perhaps *he* would bring meat, perhaps, come to check on her. For some strange reason…thinking of *Mr. Tallman*… caused great pain… tears welled in her eyes and she fought them back.

She should hold the girl close to her—she knew she should—to shelter her, to care for her, to comfort her. Yet the pain in her shoulder was so horrendous, to lift it was excruciating. She could feel her remaining teeth chatter, the front ones all missing… "The better to suck my cock with," he had said.

Agnes thought of Amelia and the tears rose in her eyes. She swallowed hard and quickly pushed at the thought—Amelia knew nothing of her older sister's life; their father was dead by the time Amelia had been born.

She thought of Elisabeth and wished she had gone with her, for refuge, for escape…only her pride had kept her from accepting the proffered help.

Agnes thought of Eleanor and her often deranged mind, even she knew Eleanor was not right in the head, that she was planning to go live permanently with the Indians, was it the Crow, she couldn't remember—only that Eleanor thought it would be better for Joseph if she left him… He could then find a new wife, a wife who deserved him.

Was she, Agnes Corrigan, to leave this earth having felt no love, no comfort, no home? She breathed deeply of the foul air and thought of the greenness of the land they had come from, of her mother, of her sisters, of her father—*may he rot in hell!* A tiny fire of anger at the thought of her father rose in her… She could smell his foul breath; feel his hands and fingers as he had probed her small body, pushing his great penis in her lady parts, in her anus. She felt once again the spray of his seed as it spewed over her naked five-year-old body; as quickly, she could feel the slap of her mother's hand across her young face, the harsh words of *"liar, slut!"*—the banishment to the attic. The anger that had festered in her these many years, near quiet now, at nearly fifty years of age; she had worn it out—used it up. The thought of her sisters brought little feeling, if any at all. Emotions of longing and love having long ago left her soul. Had she, Agnes, made those decisions or had a higher power deemed she was to be the scapegoat for all mankind? She didn't know and found *she no longer cared*. She had done the best she could. She had always known she had a jealous heart, a spiteful side, a cruel and sarcastic tongue, and yes, a deep abiding fear. If that alone drove all the rest of the sins she exhibited, it was best she die.

Where would she go? Was there an afterlife as the Mormons said, or would her soul perish? What of the girl, would she simply return to dust? It would be better should that happen, better than living *this* life. She had never felt love for the girl, or for this child she carried. She had shared this information with no one, other than Eleanor and Eleanor had not been at all shocked. She remembered now the look in her small dark eyes as she had related the incident of the last child she had given birth to. Agnes smiled a small heinous smile. *Oh, could I tell Joseph some things about his precious wife!* But she wouldn't do that, Eleanor was her only friend, perhaps not friends—rather co-conspirators—they had secrets they told no one else.

Would she do *that* to this child she carried? Something as important as a child had died with Eleanor in those hours, those weeks prior… Eleanor had said, "It *had not taken long.*" That "it"—*the thoughts, the solution*—had come in the last few weeks of her time, that she had thought of the pain and of the child, of "it" taking Henry's place—*her own place*—in Joseph's heart. Eleanor had been somewhat pensive, as she had continued… "All that blood—it was disgusting. Joseph did leave me—how could he have done that?" Agnes thought about it now—though it had happened years ago. She remembered Eleanor's voice as she had described her thoughts. She had said, "She knew it was not right, yet everything she had done those weeks before giving birth had led up to it. She had planned it, she had sent Many Hands away, back to her people, had ordered Wil to go to town; she would not be needing him. She had locked the door of the house and waited. Waited with the laudanum she had hidden."

Agnes understood; strange though it may be, Agnes understood Eleanor's fear. She herself felt no fear—*that* emotion, too, had vanished. *Perhaps if she and the girl could but go to sleep.*

Should she live through the winter; in the spring, she would take the small piece of gold Mr. Tallman had given her for her land. He had physically forced her to sign the deed for the many acres of her land over to him, breaking her leg and dislocating her shoulder—breaking ribs—it had taken her month's to mend. She could buy flour and rice and ammunition. Yes, in the spring she would do that.

Should her circumstances not improve perhaps she would go to Amelia's. She would perchance learn to love the girl and the babe.

Disgust and malice rose in her mind as she thought of Amelia. "Such a sweet, kind girl," her mother had said of Amelia. Had she ever said those things to Agnes or Gwendolyn for that matter?

She looked down at the girl; they would both be better off dead—the babe as well. They lived no better than animals; were treated no better than animals. If she could just sleep…go to sleep and never wake up.

She and the girl had each repeatedly urinated and defecated in the corner of the tent. The snow had drifted high above the flap, making it impossible to leave. The fire would soon go out and they would die, free from the cold, free from the noxious odors, free from the hunger and the beatings, free from their miserable existence. *What a blessing that would be.* Would *he* grieve for her and his children? Sadness filled her, grief for her lost life, for her lost dreams. She felt sadness for the girl, this child she had birthed, the girl had known nothing but this—this….

The sins of the fathers. She found she was grateful for the grief she felt. She had felt nothing in such a very long time.

There lie within her no concept of survival; she had long ago accepted that she would die out here in this godforsaken wilderness, this land that was filled with animals that preyed upon you. In this cold, lifeless world, the weather was harsh beyond measure, the river just at her doorstep, adding more danger than comfort, ice chunks as big as her tent pushed slowly along the river by the diminished force of the current.

The river…if she could just make it to the river…

Respite

Jamie sat rocking slowing, the rocking chair making quiet, rhythmic, peaceful sounds in the warmth of the their home. The flickering light of the fire cast shadows within the room. Ellie sat upon the floor, a wooden puzzle before her. Little Jessie—Justine—slept peacefully in the cradle.

Jamie puffed at his pipe and looked over at Elisabeth, her head bowed over the needlework she employed. Her perfection undaunted by both time and circumstance, her hair as luxuriant as time immortal, the candle glow played upon her image, giving her a somewhat unearthly, angelic image of perfection. *Lord, how did I get so lucky? Let me never take this for granted.*

Mon chéri ne Elisabeth, vous savez combien je t'aime beaucoup comment? (My darling Elisabeth, do you know how much I love you? How very much you mean to me?) The language of the French something they shared between them. A language they spoke often.

Looking up from her needlework, "*Pourquoi Jamie bien sûr que je fais.* Why, Jamie, of course I do," she answered. *She* took not one moment for granted. This peaceful respite in their lives, this element of family and generosity served up by the gods. She looked at her husband and saw the graying at his temples, the structure of his sun-browned face, even in the snows of winter the sun was vibrant in this land. She saw the breadth of his shoulders and the bulk of his muscles, the leanness of his body through the muslin of his shirt. She rose and bent to kiss him, his hand reaching up to caress her face. She heard the titter of Ellie, "Mama, Papa." Most of the child's words were still unclear, but not these—these words came from the child's heart. Elisabeth felt the joy that filled her soul, such beautiful children; these children of theirs. *Thank you, Lord! Thank you!* "Would you like some tea?"

"No, I think not, but thank you, my darling. I think I shall go tend to my bookkeeping, although I must admit this is the most idealic of scenes. And to think—it is ours, yours and mine. Elisabeth I shall never be possessed of the words to tell you how grateful I am for you, for your sacrifice, for your love. You, you, made all this happen."

She laughed. "How you do go on, James Martin! Why, you built this house, you purchased this land, in fact, my handsome husband, without you there would be no lovely daughter's either." Standing behind him, she nuzzled her nose in his hair, the scent of him bringing with it a mirage of sentiments to rise within her. Comfort, peacefulness, love, and dare she say *lust*. "Thank you, Jamie," she whispered softly.

His hand rose to caress her face, raising his head, he kissed her. "I shall see you shortly *Madame, dans le chambre à coucher peut-être.*"

"Indeed, sir." Elisabeth laughed and ruffled his hair. "Shall I be surprised, Mr. Prescott?"

"Perhaps, Mrs. Prescott...perhaps."

Elisabeth looked into his eyes, watched as his soulful amber eyes darkened with desire and felt her own yearning for the promise they held. The near jade green of her own eyes, flashed lasciviously, eyes that, at their depth, were filled with love and longing.

Opening the door to the library. Looking about the rooms he had added to the house, he felt abundant gratification. He planned to add a Parlor this summer—although he had not spoken to Elisabeth concerning this, he felt she would be pleased. He had done an astonishing amount of work on the house since his return from the battle at Gettysburg. He had built two additional rooms to be used for bedrooms for the girls and perhaps, rooms for help for Elisabeth, or perhaps more children. A smile crossed his face as he thought...*and I thought she was barren*, he'd not soon forget the look on her face as he had said those words to her...but then there had been other more dire circumstances involved. He ran his hands through the thick ebony of his hair and looked at the maps and journals that lined the shelving. *This* had been a learning process, one of great magnitude; the transportation of the cattle to the railroad, the branding of the cattle, the castration—Lord God Almighty, what would he have done without Joseph and his fondness and knowledge of the beasts? Then there was the construction of the many buildings. In truth, it had been the greatest of adventures—the adventure he had sought. *James Martin, you lucky bastard you.* He thought of Elisabeth and smiled, thought of his daughters, of the horses and the cattle, the land, and of Joseph and Mack—of Josiah. He had all a man could yearn for, and he took none of it for granted. He sighed and sat down at the table he had fashioned with his own hands. *Never thought I'd be a carpenter...* He laughed. Necessity and desire. *In truth, I never thought I would own thousands of acres of land...nor have a woman that I loved so deeply or had dared to dream that love would be reciprocated.* Yet here he sat.

Niggling thoughts of the war tried with some success to disturb his cognizance, and he pushed hard at them, those thoughts pushed back. He pulled the books of geography from the shelf and lit the candle. Where would they be now, the Union and the Confederates? Was it over? Was the country now spilt in two? Perhaps should tomorrow be a fine day, he would take Elisabeth and the children into St. Helena and find a newspaper...perhaps telegraph his father in-law, or Josiah...even Seward... Surely they would know something. Opening the book, his fingers traced the battlefields, pondering the King family. He recalled the raucous laughter of Richard King, and smiled. A fine man! Would Texas indeed be an individual country as they had proclaimed? From what he remembered of his journey there, it seemed Texas was many, many miles from the other southern states. Yet as he looked more closely at the maps, he could see the Louisiana Territories abutted them.

What would happen to Montana and the territory of Oregon and California? He loathed to consider these questions.

Perhaps while in St. Helena he would go speak with Harold Baumgartner. These Western territories needed leadership should the Confederates win this war. Other than the battle at Gettysburg…they damn sure gave every indication *that was going to happen!* This *new country*—America, would be as Europe, a nation of small countries, each governed individually. The thought did not bode well in his mind, nor in the mind of Josiah. Consolidation of the states, states that were united in one common foundation, gave strength to a country—as well as a family. The Union held many advantages over the Confederates…yet *one they did not hold* was Robert E. Lee, perhaps as great a warrior as the Americans had yet to see, perhaps as great as Saladin of Arabia or perhaps Gaius Julius Caesar, or Alexander the Great… Napoleon… The poetic heart of James Prescott had surfaced— he thought of the great battles throughout the ages. Why was it man was not content to simply *live and to enjoy* the fruits of the world around him? A question that had been queried by men with far greater intellect than himself.

He thought of Lincoln's pleas for Lee to lead the army for the north, pleas that fell on deaf ears by Lee, as Robert E. Lee was a Virginian, heart and soul! He held slaves and in his words, "I feel there be no need for the apology concerning such. No. Thank you, I shall fight for the right to retain my way of life."

The telegraph communication was no replacement for General Robert E. Lee, yet it was something that could and did, keep Lincoln abreast of the goings on within the war. The Confederates had no telegraph lines; they employed the use of hot air balloons to survey the position of their enemy's armies.

Jamie knew that Lincoln had spent the entire night in the telegraph office over the course of the days during the battle of Gettysburg. He pondered on what, if anything Lincoln would do about McClellan, he was a brilliant engineer and highly capable organizer. Yet George McClellan simply was not up to the duties of an army commander. Jamie could most certainly understand that. The vision of the dead—of the dismembered limbs, of the twisted corpses, his countrymen—rose in his mind and lay upon his heart, the sounds of Shubert's *March Militaria*, thrummed there as well—yes, he could understand McClellan's distaste for war.

He had heard the Revolutionary War hero, Paul Revere's grandson, had been killed at the battle of Gettysburg… He shook his head, as if that would clear his mind of the cruelty of men. Should he return? *He abhorred the very thought*, yet it was as a gnawing within his soul. No, his place was here with his family, *this* gave him peace… If he was intent upon a political career, he was needed here in the west as much as in the east…with far less opposition. Yes, should the morrow dawn a fine day, he would take his family to St. Helena, pay a visit to ol' Harold! Perhaps even give him a stout uppercut to the jaw for all the leering looks Mr. Baumgartner had held in the direction of *his* Elisabeth! As the Great Sun Tzu of 400 BC said, "Keep your friends close and your enemies closer." He smiled; *truly* there had existed great men in this world.

He thought of Elisabeth…the promise the night gave them. *How blessed could one man be?*

Returning to his bookkeeping, he stopped and made a note to himself, to go on up and visit with Tallman… He had heard from the hired hands there were Crows in the area, the Crows were notoriously combative and damned dangerous. He was in hopes that Jeff Tallman knew something of their intent. He would bargain with them, even offer them food, if that was what they needed. Cattle or pigs, perhaps even corn or wheat. Those things he had in abundance. But he would not stop at introducing a well-placed bullet in their heads, should they not be willing to make some agreement.

Entering the figures of sales and the birthings of the cattle, he was once more astonished at the accuracy and detail Elisabeth had maintained of the records in his stead. They had branded their cattle and Joseph had numbered each of his cattle and that of Jamie's and Elisabeth's with a tag in their ear. As each gave birth, the calf would be given the number of the mother plus a letter—quite an ingenious way of determining the many events that transpired, the loss of a member of the herd, the count and age of the herd. As Joseph had mainly milk cows, it was not necessary to distinguish those, but there was Jeff Tallman's herd of cattle that simply ranged at will, him seeming to have no desire to accomplish a system of relating to those cattle he owned, absconding with Jamie's and Joseph's livestock at will, with the ever non believable apology. The horses where treated much the same way, with Elisabeth having deduced a method of listing the sire and mare of each foal… Although he had no idea how she determined the sire…yes, she was quite a remarkable woman.

"Jamie, come to bed, it is late."

"Yes, yes, I thought perhaps…" He stopped mid-sentence… as he looked up from the pages of his journal to find a vision in white. The exquisiteness of her hair shimmered from the nightly brushing and fell about her lovely face. Time had made her more beautiful than the first time he had met her. He smiled at the implications of that thought, for she had been the most stunning creature he had ever looked upon, rivaling the women in Arabia and Europe. The dressing gown she wore, one made by Grandmère of the finest batiste and sewn with ribbons and lace inserts. The sheer fabric shown full, heavy breasts, the darkness of the nipples held a mere shadow beneath the gown, with the firelight in the room revealing the smallness of her waist and the firmness of her body. The black of the bush that covered her

Mound of Venus revealed temptingly at the base of her torso. He swallowed hard. The lump in his throat caught by the beauty of the woman that stood before him. This woman was his wife, the mother of his children…for a brief moment in time, he wished only to kneel at her feet, to worship her.

"Jamie…?"

He watched as her small hands rose to her throat, marveled at the length of her slender fingers that had begun unbuttoning the gown. Observed in awe, as she revealed her breasts, the glisten of her ivory flesh revealed to him. "Jamie…"

"*Mon Dieu Elisabeth, quel un divin* creature you are." He felt the shallowness of his breath as he rose from the chair, felt the beating of his heart and the rising of his cock. *Christ, have mercy, Lord, have mercy… Thank you, Lord…*

He quelled again the desire to kneel before her, and standing, he walked to her. He lifted the heaviness of her hair and could smell the fragrance of it, the sweetness of it. His speech faltered as he bent his head to kiss her forehead, his nose to nuzzle her neck… There lay within him the male desire to crush her to him, to take her fiercely and yet, and yet the love he felt for this woman, this incredible creature, demanded passion, passion and reverence, love and respect. His lips brushed hers and he felt the gasping of her breath. Down the length of her elegant neck his kisses were placed and he heard the thunder of her beating heart, felt the rise and fall of her breathing, the utterances of a fierce wantonness, felt the agony of waiting. He placed kisses upon her heaving breasts and suckled the hardness of her nipples, tasting the richness of the milk they secreted. He knelt before her exquisite body and probed the innermost parts of her sex.

"Jamie… Jamie…"

He felt the heat of her body and the sweat that glistened upon it…the near torturous desire that melded their bodies, their minds, and their souls. Rising, he lifted her into his arms…and thought of their wedding night. "I believe we have a bed, Mrs. Prescott."

She smiled and her small white teeth bit at her full lower lip, the green of her eyes appeared mystical in the firelight. He felt his heart race.

"Jamie…"

His mind ran to the tantric sexual practices of the Eastern countries, and he smiled. *Dawn was a very long way off.*

The Decision

Danny circled in anticipation of what was to come. The thunder of hooves that reverberated from the earth of the green plains could be felt throughout Jamie's body. Jamie looked at the cattle and saw a moving sea of brindle and white. He could smell them; he could sense their excitement, their fear. Once moving, it would indeed take a great effort of will to stop them.

It was late afternoon and the sun shone on the western most side of the Rocky Mountains. The emerald green ruff of trees that lay at their base, added softness to the decent of their rugged snow covered peaks. The prairie grasses sparked a measure of white in the wave of but a gentle breeze that rippled across the land and the newly formed leaves on the aspen and cottonwood shimmered and danced. He knew, that should the world around him still, he would hear the sounds that these strange leaves made. The Missouri River ran fast and deep within the gorge to the west of him, their waters were the deep blue of the evening skies, the walls of the gorge scattered with young and old trees that fought for a foothold within the earth. He looked at the forest that lay beyond the river, a forest dense and thick with cedars and spruce—alive with wildlife of every genus. The earth had awakened from its snowy slumber and all that had retired in dens of their own making, reached now for the bark and leaves of the trees and berries of an early spring—not yet here.

Danny again circled, whinnied and tossed his head, his knowledge of Jamie was innate, and the horse knew he was not paying attention. Jamie pulled him up short, dropping his lariat to the pommel of the saddle. "Steady, boy, steady," he whispered to Danny while patting his neck. Jamie's eyes were intent on the striking image before him. Across the breadth of moving cattle he watched as Elisabeth rode atop Mercy, the stark white of the horse stunning against that of natures newly formed, vibrant hues of spring. Mercy's mane of white flew horizontal with the speed of her hooves, Elisabeth's lariat hung in the air above the horse's head. Elisabeth rode not unlike the Indian Braves they had seen on the plains as they had traveled over the Oregon Trail, her torso bent ever so slightly over the pommel of the saddle, intent on the destination of her rope, the circle of the lariat caught in midair by Jamie's gaze. Her buckskin coat open by the wind made from the swiftness of Mercy's gallop, her hair black and shining against the rays of the sun. Her lips were parted and although he could not hear her words, he knew she was echoing his own, as he had ridden this side of the herd. "Hah! Hah!"

His Danny pranced in anxious determination to resume what they had started. Jamie sat—mesmerized into stillness, in awe struck love and yes, admiration. She looked as if she had been born to do this very thing. He grinned as he watched her, delight at just being here with her in this moment, and thanked God for his luck—this woman, this remarkable woman, loved *him*. Would he never be allowed to see the depth of her? Was there always to be something more, would she always *rise to the occasion*? He had read once that *the character of a man counted more than that of his words*. His Elisabeth had character that was the embodiment of strength and courage, of faith and determination. He watched as her rope flew to its mark and for a moment in time, he thought; what a phenomenal painting this would make, the paintings of other great events in his life flashed before him...as well, a poem by Elizabeth Barrett Browning rose within his mind:

Earth's crammed with heaven
And every common bush afire with God
But only he who sees, takes off his shoes.

At that moment, Elisabeth looked over the vastness of the cattle and smiled, he grinned and tipped his hat to her. Turning Danny, he resumed his position and pushed the horse to a gallop, running along the southward side of the herd, their goal, to fresher pastures.

He stood now currying the horses, thinking of the telegraph, of the letters. Of information he had not yet shared with Elisabeth. Information he had neglected with purpose, was that purpose to spare himself, or Elisabeth? Perhaps he could attribute his failure to Agnes and her daughter? He had a hundred and one excuses, none of which Elisabeth would accept, he knew that, he knew she would be right to not accept them. He also knew that putting it off was going to make it worse, oh yes, with Elisabeth...*far worse*.

Jamie had taken his family; Elisabeth, Ellie and little Jesse to St. Helena for the purpose of visiting, shopping; and he must confess, to contact someone with information that was current, concerning the war that raged in the east between the Union and the Confederate armies.

He marveled at the change in the city from whence they had arrived some six years previous. The city building's were often new and sheeted in granite, grand edifice's had replaced wooden structures, the streets paved in asphalt and some in cobblestones, intended to mimic the eastern cities of the *United States*—or should it be *America*—the mere thought aggravated him.

They had first stopped to visit Ma and Pa Parsons and their growing children, Ma, as always—her kind and effusive self. She was more than pleased at their visit, offering food and drink and begging Jamie for details of the war. She had not heard from either Tommy or Micah for "nay onto six months" and was more than a little concerned. Jamie tried desperately to assure her that 'they were fine or she would have surely heard. Yet he, himself, was not at all convinced of his own words. His memory of the men—thousands of dead and wounded, played upon his mind. Pa was well—Pa— quiet, with a peacefulness that radiated from within. Thinner than the last time Jamie had seen him, his dirty trousers hung more loosely; the suspenders now necessarily, hung upon his frail shoulders, his ears somehow larger, his pate bearing less hair, yet the ever-present pipe hung in his mouth and his eyes twinkled.

"Jamie, me dear boy, iffn' ya go on back, could ya look fer m' boys?"

"Yes. Yes, of course, Ma, you know I shall." He caught the fleeting look of Elisabeth as he said the words and quickly looked away. It was a subject that they in silence, had agreed they would not discuss. *He prayed it would not be necessary.*

From the Parsons' home they went on to Sally Susanne's. The storefront was now embellished with Victorian ornate festoons and carvings, the paint, stark white and new. He chuckled to himself thinking, *regardless of where you lived, spring was a time to repair, replace and enhance what the winter of Mother Nature had set upon to destroy.*

Caroline's back was to them as they entered, she was dusting furiously while singing a lovely gospel song they had heard her sing on the Oregon Trail, her children playing hide-and-seek. The children saw them first as they all strode through the door, the little bell announcing their visit. Caroline and the children all squealed with delight. "Lordy, Lordy! I's so glad ta see y'all! My, don't y'all look fine, and Lord have mercy, le' me take thet' prutty chil'. Chil'un' y'all come! Say hello ta Mista an' Miz Prescutt! Youse come *now*." The pretty mulatto woman scurried after her small chocolate children; the chil'un', of Tobias and Caroline running from her and the persons calling; running to the back of the store that was Sally Susanne's work room, hollering, "Miz Sally! Miz Sally they's hair'!" Right behind them ran an equally enthusiastic Ellie. "Aunt Sally! Auntie!"

Jesse squirmed in Elisabeth's arms and peered through thick black lashes at what appeared to her to be quite an adventure. At nearly six months old, she was crawling on the floor—if one could call it that. She simply scooted across the floor on her bottom. A bottom made quite round with diapers and soakers.

Sally Susanne *and Petra* came running from the back room, both women gleaming in absolute pleasure at seeing Elisabeth, Jamie, and their daughters.

"Why what a most delightful surprise! I have been thinking of you for days now! Near constant you have been on my mind! Oh, dear Jesse, come to Auntie. And Ellie love, how beautiful you are." Sally loved Elisabeth and Jamie's children as if they were her very own. Quite suddenly, a fleeting knowledge presented itself. *She would never have any children of her own.* This did not surprise her; as if she had always acknowledged it to be truth. She was after all, the consular to many—to many, the consoler. Perhaps children of her own, she did not require. Strangely enough she found herself to be engaging in conversation all the while this phenomena took place. But then, this was often the situation. The sounds of the *voices* were but rarely quiet and should they ever become silent...*Lord, how she would suffer a great injury to her very being.* With the tiny, fat little Jesse between them, Sally reached out and hugged Elisabeth, amazed, as always by her beauty. "You, my friend, *why, you look wonderful*, as always. I am so happy to see you. Come. Come sit. Would you like tea, coffee, and scones? They are fresh from the oven this morning..."

Petra gathered Elisabeth in her arms, as pleased to see her as Sally Susanne was. Petra reached for the baby, "My word, how she has grown! Elisabeth she is the spitting image of you!

Sally Susanne reached up and hugged Jamie and was yet again amazed at his resemblance to Josiah. *Josiah.* She indeed missed him. She felt the letter in her pocket. With her arms around the shoulders of James Prescott, upon the moment of physical contact, her senses became overwhelmed with a strange absence, a sadness, a sense of loss—an image of golden summer grasses, of his blue uniform...of pain, fear, and desperate despair. She swallowed hard and patted him on the back, her hand still resting on his arm. "You, too, look wonderful Jamie. The ranch agrees with you, family life agrees with you." She saw the smile on his face and the new crinkle about his eyes, again reminding her of Josiah.

The *image*—she had not an inkling of its meaning, but she had no doubt as to the truth of it. *It* had been taking place near constant since yesterday, images of stark clarity, emitting fear and feelings that she had quickly pushed aside. Now she knew they to be associated with James Prescott. She did not doubt the truth of them, the *voices* and the *images* had been happening since childhood. The longer she held to him—the more vivid the voices and the images became... fear, despair, physical pain, disorientation... She pulled back quite suddenly, too quickly she feared, certain Elisabeth would take note of her strange behavior.

"Sally? Sally Susanne, what is it?" Elisabeth's green eyes flashed in the direction of Sally Susanne. "What is it?"

"Whatever to do you mean? Come, the lot of you, what do you fancy, coffee or tea, jam or honey?"

Petra placed small Jesse upon the floor. "No, no, thank you, I must return to my office... I am certain I have patients waiting." Petra was about to leave when she suddenly said, "Oh, by the way, Ezra has gone on up to a small valley... I believe it is called Snoqualmie Valley, up north of Walla Walla. I expect him home in the next month or so and I thought we should have a party. Perhaps a Fourth of July picnic again?"

Elisabeth's eyes lit up! "That sounds wonderful, Petra!"

Jamie laughed at his wife's enthusiasm; actually she was enthusiastic about all things. Within this woman he loved lay exuberance for life he had not thought possible. He looked at her adoringly, "I quite enjoy our picnics. We shall have one at the house at harvest time. Listen, you lovely ladies…" He reached over and squeezed the shoulders of Caroline, causing her to blush a radiate umber color. "Ah…Mista James, how y'all go on."

"I am off to pay a visit to Harold Baumgartner. Thought I'd see about some public office here in St. Helena. You ladies enjoy a pleasant visit and I shall return for my lovely wife and we shall procure our staples from Ben's mercantile. Is that satisfactory, Elisabeth?"

"Yes, of course, Jamie." Standing on tiptoe, she placed a kiss on his cheek.

Jamie turned and left, with Petra at his side, both leaving and chatting as they did so.

They had scarcely exited the seamstress shop of Sally Susanne when Elisabeth's hand was on Sally's shoulder. "Sally, Sally, I must know!"

Sally Susanne watched Caroline as she gathered the children and began climbing the stairs to Sally's living quarters. She felt Elisabeth's anxiety and looked at her dearest friend. Would she tell her, she simply could not…perhaps she was wrong…perhaps the summer grasses of the images were of the golden pastures of grain on Jamie and Elisabeth's ranch…yet the blue uniform… Oh dear…

"Sally, I *must* know."

Sally stopped, "Elisabeth…"

"I must know of Josiah! What do you intend? I simply shan't stop until I have heard all!" Sally smiled at her friend. *Thank goodness romance was far more important to Elisabeth than that of the startling look on her face as she had touched Jamie. Thank you, Lord!* Sally Susanne hugged her friend, "Elisabeth, my dearest friend, you are such a romantic! I am so very grateful for your visit… I do have a letter from him." She reached down into her pocket and handed the letter to Elisabeth. They held no secrets twixt the two of them…well, perhaps a few… The letter was most affectionate; Josiah had said *he loved her*. He had asked her to join him in Philadelphia. Sally Susanne watched with a small smile on her face, as Elisabeth read the very intimate words of Josiah. She, with fascination, observed as the smile on Elisabeth's face grew more effusive, with her lovely eyes widening and now her mouth agape. Was she going to scream? "I simply shan't wait to tell Jamie! Are you going? Oh, I shall miss you so! Oh, Sally Susanne, I could not be more pleased!" All the while dancing up and down in glee, one minute filled with joy, the other with eyes filled with tears and hugging Sally. "Whatever shall I do without you?"

"My dearest Elisabeth, I shall not go. If you recall, I am still the wife of Thomas Sullivan, regardless of where my heart lies. Too, I must say, it would be difficult to leave this, this life I have made for myself, to leave you and your children—as well as Caroline and Tobias—their children. No, I shall perhaps visit him soon…" She knew her voice to be wistful, and as she looked into the eyes of Elisabeth, she felt the tears spill from her own. "Oh dear, please, please, pay me no mind. It is, it is, I… had not thought I had made up my mind. I miss him terribly *and* me mum." She felt the arms of her friend about her and the soothing words of comfort. "I am so sorry Sally, perhaps you shall change your mind. Perhaps? Oh, I so wish for you to be happy, truly so. Do you recall, you may extract a divorce from Thomas in Canada! You *could* do such as that. Try to remember, you do have options. To love someone as wonderful as Josiah, to be loved by him… Sally Susanne, you deserve to be loved, to be cherished. Cry, my dear friend, cry your heart out. You are not alone! I shall always be your bosom friend. Always…" In all the years they had known one another, in all the dreadful experiences they had shared, never had Elisabeth seen such emotion from Sally Susanne. It broke her heart. She held to her friend tightly and let her cry.

Having left Petra to attend her patients, Jamie walked to the telegraph office and sent a telegraph to Josiah and Seward, one to

Lincoln as well. He thought it best that he should not depend on any one of them responding over rapidly. The clerk told him he would receive confirmation within the hour. Jamie thanked him and determinedly set out for the office of the mayor.

Harold Baumgartner stood behind his lavishly appointed desk; he was a strikingly handsome man, with golden locks, fine patrician features and clear, intelligent blue eyes. His clothing was immaculate; his suit of worsted wool was of the finest tailoring, and was the color of the evening sky. His shirt white and the collar and cuffs, crisp and clean. He stood as Jamie entered his office, his hand outstretched in greeting. "I say, James, what brings you here today. A problem with that pesky neighbor Tallman…?"

Jamie smiled. "No. Tallman and I have long ago agreed to disagree. I thought perhaps you could advise me of a position open here in St. Helena."

"Indeed, Prescott? Do you fancy yourself to be sheriff? We could use a good one. Perhaps sit on the counsel. How about mayor? I believe I shall run for governor as soon as statehood becomes a possibility."

"Is that so? And do you know when that would be?"

"No, I do not. Thought perhaps you would know, since you are in tight with Lincoln and Seward." For a moment, the room was filled with a most uncomfortable animosity. Jamie rose from the chair in which Harold had allotted him, and began pacing the floor, gathering his thoughts and his emotions. He did not like this man…other than Harold's amorous attentions to Elisabeth; he had no reason—he simply did not trust the man. His allusion to Jamie's *in* with the government was not made with admiration or interest, but with a sarcasm that dripped of envy and irritation. Would he, James Prescott be comfortable to live with those sorts of constant references this man made, each and every day. *Would he, could he, work for this man?*

"How is Elisabeth?"

"*Mrs. Prescott* is very well. I thank you, Harold. However, I believe I must attend to an errand of some import, perhaps I shall see you again soon." He placed his hat on his head, looked askance in the direction of Mr. Baumgartner and strode purposely from the room. *No. He could not work for or alongside this man. He would do better at opening a saloon or simply playing cards. As far as contributing to the community...well, he would think about that.*

Jamie stood at the far end of the bar in the saloon, happy amongst the men and the sounds of the piano, the cacophony of card players, the sounds of billiard balls being struck. For the second time he read the telegraph message...mulling the contents over and over in his mind.

Lincoln has turned to Grant and Sherman—stop. They will cripple the South—stop. Take Atlanta by storm with Sherman in charge—stop. It will be over, need as many men as possible—Come now—stop.

He folded the telegram and placed it carefully within the inside pocket of his vest. He took a deep breath and tossed the remaining whisky back. He felt the familiar sting as it traveled down his throat. *What the hell do I do now...?*

Having procured the necessary items from Ben Parsons's mercantile, Jamie and Elisabeth and the children traveled in the direction of home. It was early yet and the day was a fine one. It would be a rather circuitous route, but still, perhaps Elisabeth would enjoy it. "My dear, would you like to pay a visit to Agnes? It has been some months since I have heard from Tallman." Jamie very seldom gave thought to the man, yet today he had heard mention of his name twice. "Or have you something more pressing?"

"That would be very nice indeed, we needn't stay over long. I do have to feed the children."

"For a brief visit then." He turned the wagon toward Jeff Tallman's land, to the small valley that lay northwest of their own home, as their acreage abutted one another. He was reminded of the days he and Elisabeth had spent staking out their claim of land, with Jeff hovering and tracking them—so bent on having his land right next to the Prescotts and the MacKenzies.

The wagon rumbled over rocks and good-sized limbs, downward to the open valley, the rivers edge coming up to the top of the land itself. The forest was dense and offered shelter from the western elements of Mother Nature, yet the wind and snow coming from the North, filled it like a bowl in the harshness of winter.

The scene before them was one of irrefutable abandon, shocking both he and Elisabeth. The top of the tent like structure rippled in the breeze, remnants of wood, split and ready for a fire lay strewn about the small, disheveled structure, a structure surrounded by heavy drifts of snow frozen in place from the long harshness of winter. A galvanized pail and a cooking pot lay overturned within the confines of the ash in the fire pit, the lean-to leaned heavily towards the east. A garden fence lay towards the earth with dried and desiccated vines of pole beans and peas.

He felt Elisabeth's hand upon his leg and he pulled at the reins of the horses, pulling the wagon to a stop. He swallowed hard and felt the eeriness of the scene in his bones. "Elisabeth, when have you heard from her last?"

"Why, why, I believe Joseph said…I daresay—it could not have been more than a month…but surely Jeff has… Oh, Jamie, perhaps, perhaps she has gone to stay with Jeff. Surely she and her child cannot be *here. The weather…the temperatures* have been far below freezing. Would he have left her? *Oh, Jamie.*"

"Has Eleanor been to see her, do you know?"

"I daresay. I doubt it. Joseph said Eleanor has sequestered herself in the house…the laudanum…and…I believe Petra has given her that new drug, morphine for the ghastly headaches."

"Morphine…?" He thought of the *soldiers sickness* caused by the morphine. "Stay here with the girls, Elisabeth. I shall go have a look."

"I'll not stay here! I will come with you, the girls shall be fine!"

"Elisabeth, what of the Indians. The animals. Certainly you don't wish to see…"

"James Martin, do not tell me what I wish to see. Of course I shall come with you."

Jamie slapped the reins on the back of the horses and they pulled the wagon closer to the scene of desolation and abandon that lay before them. Fear and dread lay on the hearts of both of them. *Surely Jeff…* Jamie could think of nothing less… *Surely even Tallman…would not have left her.* He thought of the conversations within the saloon. Information passed along, information from the long winter months that had isolated them from one another. He heard now the words of the fellow Culver; was that his name? He couldn't recall for certain but he thought Culver lived north of Tallman and his squaw, Jamie recalled now, Culver saying, "Tallman and his squaw had gone on up to the village of her people for the winter." Had Jeff Tallman left Agnes and their child alone over the long winter months…*surely not?* Jamie looked at Ellie, "Ellie, stay with your sister, Mama and Papa will return shortly. *Do not* get out of the buckboard. Do you understand?"

"Yes, Papa." Her amber eyes darkened by the fear she felt in his voice.

Elisabeth lay the sleeping Jesse on the floorboard of the wagon, and they climbed down. They were mere steps from the hovel that housed Agnes and her daughter. Jamie reached for his rifle. "Do you have your knife?"

"Yes, Jamie, I always have my knife." Her mind flashed to the young Indian brave she had killed on the plains above Texas. The knife had saved her life; she would go nowhere without it.

"Very good." Jamie hollered, "Agnes…Agnes! It is James and Elisabeth Prescott, come to call. Agnes?"

Nothing. He looked at the sky, the sun rode midway between the mountains and the height of the sky, it was nearing three o'clock, listening, he could hear nothing more than the bubbling of the river, the sound of birds in the trees, the scurry of small rodents and rabbits as they sought shelter from these human invaders. He watched as Elisabeth made the sign of the cross. "Stay behind me."

Within ten steps, they were at the flap of the tent. It rippled ever so slightly. "Agnes! Agnes Corrigan!" *Oh dear God…the only words that came to mind.* He cocked the rifle and entered the tent.

Emotion welled within him as he viewed the scene before him. *Praise the Lord above…what have you let happen here?* The odor was slight, yet pervaded the air. The cold having created an atmosphere that was frigid. The gray of Agnes's head hung at her chest, her hands rested on her stomach, a stomach large from pregnancy. The girl, *what was her name*, leaned close to her mother, her small hands gaunt and purple clutched at the remnants of Agnes's tattered clothing.

"*Lord, have mercy, Christ have mercy…*" He heard Elisabeth's words and reached his arm about her shoulders. "Oh God, Jamie! Oh my God…" She felt her chest tighten and wished desperately to scream.

The ashes on the cold fire-pit were frozen in place and as she gasped she could see her breath. Jamie looked at his wife, the color having drained from her face, her eyes welling in tears.

Sorrow mixed with anger engulfed him. "That little fucker… that fuckin' Tallman…" Jamie wanted to beat him to death. They should have done it long ago—he, Mack, and Joseph! They all knew, they had *let* it happen. He sighed. "Elisabeth, Elisabeth? Are you all right?"

"Yes. Jamie, yes, I am. I am. I shall be—we knew this would happen…I, I…" The tears spilled over. Again he sighed. "I shall take you and the girls home, then I shall come back and get them."

"Jamie, you mustn't do this by yourself."

"I'll ride up to Joseph's and Mack's—let them know, then come back and bury them."

"Shall we look for Jeff?"

"No, not now, would do nothing for Agnes or the child and—and I just might resort to murder. No, come, let us be going home."

"But…but we shan't just leave her!"

"Elisabeth, darling…she has obviously been here for some time, a few more hours will do no more harm."

The ride home had been silent, with Elisabeth saying only, "Jamie I think we should bury them on our land." He had merely nodded his head. Rather than grief, he felt immense anger!

He tied the wagon to the hitching post in front of the barn and saddled Danny, they would stop back here and take the wagon to retrieve the remains. Tomorrow they would bury them.

That evening, he and Elisabeth designated a small area of land for a cemetery plot.

The burial day was blustery and dark; the snow fell on the dead and those who came to mourn. They buried Agnes and the small child together. The mourners were but the Prescotts and the MacKenzies, Charlie and Little Flower. The hearts and tongues of the mourners could be heard across the plains on the chill of a winter's day as they chanted the Lord's Prayer. Ilene's voice echoed to the mountains on the wings of angels as she sang "Amazing Grace."

Eleanor clung to Joseph's arm and sobbed; the first time any of them had seen her cry in years. Strange as it was, she allowed Elisabeth to console her, sobbing against her shoulder, she uttered over and over… "There is nothing more for me here now, there is nothing left to lose. I should never have come."

Were any of them going to tell Jeff? Not one.

Jamie continued to curry the horses as he thought of all that had transpired. *Life was damned hard!* The last days had been filled with grief, loss, and for the men, anger. It was difficult for them not to hunt down the bastard Tallman, for Mack in particular.

Was he, James Prescott, to be as guilty as Jeff Tallman? The gnawing fear pulled at his heart. Try as he might he could not push aside the words of the telegram or the feelings of patriotism and obligation to his country.

It would be but *four months* out of their lives. It was spring, the hired hands and Joseph, as well as Mack and Duncan where here. *And Elisabeth was most certainly not Agnes.* If only the railroad were finished... *He would take her to her family in Philadelphia.* He thought of their day of riding herd, at the resplendence of Elisabeth astride Mercy, an image that would be with him forever.

There was a shallow pool beside the river, the very same pool where they had bathed after the birthing of their first cow. The bonfire he had built that night was still evident in his mind, as was the bitter cold of the night so many years ago. It had become a habit of theirs to come of an evening to bathe after the chores were finished and the girls lay sleeping. Even in the bitter cold of winter, Jamie would build a blazing fire and they would run naked to and from the house, to make love and to bath in the whirling chill of the water.

The skies were clear and the stars hung as crystals about the full marble of the moon. Moonlight cascaded over their naked bodies. The waters chill no longer evident to either of them, spent as they were. His hand caressed her breasts, and she leaned to lie against him. They had bathed each other and explored each intimate feature as if for the first time. The desire and passion within Jamie ached to be expressed, the fear of what her reaction would be to what he must tell her, causing him to near ravage her body.

Elisabeth turned her head to look up at him, her lashes wet and spiked, black against the ivory of her skin, her lips swollen from the many kisses Jamie had placed there. "Jamie, tell me... what are you thinking? You are miles away from me."

"Never, my darling, never."

"Tell me, Jamie, where are you?" she snuggled closer to him and bit his arm, her sharp, white teeth causing painful ecstasy.

He chuckled, so like his Elisabeth. They shared a bond so deep he could not hide his emotions or his intentions from her… strange…*as to this moment he had not known what those intentions truly were.*

"James Martin?" She pulled from him, remembering the passion, the devotion she had felt. *He was saying good-bye!* "You are going back aren't you? *You are!*" She rose naked from the pool and he watched as her green eyes shot fire at him. He saw her hand as it rose and felt the sting of her hand on his face. He watched as her breasts heaved, watched as the tears streamed from her eyes and rose to reach out to her. She pounded at him with her fists, all the while screaming, "How dare you! How dare you leave us again…this was *your dream,* Jamie! *You were mine…* you cannot go. You must not go…*how dare you!*"

He caught her and pulled her tightly to his chest. "Elisabeth, Elisabeth, please, try to understand. I love you so…please try to understand. I, I feel I must do this. I am so torn… *Please!*" He felt the heaving of his own chest and realized he too was sobbing…

"*Oh my God, Elisabeth, please.*"

Southern Gentlemen

The ropes bit at his wrists with each faltering footstep, the soles of the shoes of the man shackled in front of him flapping beneath each footfall.

So he, James Martin Prescott, was not the only one in need of new footwear.

Christ how in the hell did this happen to him, of all people? The years he had spent fighting in the Foreign Legion… He had never even been wounded. Now in his own country, here he found himself being dragged and fettered, to *a Confederate prison*! At least he hoped that to be their destination. Better that than a round in the head.

His leg hurt like hell, making the pain in his wrists and shoulder seem inconsequential. He could feel the dribble of fluid that ran from the wound. Shit, he hoped it was not sepsis.

The sounds of the shuffling feet of those who followed, gave him only a sense of foreboding. God, how he wished to scratch his head and face, he itched all over; the lice that permeated his hair and beard long since having become part and parcel to his miserable existence.

He thought he could discern the sounds of a river. Lord, let it be true. Christ, he was thirsty. Who among them was not? They had been offered very little water and no food in the days since their capture. For the life of him, he couldn't remember when that was.

He listened to the barking orders of the Confederate soldiers as they shouted for the prisoners to *step it up*. The sounds of whips that whistled through the warmth of the Southern air as they cracked across the body of someone who had fallen, someone simply too exhausted to carry on, *someone wishing for the release of death*. He could understand that. But it would not be so with him, he would fight to live. This was a mind game and he meant to survive. If not for himself, then for Elisabeth, for their children, his hopes and dreams.

He had no fear of death nor pain. Being enslaved without freedom; hell, now *that* was another thing altogether. Neither these men with their whips and guns could do that, nor anyone else. He *would* survive this. He was young and strong. *They would not break him!* A bitter smile crossed his lips as he thought of his capture. So often had he thought this war to be over, yet the *Southern gentlemen*—and he had to give them that, *just did not give up*. What was it about them that strove to separate themselves from the Union, to cripple a nation?

He knew the British were providing guns for both sides. He knew the French had offered their assistance to the South...only to recant after Lincoln had blockaded the southern ports. Lincoln was hell bent on keeping all other countries from interfering; while the Confederacy was entreating them to assist.

With Maryland a slave state the battles continued to be dotted about the landscape of the country. He and his men had been sent down to Columbia to assist Sheridan. Of all the battles he had been subject to, this had seemed to be the least dangerous—*go in, get out. Hold the line.* Those had been their instructions.

But General Robert E. Lee had a surprise in store for the likes of the feisty general from the Union, Philip Sheridan... He had sent Wade Hampton to intercept the threat...in the stead of Jeb Stuart, whom Sheridan had killed in Richmond.

They had had word that Lee was planning on doing such as that...but the name Hampton meant nothing to them, and their

Intelligence was by now limited to information that they had gleaned years previous. Intelligence personnel were in constant danger, not only personally, but for the Union as well. A man beaten long enough gave *some* information, and quite simply these men were needed at the front lines.

This had been a costly war both in terms of lives lost, wounded that were now unable to care for their families, *and* money. This war of Lincolns had now lasted four long years.

The thought turned Jamie's stomach. War, and what it meant, no longer thought to be such an appealing consideration of adventure and excitement. Had he grown up, or had he given up?

The bodies of his fallen comrades, flashed before his mind... Tommy and the crippling injuries of his men, the years of blood and fear having taken any romance that had existed, from his mind. That lust for adventure, that thrill, had left him.

That he felt certain, was the reason he followed now in this line of prisoners to Fort Sumter. They, too, had lost the burning desire to run head long into battle; to give their life for their country. The lot of them were *tired and weary*.

Wade Hampton was most *obviously not* tired nor weary; he was not even militarily trained to Jamie's knowledge. He was a South Carolina plantation magnate with the spirit of a warrior. Jamie and Sheridan both had been eyewitness to his skill with the sword, his marksmanship with the pistol, and his fine horsemanship.

Lee had sent Hampton with two thirds of his mounted force; among them the Sixth South Carolina Cavalry, along with the Citadel, South Carolina's military academy.

The Union Army was out numbered, out flanked and outfoxed by Lee.

Hampton was brutal, and if he had no experience, it damned well kept him from being cautious or afraid. Jamie had watched as Hampton had himself, led the dramatic attacks. Fresh blood and enthusiasm were needed to finish this war and Hampton had both.

After two days of bloody, close quartered fighting, General's Phillip Sheridan and James Prescott decided to make for a wide sweep back to Grants army—*there were times*—it was best to turn tail and run.

Jamie had turned from the blood and gore of the severed mans head and prepared to run for his horse when the heat in his leg burst. At first shocked, he had staggered, glancing about him for the culprit that had caused the attack. Determined to make it to his horse, to flee with the others. The burning had turned to searing pain, and he had stumbled to the ground. He heard the shouts of those around him to *get up, to run*. He heard the sergeant major shout at him. "Come on, General!" Jamie had seen the sergeant's extended hand and reached for it. Caleb had made every attempt, but the weakness in Jamie's wounded left arm was still apparent. The blood of his most recent kills had coated each and every part of his flesh, the slickness of the warm blood making it impossible for Caleb to pull him to his horse.

"Get out of here!" Jamie had shouted at him. "Go! I can make it." He had risen, staggered, watched with near surreal interest as his company in the command of Sheridan had thundered off.

The heat in his leg—now one of excruciating pain. He could feel the blood as it filled his boot. He had reached for his belt to make a tourniquet, he damned well didn't intend to bleed to death.

For an instant, he looked about at his surroundings. The battlefield was a mass of bloodied men, the ground shown to be a virtual open graveyard. The heat and humidity had risen to astronomical heights, causing a stench beyond imagination.

His sword hung from his hand, his pistol lay where he had fallen. Few men in "Blue" stood, perhaps thirty, perhaps twenty.

The Gray Coats were coming now.

Could he make it to the copse of trees, the land was open and exposed? Think, damn it, think! Should he lie down and feign death? The battle noises around him were deafening. He heard the pistol fire and thought better of that. As they, the Union Army had done; the rebels were shooting those that moaned or showed signs of life. Be it for reasons of humanity or simply to eliminate the Yankees... *No, feigning death had not been an option.* He had tightened the tourniquet, picked up his pistol, turned, and ran. He held no feeling of cowardice; a dead man can do nothing. To be captured was not something his mind had entertained. Those who had served him, which had been captured—had not returned. Would Josiah Piedmont, general or not, have the power to provoke within the military, an exchange of prisoners for Jamie? At this moment, he found that hard to believe. He thought of the conditions surrounding such an exchange; a general could be redeemed for thirty-two privates, but he also was aware that Grant and Stanton were opting to halt this practice, knowing it would further cripple the manpower of the Confederacy and the Union.

The grasses that had become saturated with the blood of many made the ground slippery beneath his feet as he struggled for purchase to climb the small hillock that led to the copse of trees. He felt the sweat run down the backs of his ears, knowing that there was as much blood in it as perspiration. He had seen the others, their faces and uniforms covered in another man's blood. He knew he was not distinctive in that. The hair on his head wet and matted; his armpits and crouch awash in the sweat and stench of a near three-day battle. His stomach growled and he smiled to himself. Some things were a constant.

Such as the blood that seeped from his body.

He had heard someone shout, "I got you covered, General. Run!"

Looking over he saw one of his men. "Are you hit?"

"I am. Already a gonner. Run like hell."

Jamie had heard the shots and the footfalls of those that had been caught in the act of fighting when Sheridan had made the decision to retreat. It was his own damn fault; he knew Sheridan had planned on retreating—they had discussed it! He should have been on his horse, *instead of killing one more rebel! If he hadn't left Danny home*…to have his beloved Danny shot from beneath him—eaten…

The horse he rode made no response to his whistle.

By nightfall, Wade Hampton and his men had gathered them up with expediency, as if they had been naught but school children. They had stripped him of his weapons and offered to cut off his leg. They were *Southern gentlemen* to the end.

Now days later, they stood at the crest of a barren landscape that was the newest prison constructed by the Confederates. "Andersonville" they called it. Fort Sumter it had been. Or was this some new place?

The prisoners stood in single file at the crest of the hill, their chains dangled, the blood from their wrist's dripping steadily to the hot, golden, trampled grasses. The sky was clear and blue, the sun a hot ball, hung overhead to the west. He figured it was near six o'clock in the evening.

The man who stood next to him was someone he knew from his regiment. The previous one having fallen too many times for the patience of the *Southern gentlemen*. They had shot him. A round hole had gone into his temple, quickly exiting on the opposite side of his head.

Jamie had not been mortified by the act of brutally, mortification within him coming from the observation; *that it had made no difference to him. Now, at least the man would not continually put him in harm's way.* Oh, God, what have you made of me?

The prison was *massive.* His thoughts running to Elisabeth and her expectations of Fort Laramie… A smile crossed his lips and he pushed at the thought of her. *Weakened he could not be.*

With love in his heart and fear of his death on his mind, he would be a man afraid, and *that* must not be. Not if he wished to survive.

He heard the words of Hamptons' man, as he shouted. "Y'all be livin' down there fer the rest a yur lives, best git used to it. Now git on down thar. We done been bringin' some four hun'red men a day, an' they all gonna die here."

Four hundred men a day, surely he had not heard right. Jamie looked about him—some fifty men, prisoners of war, looked back at him. The eyes that looked into his own held a myriad of emotions. *Fear, grief, sadness.* There were those that possessed but a bland, blank stare. If *he* could master that, live only within his mind, he could do this. Or he could make a run for it now. He knew it would be over then. But didn't he owe it to Elisabeth, to his daughters, to survive?

The droning sound of the rebel went on, with Jamie often unable to fathom what he was saying, the man's southern drawl so extreme as to ring in his ears as a foreign language, one he could not comprehend.

"Escape is not an option. Them logs is some six feet deep into the groun' an' there are these fella's down yonder, ya see with them cannon's..." he heard the soldier shout. "So git thet dumb idea out a' yur mind."

Had the soldier read his mind? *Escape was always an option.* He knew several of these men and he felt certain they would follow him. A tremor of hope rang in his mind, making his heart leap with courage. Suddenly it was clear that this was the best view he would ever have of this place they were taking him, he thought of Ezra and his ability to observe and absorb the most minuet details—*Ezra, help me now.*

Standing on the precipice of the hill he could see that the "Pen" covered about sixteen and a half acres of land, which was enclosed by an immense twenty-foot high stockade of hewn pine logs. He could also see that they were enlarging the space by what appeared to be another ten or so acres. Thank God, he had had to claim all that acreage in Montana and knew what the size of an acre was. The stockade was in the shape of a parallelogram, and looked to be approximately sixteen hundred feet long and perhaps eight hundred feet wide. Sentry boxes, or "pigeon roosts" as he had heard them called, stood at about thirty yard intervals along the top of the stockade. There were two hills with a valley between. Flowing through the prison yard was a stream.

There were two entrances, one at the north and one at the south of the west side of the stockade. Eight small earthen forts located around the exterior of the prison were equipped with artillery. There was no doubt in his mind that they were intended to quell disturbances within the compound and to defend against feared Union cavalry attacks.

The interior was dotted with what appeared to be shelters of some sort, with a *mass of humanity* that seemed to fill the entirety of the vast space. From where he stood, it looked as if many of them were without clothing. He felt the rise of panic within his heart, felt his gut wrench, and swallowed back the bile that rose.

Standing on either hill within the prison, he could see the camps of the rebel guards, their battery of artillery trained at enabling them to rake the prison at all points; the line of rifle pits on the north side more than likely used as a means of defense by the guards, should they be needed to repel an outbreak within the prison walls.

Jamie heard the sound of a train and looking toward the sound, he could see a railroad that was nearly half a mile away, winding its way through the picturesque Georgia Pines.

"Thet there train be bringin in 'Fresh Fish,' y'all know; more o' you Yanks."

The man in charge and those that were his underlings gave off a great guffaw. "Yeah! 'Fresh Fish.' Once more their bawdy laughter rang through the air.

Jamie heard the frightened sobbing of the man behind him, gut-wrenching sobs that came from deep with in his chest. He knew he should not—yet he turned to look at the man, was it one of his men, was there anything he could do for him...

A shot rang out, the round pierced the sobbing man's head.

The sobbing was no more.

To imagine oneself a prisoner of war was particularly compelling; a captive soldier is in a liminal state, vanquished in battle but not yet defeated by death. Away from home and in all likelihood away from his comrades as well. Unable to fight or to flee. He could not remember where he had read that. He took a deep breath.

It had begun.

Inside Andersonville

The proximity of the men had tightened. Fear permeated the air. Its acrid smell, one Jamie recognized all to well.

The Confederates had eliminated three more men within the group of prisoners they had marshaled from Virginia. Given the odds, Jamie thought it to be a small fraction. Tears or anger had brought them only a bullet in the head.

The remainder of them seemed to have received the message; they stood quietly, docile now, in solid lines, some five feet across. The slain men having been drug to the front of those remaining; the better to look upon their assassinated comrades; to reinforce the punishment for poor behavior.

The Confederate soldiers no longer appeared to be as *genteel* as Jamie had thought.

He took the opportunity given him to search the faces of the crowd. He saw among the throngs of men the faces of Colin, Liam, and Mathew. These men were among those that had accompanied him; these were *his* men. He knew them and trusted them with his life. He wondered if they would say the same of him. They were now prisoners of war because of him. Perhaps they would not be so willing to follow him now. The shrill sound of the train whistle brought him from his contemplation of escape, and he watched as blue-coated Union Army men climbed from within the length of the train. Sunlight bounced from the shackles and chains upon their wrists and ankles. Confederate guards in profusion, stood en'guard as the Blue coats filed through the lines of gray and butternut.

As the Union men exited the train cars, many stumbled and fell. The Confederate guards appeared to have an internal time table as to how long the Union man had prior to standing; as those that tarried on the ground were executed.

He could feel his resolve lessen, his courage falter.

The Union men, *Lincoln's* men, were marched across the plain and up the hill to the Confederacy headquarters. Rebel troops from the camps on the hills turned out in force; rifles and pistols drawn in plain sight, clearly meant to prevent any attempt to over throw the guards.

As the line of the men from the train lessened, twilight set across the valley and Jamie thought of the beauty of this Georgia landscape. Such an incongruous thought. He was about to be imprisoned for life and he was contemplating the beauty of God's creation. God…would his faith help him through this? He swallowed the mounting emotions that rose in him.

They now had been standing in one spot for over three hours, those men that fell continued to be executed.

Endurance was tantamount.

He heard the heavy southern drawl of barking orders "Y'all march! All o' y'all on down t' the *Brush Dead House*. General Wirz, he be the military commandant, he'll damn sure sit ya straight." Again the bawdy laughter. "Git now."

Directly opposite the south gate, the one-story house that was occupied as headquarters by this fellow General Wirz appeared to be where they would register you, perhaps see to your wounds.

Jamie had no idea what to expect, he didn't want them to take his papers—his letters from Elisabeth, his military identification… Hopefully, there were so many prisoners they would search only at random.

As with those that had disembarked the train; they were surrounded by guards. Guards that poked and prodded them with rifle butts and swords, by the time they arrived at the "Brush Dead House"—*Where the hell did they get that name?* he wondered—if they had not been wounded before, they were at the very least bleeding now. How could he have ever thought of these men as *genteel?*

They were led into the main headquarters. No officer sat at the desk, only a young boy that looked weary beyond his years. "Have y'all searched 'em?" the boy asked of the lead guard that had marched them from Virginia to here.

As the thought struck him, he was shocked; it must have been weeks since they had been captured. Perhaps not, they had been shoved in cattle cars and transported by rail for several days, with Jamie fitfully sleeping most of the way. He thought of the lard they had offered them as nourishment, at the disgust with which the prisoners received it. He had said not a word; they had given their horses such as that in Arabia. It would be of some nourishment.

"Yes, sir!" the guard replied. "Thet' we did, sir!" His hand raised in salute.

"Did y'all take their weapons?"

"We did, sir!"

"Good. Divvy 'em up and git 'em in the *Pen.*"

Shocked by the lack of protocol, shocked at the lack of scrutiny, at the sight of a boy no more than fifteen in the stead of the General. What sort of facility were they running here? But then, *he* was captured, *he* was being held prisoner. *They*—the prisoners—were surrounded by armed and *very* dangerous men. Men fit for this position—angry, mean, and spiteful. He should be grateful. His papers were still in his possession; they had not strip-searched him. They had taken nothing from him thus far; save his weapons…and his dignity.

Again the prisoners were commanded to march. Nearly halfway down the hill he heard one of the guards say, "What the hell Wirz's kid doin' there. Ol' man Wirz sick or sumpin'?"

"Naw, just went on home ta git some vittles. Been at it all day."

So it was true, they were bringing at least four hundred prisoners a day to this *Pen*.

The guards pushed at the gates and the interior was exposed. The full moon in the dark, star-studded skies cast a shadow upon the Confederate flag that flew. They called it the *Southern Cross*.

Jamie knew they had changed the configuration countless times over the years; as one after another, the Southern states had banded together. He knew, too, that Texas had sworn their independence from both the Union and the Southern states.

The moonlight shown clearly the masses of men that stood slumped in a posture of defeat, their eyes glazed, their demeanor one of rout. More than half of the men stood or crawled naked. Bones protruded in the most repulsive of ways, flesh hung on their skeletal forms. Many stood clinging to another man's arm for support—physically or emotionally? Jamie felt certain it would be both. The mass of men that stood before him was untenable. The stench of the *Pen* unlike anything he had before experienced. Makeshift shelters, looking much like tents cluttered the grounds, with the masses of humanity and the shelters, Jamie could not fathom how it would be possible for them to traverse further inside the *Pen*.

The guard dismounted his horse. Standing just within the gates, pointing to a simple fence-like structure, he shouted, "This here is the *Dead Line*, means jus' what it says. Y'all be crossin', we be killin'."

Guards sat near the stockade walls, perched in sentry boxes, their eyes and weapons aimed at the *Dead Line*. The *Dead Line* nothing more than a small structure of flimsy lumber, yet it struck fear into the hearts of those gathered there.

The new prisoners now stood some twenty feet inside the stockade, each of them involuntarily backing away.

A rifle shot ricocheted from the stockade wall, immediately halting those that were prone to move in any manner.

One of the new prisoners—not entirely within the gates—turned and attempted to flee through the Calvary of horsemen.

Jamie heard a swooshing sound and a thud.

They had beheaded him.

Every bone and sinew in his body felt only fright. Some innate knowledge told him he would never again see his wife and children. The oppressive heat gave no credence, as the chill of his flesh rose in fear to wash over his body. This was real; this was a fight to the death. He had no weapons, only his cunning, and his will to survive. How best to do that…time would tell.

Initiation

Sounds of moaning, the shuffling of feet, the stench of unwashed bodies—of offal, of sewage, was the most prevalent sensory images that registered with any accuracy in the mind of James Prescott.

Anger penetrated each and every thought within his mind. *Better than fear,* he was certain of that. Looking about his surroundings, the paradox that surfaced was indescribable; disgust tantamount in his mind. This was despicable!

Were the prison camps of the Union Army as merciless? What sort of inhumane minds created such as this?

The newest *guests* of the Confederate Armies, *Andersonville Prison*—the *Pen*—were pushed and prodded to form a single line of frighten new inhabitants. The hospitality and civility they were to expect, evidenced by the feces that hung on the naked buttocks of those prisoners that stood gaping at them. The gauntness of their skeletal forms, a sight inconceivably grotesque! How this had happened, Jamie had no idea. How did one become so extremely emaciated in but a few short weeks. He thought this was a *new* prison.

The darkness was a blessing, and he was fully aware of that fact. His mind deriving to assimilate all the information that lay before and about him. Once more his thoughts ran to Ezra Gilky.

As they filed before the Confederate guards, they were given one tin cup, a spoon, and a tin bowl, as well as a number, ripped unceremoniously from a tablet.

The bowl was filled with…could that be correct—*peas*? The stench of them sour, and his first reflex was to gag. *Yet it was food.* He would force himself to eat it. He looked at the number on the paper, expecting to see "666"; however, it was 15,985. Could that possibly be the number of inhabitants within the confines of this stockade?

He looked about for a place to simply sit down. Hesitating, he waited to be assigned an area. He had no intention of becoming the butt of ire from the guards.

Within the soft glow of insignificant campfires, he could discern just enough to navigate within the small spaces unfettered by humanity.

They simply pushed him aside.

He looked for the faces of Colin, Mathew, and Liam; only to find that they had disappeared within the throngs of the masses. He turned to find a place to sit down, to rest, and to eat this revolting mass within his bowl; doing so, he was assaulted by emaciated, skeletal forms. Against the firelight, they appeared so thin as to cast the shadow of but one man. Yet there were five that surrounded him. Hands reached out, grabbing at his bowl of peas. Fawning hands, hands that stroked his jacket and his hat in a most coveting manner. Disorientated emotions rose within his heart and mind. He needed to protect himself, but, *my God, they are all starving*. Unclothed and starving. He looked at the man closest to him, and *rage* warred within him. The man was about five-foot-ten, weighing perhaps sixty pounds. A thin rag tied with a shoelace covered his genitals; he wore nothing more. His hair sparse with huge patches missing. Flesh wounds of open sores showed in the scant firelight, sores that appeared to cover his entire body. His hands filthy, fingernails that curved like talons at his fingertips, fingertips that clawed at Jamie's food and clothing.

Out of the darkness approached a figure of the same skeletal proportions—eyes set deep and dark, skank, filthy hair and beard covered his head and face, the jacket of a Union soldier hung on his frame, pants that rose to just below his calves, the rope that held them in place, frayed. His voice weak and tenuous, "Come stay in my home."

His home. Jamie looked into the man's eyes and saw only madness and greed. In this man's *home*, he would be stripped of clothing and food, of life itself. This was *war* all over again, within the ranks of his own army. The Bedouins came to mind, and he thanked the man graciously and pushed himself clear of these shadowy ghosts.

"General. General…" he heard the voice of Colin.

"Don't call me that. Come with me." Although he hadn't an inkling as to where he was going. His intuition told him, *to the least inhabited area would be best.* Looking about at the sea of persons, the audacity of such as that was not lost on him.

The four of them settled in the area to the north, huddled against the great stockade. Jamie wondered at the lack of persons close to them. Ah, the guards, the sentry stood just above them. In plain sight—to hide in plain sight—*that* was always best.

The unbearable heat of the day had diminished with the darkness. The night sounds of mosquitoes as they made their disquieting buzzing, the flicker of lightening bugs, as they bounced about the night air. The sounds of bickering, the moaning of frightened humanity and all it implied, overwhelmed his senses; he clung to what remained of his rational mind.

"We have grave concerns here, and it would be best if you each decide which it will be, we stick together or we go it alone. I do take full responsibility for our capture." The sound of his own voice astonished him, as there lay no fear or hesitation there, only calm assurance.

"No, General, we were told to go, that we were retreating, but we saw you fighting on and we… We just wanted to…" Colin's voice faltered. The glisten of tears present in his eyes.

Jamie looked at him. He was just a kid, no more that sixteen or so. "So we stay together then?"

There was always safety in numbers.

"Yes, sir," all three said in unison.

"No more *sir*. No more *rank*, I am Jamie to you, and each of you are to be called only by your Christian names. That understood? It will keep us safer. Now, first things first, in the morning we will see what we make of this. I do think escape to be an option. Right now, let's get some sleep. Colin, you take the first watch, Liam, you next, then myself, and Mathew. I think the others are so exhausted they will not be bothering us. But better to be watchful. In the morning, we can tell more of what lies in front of us. For the present, I think our brothers in combat have turned and will do anything to survive. Be it kill their *brothers in arms* or not." Yet again he thought of the treacherous nature of the Bedouins. He would not sleep, of that he was certain... He had to do something to remedy the infection in his leg and see if the others had wounds. How was it he had thought there would be a doctor that would see to their wounded bodies? In all fairness, they *had* offered to cut off his leg. Again he thought of the Bedouins... They urinated on anything that was the least bit infectious. He swallowed hard and tried to imagine how he was to remain with his dignity intact when he asked one of them to urinate on him.

He was awakened by Liam from his restless *sleep*. "Jamie, it's your turn. It's quiet out there, just moaning and crying. My Christ, this hellhole stinks."

Jamie rubbed his head. Christ, he had the worst headache. His arm hurt like hell and his leg was throbbing as if it had a heartbeat of its own. The pit of his stomach made sounds of discouragement, feelings of actual hunger having lessened with each day without food. Dysentery followed next... The mere thought frightened him. He thought of the skeletal forms of those individuals they had encountered and swallowed hard.

Perhaps escape was not possible. Quickly he pushed the thought aside.

He looked to see the rays of morning light begin to peak in the east, surprised at how quiet things were.

"So do you have a plan?" Liam's voice a soft whisper, his face lined with all the emotion's one could fathom. Already thin, his tall sinewy frame, nearly the height of Jamie's own; he could not stand to lose more weight. His dark hair was matted and stringy, his beard now several weeks old, giving him a grizzled look not to be opposed. Jamie had no idea as to the age of his second in command, but he knew he had a wife and children in Ohio, and he knew him to be a lawyer.

That momentary lack of fear, the feeling of grace that one has immediately upon awakening, before reality sets in, now having disappeared, replaced by a fear he had never before experienced. Jamie looked into the eyes of Liam. "We escape." Quickly looking away to the scene below them. Had Liam seen the fear? "But for now, we observe."

They sat now in the early morning, the sunlight only a glimmer in the eastern skies, the slight hillock they sat upon, giving them a view of the entire stockade. They could see that the swamp appeared to cover approximately six acres. It was the receptacle for most of the filth accumulations of the prison; the deadly stench that surrounded them was coming from there.

There was the branch of a river, approximately four to ten feet wide and about six inches deep; it appeared the men were gathering there in an act to secure water that would be clear enough to drink. The crowd surged up near the little footbridge close to the *Dead Line*, reaching with a cup or pail to where the water looked to be the clearest.

They heard the shots ring out and watched as the poor fellow fell dead from the footbridge. The sentries had shot him for reaching his hand under the *Dead Line*.

Again…despair and dreaded fear rose in him. In light of day, Liam and Jamie could clearly see the "Dead Line," shocked by the insubstantial substance of it. It consisted of thin strips of fails—or wood so very thin as to be inconsequential—nailed to stakes driven in the ground, and was but three feet high.

As the four of them viewed the scene of the prisoners awakening to daily life, each became sated with a cloying fear; in reality they were now one in congress with this indescribable condition. As the morning progressed, from their vantage point, the scene below was one of confusion among the prisoners. Jamie, Mathew, Liam, and Colin watched men in every imaginable position, standing, walking, running, arguing, peddling, gambling, going to or coming from the branch of the river with cups, dippers, canteens, or rude pails with water.

Some were lying down. Were they dying? Many seemed to be praying, many giving water or food to the sick, crawling on hands and knees, on hunkers. Some making fires and cooking rations, splitting pieces of wood almost as fine as matches.

"I wonder where we get rations? I think it best we bury our clothing and any valuables, even our bowls and spoons, and go down and speak to the guards for rations." Jamie watched the look of fear cross the faces of the younger Colin and Mathew. "They are just men with guns. Be humble, be frightened. Men with guns expect that."

"Thet'll be easy 'nough. I'm scared shitless."

"We all are, Mathew, we all are." Jamie looked to see the tears of young Colin as they spilled from his eyes. Reaching over, he patted his shoulder. Colin quickly dropped his face into his hands.

Jamie went on. "Then we slip in and mingle with the other prisoners. See if you can tell if any one of them has instigated an escape. But be very, very cautious. Say nothing, only listen with encouragement." Jamie had no idea how long they would have the strength to do such as this, or the candor. "Then we see to our wounds. It is my intention to ask the guards for medical treatment."

They heard howls of derision from the prisoners below and looked to see the "Rebel Flagstaff" being hoisted.

Shots were fired from the sentries above them warning the prisoners to cease. Guards suddenly appeared at the gates, with the prisoners quickly gravitating in that direction. The guards poked and prodded them with rifles and swords, warning them to stay back least they be shot. Pail's filled with a gruel like substance were being carried in by other Confederate soldiers.

Prisoners—Union men—were now filing towards those pails. It appeared they were issuing, and dividing rations.

"We better get down there. I don't think we can afford to miss a meal. Eat, mingle, and come back up here. Remember, get more spoons if you can. Tell them you didn't get one."

They watched as the Confederate sergeant of the mess divided the rations, dividing them in piles spread out upon a piece of cloth, nothing more than a rag to Jamie's eyes. He watched as the mess sergeant looked to those standing about for approval.

"Even enough," one prisoner called out.

"Call off!" the Sergeant shouted.

Each man sounded his number, the prisoner stepped forward, reaching for his ration; he ravenously devoured it. Again the sergeant shouted, pointing to a pile of what would be said as food, "Who'll have this?"

Jamie heard his number called, only to see a tablespoon of gruel left sitting on the filth of the cloth. Quickly he reached for it. Worms wiggled from the mass he held in his fingers, he opened his mouth and swallowed hard and fast. He felt a hand on his back and swiftly turned to see the man of last night staring at him with those haunted features. "You'll learn to relish the worms. Lots of protein."

Jamie said nothing, wiping his mouth with the back of his hand.

"Come, I'll show you around. Tell ya some things ya need to know."

He followed the man. There was naught to do and in the light of day he felt more comfortable with this man.

"Over there now is the Sutlers. They are wanting to sell you something."

"For what? I have no money."

"Oh, hell's fire, they will take your jacket, your hat. *Your meal.*"

"And what do they have to sell?"

"Matches, roots, medicine. Free passes not to be raped or vandalized."

Jamie felt the shock of reality coarse through his body! "Do we get more food?"

"Yep, evening meal, same as breakfast. Sometimes some old vegetables, roots, that sort of thing."

"My gawd, how have you survived?"

"Most don't, look over there."

Jamie could see a wagon filled with the bodies of corpses in all manner of decay. The dead were thrown promiscuously upon a wagon. The same as you would cord wood. However the body had fallen, it remained so, heads, legs and arms, hung over the sides of the wagon, many entangled within the wagons wheels. His stomach wrenched. "But why don't they bury them?"

"Oh, they will, when the wagon is full, about once a day. 'Take them to the cemetery. On up that hill there. They dig a trench 'bout one to three hundred feet long 'bout two feet deep, lay 'em out like clothespins."

"Does anyone know or care who they are?"

"Yep, they label them with little sticks—name, rank, and number of bodies. Then they deliver our food in the same wagon."

Jamie stood mortified. Trying desperately to assimilate this information and still maintain his courage. "How long have you been here? I thought this was a new prison."

"Oh, it is. Brought us down from the one in Carolina, not much better, starving is starving, an' beatings are beatings."

"Has anyone tried to escape?"

"Hell yes. Lots, they're in that wagon. Some tried to tunnel out. It goes on all the time. Others so plum crazy, just try to run out of the gates. Death by soldier my guess is. They figure they're better off."

Jamie walked with the man, as they zigzagged through the vast despairing humanity. Strange, no one approached them.

Looking out across the vastness of the area you saw any manner of shelter; tents made from clothing, some from nothing more than rags held up over two poles. Made to either cover your head, or often an effort was made to cover a prone man's length.

This strange emissary began again. "There is a railroad out by Andersonville, but you don't want to hop on it. The damn Reb's run it night and day, bringing in new prisoners. The best hope we have is for the damned war to be over."

"And you're just going to wait for that? How long have you been a prisoner?"

"A year probably, time is of little consequence here."

"What of these dead bodies? Is there nothing we can do?"

"You'll get used to it, and be damn glad it isn't you. Too, sometimes they have things you'll need."

"You mean, you steal from the dead?" Jamie was shocked by his own naivety. He had been at war before…but…this was… *not American.*

"Oh, your idealism is so fresh and sweet." The man's mockery thick, lacing each word. "Do you really think they need it any longer? Do you want to survive?"

The two of them continued through the throngs of putrid odors and burgeoning men.

"That over there is the 'Branch.' Just a shallow brook—a *swamp* in truth."

Prisoners, nearly naked, were wading through this hideous mass.

"What are they doing?"

"Searching for roots and whatever else washes down from the river outside the stockade."

"Do they eat them?"

"They should, but most often, they dry them in the hot sun, and use them for fuel to cook their scant rations. I eat mine."

"And that?" Jamie pointed to a pile of near corpses with men hovering over them. Many of them wandered aimlessly.

"Our hospital. All manner of disease and disability available—*without request.*" He chuckled, his manner of acceptance disquieting. "Scurvy, diarrhea, which rapidly turns to dysentery. Gangrene, dropsy, fever. Some just plain mad—crazy. Others, their mind just plum gone."

"Sweet Jesus. What can you do for them? What is wrong with his arm?" Jamie could see the glittering whiteness of the bones of the hand and forearm of a man lying on the ground beneath the blazing sun.

"Gangrene, not much but tobacco juice and sumaches berries to treat any of it."

They walked awhile longer. Neither saying a word. The man seemed comfortable with that and Jamie was mortified beyond speaking. *Was* escape possible? Was this man right? *"Just wait until it was over"*? Lincoln never intended for it to go on more than a month, let alone five years. What of his family? What of… he could not bring himself to even as much as think *her* name. *Her* face rose before him and he fought to stand upright, to continue walking with this person, within this hellhole.

Elisabeth. Elisabeth. He felt the tears as they slid unbidden from his eyes and felt his nose begin to run. He reached up and wiped it with his hand. This man perhaps would understand.

Raising his head, he looked about him.

The "emissary" had disappeared.

William Tecumseh Sherman

Josiah lifted the canvas flap from the tent, ducking his head as his hat skimmed the harshness of the fabric; he was relieved to be exiting the tent. Tired of the politics and the inane strategic elements of those in charge. They had lost the last three campaigns in Missouri and one in Virginia, several in Tennessee. All within the last couple of months and now Sherman, with his idea of burning Atlanta stuck in his craw. It certainly did make Sherman appear like the *lunatic* they often called him, but he was brilliant and determined. "Total war!" Sherman had said this morning. Further exclaiming that "*War is war*—not the seeking of popularity!"

Josiah cleared his throat, thinking of what had transpired within the confines of the "war tent"; those that sat about the tables and stood, smoking cigars and pipes, readily understood that Sherman, as well as Grant, were as *hell bent* on winning this war as Lincoln himself…for that reason and for many of them, *for that reason alone*, they sat or stood and listened. They were tired and weary—*it* needed to be *finished*. It wasn't as if Sherman did not know the enemy. William Tecumseh Sherman's early military career was a near disaster, having to be temporarily relieved of command. Josiah snickered to himself at the irony of life.

Josiah had heard Sherman had graduated in 1840, sixth in his class, certainly that would indicate him to be highly intelligent. He took a deep breath of the biting coldness of the air and pulled his greatcoat closer to his body. *Damned nippy*, he thought to himself. He could not seem to shake the niggling thoughts concerning Sherman, but then who in their right mind would not question these men? Sherman and Grant seemed to be orchestrating this war... Grant, a renowned *drunkard*, and Sherman termed a *lunatic. Now don't that just beat all.* Again, he laughed to himself at the audacity of it all. His thoughts further examining the career of Sherman. Why? He looked out at the men and tents sprawled across the pastures and knew these men's lives rested in the decisions that Sherman and Grant made. Surely Lincoln had something to say in the matter, but sitting in the seat of the presidency was not the same as being *here*, on the battlefields—as you watched and waited, patience giving way to anxiety, anxiety giving way to fear. Fear, man's last enemy—so many philosophers, so many poets having given credence to just that fact. He knew Sherman had first seen action against the Seminole Indians in Florida and had had numerous assignments through Georgia and South Carolina, where he had become acquainted with many of the Old South's most respected families. He had heard Sherman felt that the US Army was a dead end and had thusly resigned his commission in 1853. He had then traveled to California during the glory days of the gold rush and stayed as a banker, but that had ended in the Panic of 1857. He then had settled in Kansas to practice law, but had had little success.

Josiah again chuckled to himself. Thinking of the traveling from one place to another, not uncommon for a man of intelligence. *The striving for knowledge, for information.* Rather like Ezra Gilky, thoughts of Ezra causing a smile to cross his face. Not that the smile could have been seen; he hadn't shaved in months, to say nothing of the dirt and grime no doubt embedded within the confines of the damnable bush. Reaching up he scratched at the mass of ebony whiskers, which now held tightly to clusters of silver. His ruminations of Sherman pushing all other thoughts from his mind.

Josiah had heard that in 1859, William Tecumseh Sherman—*Tecumseh*, strange goddamn name for an Englishman... He had heard his father named him that because he admired the Shawnee chief. Sherman then became head master at a military academy in Louisiana. Heard he had proved to be an effective administrator and popular with the community. But as sectional tensions rose, Sherman had warned his secessionist friends that a war would be long and bloody, with the North eventually winning. Josiah sighed and wondered at the brilliant mind of Sherman... How the hell did he know that? *Today* it seemed he was in great error.

When Louisiana left the Union, Sherman had resigned and moved to St. Louis, wanting nothing to do with the conflict. Though he was a conservative on slavery, he was a strong supporter of the Union. After the firing on Fort Sumter, he asked his brother, Senator John Sherman, to arrange a commission in the Army. *Damned strange how life pushes you here and there.* He thought of Sally Susanne Sullivan and her beliefs in destiny—*divine destiny* at that—perhaps she was right, damn sure saw no rhyme nor reason for the way events in life gathered themselves.

He knew that in 1861, William T. Sherman was appointed colonel in the Thirteenth US Infantry, and was assigned command of a brigade under General William McDowell in Washington, DC. He fought in the First Battle of Bull Run, in which Union troops were badly beaten. He was then sent to Kentucky and became deeply pessimistic about the war, complaining to his superiors about shortages while exaggerating the enemy's troop strength. He was eventually put on leave, considered unfit for duty. The press picked up on his troubles and described him as "insane." Josiah had heard Sherman had suffered from a *nervous breakdown*.

Pushing the man from his mind, not a damn thing he could do about the likes of Sherman or Grant. Josiah took a deep breath of air and straightened to his full height. God almighty these men were stubborn. They had convened at seven this morning, and it was now nearly one o'clock... The cigar and pipe smoke had seemed a veritable cloud within the tent itself. The smell of unwashed men seemed to cling to his person. He stood for a moment and looked out across the fields, felt the whisper of wind as it caressed his face. Chuckling to himself. Damned humans are never happy with what their decisions brought them. Right now he'd give anything to be trekking across the continent. To be outside...if he were honest, *to be in charge*. Damned Sherman! The man was as stubborn as a mule. Couldn't they see they were about to be defeated? Was Lincoln a fool to have put the Union in the hands of Ulysses Grant? Josiah thought of all the generals that had preceded him, the words of Lincoln concerning Grant—*the man can fight!* He damned well could, to that Josiah could attest.

He stood now on the small green precipice. Beating his hat on the leg of his trousers, he ran his hand through his long, once ebony hair, it too, was now scattered with the same silver of his beard. His hands slid over his face, as if that would erase all the confusion and weariness that had seemed to pervade his mind and body. He had never given a thought to this war having longevity such as this. He had known nothing of the South or the Southerners—never been further south than where the Oregon Trail passed, but he had to admit them to be a determined lot. He had never seen tenacity the likes exhibited by Davis or his General Lee. Fierce men, these Confederate soldiers were.

He knew the Union had expended millions of U.S. dollars in the last—hell, he had no idea. Seemed Lincoln had had the secretary of Treasury—Salmon P. Chase put his thinking cap on and came up with the some damned creative ways to finance the war effort. Sold over a billion dollars in war bonds—fudge was there no end to the naïveté of the public? The Union had posters plastered everywhere one looked. They were printing "greenbacks" they called them; paper said to be backed by real gold, wasn't at all certain he believed that, but what the hell, could be true. Wondered where the hell they got the gold, *Prescott would know*.

Heard just this morning they had passed the Internal Revenue Act, a tax on whatever income a man earned, now if that didn't beat all. So one way or another, his men were paying with their lives and their money for this…this…*atrocity*!

His own men had not been paid for at least two months, that he knew! And he had not received a penny since…Christ, 1862, and he had invested his own monies for weapons and often, boots for his men. That, too, was part and parcel of their plan—to enlist men of name and some wealth—to provide in exchange, titles of authority.

He looked down at the encampment of men—their uniforms threadbare and filthy. The hospitals filled with wounded and dying men, disease as prevalent, hell's fire the graveyards were filled to overflowing… And should they lose, *he couldn't think of that!*

He had had just such a discussion with his subordinates, a damned long discussion to his way of thinking. The Unions enlistment of the Negro had turned the tide. Damned clever of Lincoln to give them amnesty if they signed on. Did that give them an edge? Damned if he could discern that. He looked across the fields, the leaves of the trees held a golden hue to them. The grass was the color of ripe wheat had it not been trampled by men and animals. The winter would be harsh, on his men and their animals; he could feel it in his bones. A slight shudder ran through his body.

He thought of the day ahead, at least what remained of it, what he would tell his men that would buoy their spirits and provide them with some hope of victory. Strange, the war had become only a *game* to win. The reasons for it long lost in his conscious mind. Did it make any difference to him who won at this moment…it did. Slavery of any form was out of the question… He thought of his homeland and what had transpired there, the feeling of Austria's people, the insidious cloud of fear that permeated entire villages…Lisle, his children. He brushed these thoughts from his mind, it damned sure made no sense to be thinking of such as that...strange it had been years, indeed decades and the fear, grief and images remained as vivid as if they happened yesterday. His mind wished to push them away, did no good... *They were why* he stood here today. He would fight to free the men who were enslaved and those that enslaved them. Did he think those men to be monstrous, no, simply ensconced in a world of conditioning, why hells fire, could not it be just as easy to pay a man a simple wage than to house them and feed them? Humans...he thought of his many treks over the Oregon Trail and the persons he had encountered...no figurin' the minds of most folks.

His mind wandered once more to Sherman and his *plan*—recited with great alacrity this morning.

Sherman had been hell bent on disaster—or victory—since early this summer, with Johnston and his Confederates having defeated him at the Kennesaw Mountain, and John Hood having cut him off just outside the city, it had pissed him off. Once again a smile crossed his face. Sherman had been beaten by a man the Texas Brigade had called Old Wooden Head, thinking he lacked good sense. Still Sherman had headed onward, again defeated. He had called for more troops and Josiah had gone.

Johnston and the Confederates had taken a defensive position, moving back along the Chattahoochee River. It had surprised both Sherman and Josiah.

Sherman ordered them to cut the rail lines, battling Confederate troops and laying siege. By the look of it, Josiah and Sherman thought Hood had determined the Union had retreated; instead they had gone south and cut the last rail line into the city.

On September 2, 1864 they had claimed Atlanta.

Now, this morning, Sherman told them he was going to *destroy the South and its people*. He intended to take some ninety thousand men and cut a swath of destruction through Georgia in a march to the sea; his plan was to destroy everything from railroad tracks to cotton mills. They would seize plantations or burn them, kill their horses, mules, cattle, disable bridges and telegraphs, killing all persons that stood in their way. He had said, "I know many will raise a howl against my barbarity and cruelty."

Hearing those words Josiah had stood and left. He saw no purpose in such barbarous acts against a people. It sickened him. They had captured Atlanta, why destroy it? *War is hell…he knew intimately the truth of it, in Austria and here, in America—the land of the free!* He looked up as a young man approached him on horseback.

"General? General Josiah Piedmont?" The youngster shouted to be heard above the clamor of persons, horses that snorted and the rabble of chatter about the fires within the encampment.

"Yes, yes. May I help you, Sergeant?" Josiah watched as the youngster flung his leg from the saddle and sprinted to where he stood.

"Got a message fer ya, General."

"Have ya now?"

"Yes, sir."

"Thank you, son." Josiah looked at the leather pouch, tied tightly with twine, a tattered piece of paper could be seen within its confines. Why, it must be months old, the sweat and grime having left it looking as if it should be archived. "Where and when did you receive this?" Josiah looked up at the young man, and thought him to be no more than perhaps eighteen years of age.

"Don' know where it came from, some fella down in Franklin give it ta me. Said I was ta see ya got it."

"Thank you, I appreciate it—take care." The soldier turned and was off.

Placing his hat once more upon his head he turned and walked from the cacophony of sounds. The paper, the message… he could only assume it to be a message. "Orders" he got from headquarters and he had just left their company. He swallowed hard. An intuit of morose rose in him and he pushed that sense down. *Have no damn reason to assume a friggin' thing.* He thought to himself. He had no brothers, no son, no family out there to be concerned for. He was alone. His choice—one could say, but… still the feeling persisted.

He played the tattered paper through his hands, looking at it with a sense of doom and foreboding…smelled it, shaking his head as he did so…sweat, the sweat of man and horse, onions? He smiled, chastising himself. *Open the damn thing.* Could be a request for weapons…clothing for someone desperate. But who among them was not desperate? He took a deep breath, looking across the horizon to the heavens, the sky blue and filled with the ominous look of thunderclouds.

Shit. Open the damn thing. He found the palms of his hands were sweating and trembled ever so slightly. He swallowed hard and gently unfolded the missive.

"*Prescott captured. At Andersonville!*"

Four words. Four words that made him want to drop to his knees. And weep. *God… Prescott… What the hell!* His mind filled with images of James Martin Prescott, of his Lizzie…of Sally Susanne, of the Parsons… He looked at the note again, a damned miracle it had found him. Andersonville, the biggest hell hole in the Confederate armies!

How the hell, Jamie? How the hell?

Christ!

He turned and went back towards the tent.

Anger infused him. Grief and anger! Fear for his friend! The man that was like a brother to him! The man he had shared his grief with—bared his soul too.

As he re-entered the tent, the men parted, the war tent sensing his demeanor, the size and stature of him intimidating.

"Thomas, did you know of this?" he nearly shouted, his hand held up shaking the leather bound note.

Sherman looked up from his papers and into the fiery eyes of Major General Josiah Leon Alexander Piedmont. He had great respect for this stalwart man, this man of impeccable common sense, his ability to command.

Standing to his full height of nearly six feet he looked up at Josiah. "What the hell, General. What do you mean by such an intrusion?"

"Did you know of this?"

"I haven't the most remote idea of what you speak. Come, man, out with it."

"Prescott, James Prescott! He was in your service. Do you remember that?"

"I do, lost him at Columbia."

"You *did not* lose him! He was captured! Surely you knew that!"

"I... had no idea. Figured he had died in battle, an honorable death. When we retreated, he was not amongst us..."

"Well, I have just been given this communiqué and he is presently held captive in *Andersonville*! Andersonville!"

Obviously shaken, Josiah watched as the color drained from the face of Thomas Sherman. Seated once more, he looked down at his papers. A hush had fallen around those gathered within the tent. Sherman looked once more into the eyes of his general. "It is nothing more than war, General...nothing more than war." Rising he stood and turned his back to Josiah.

"We have to get him the hell out of there, Sherman! We must!"

Sherman turned and looked up into the eyes of Josiah Piedmont. "I am your superior. Please address me as such. I do not have the men nor the time. Surely you know that to be true."

"I know no such thing. We have an agreement, *General, sir*, we have had an agreement with the Confederacy since 1862. Ten days, ten friggin' days is all they can hold them! But then—perhaps you would not be aware of that." Josiah fought the urge to throttle the man where he stood. Instead, he continued to shake the leather bound paper in the face of Sherman. "This piece of paper appears to be *several months* old. *One general for sixty privates, a major general is worth forty privates.* I am requesting one hundred of your Confederate prisoners of war to use in exchange for our men, as well as a detail to complete the mission. Sir!"

"And why exactly would you be in need of one hundred men to retrieve Prescott?"

Josiah felt the palm of his hand as it rested on his revolver; quickly he removed it. He was unaccustomed to taking orders, in particular from a man deemed a lunatic. "If they have Prescott, they have many more. Prescott is a fine strategist, supremely intelligent and equally as courageous. Rest assured he is not alone."

Jeremiah

She had slept but perhaps an hour, the day was dawning as she had fallen asleep—awake now the sun still had not fully emerged. Her eyes had near swollen shut from the tears she had shed, tears of such grief and unfathomable terror, a terror she had never before encountered. She could not find it within her to control the emotions that plummeted her heart, her very soul.

Elisabeth rubbed her face hard and took a deep breath; she looked at the table strewn with the letters from Grandmère and Papa. She leaned over and blew out the candle, there were but a very few left this time of year. She had heard that the people in the east had gas lighting in their homes now. Would not that be the most wonderful thing—to simply *turn on* a light! She rose and walked to the great flatiron stove and poured coffee in her cup. She had been out of tea far too long. Simple things—simple pleasures once taken for granted.

She felt old and weary, an unfamiliar presence in her ever-optimistic soul.

Life—what was it about? The longer she lived the more confusing that question had become. Strife seemed to far out weigh the joys, or was it simply ones interpretation that gave one that feeling? If this was a world of learning and evolving as Sally Susanne thought, then perhaps she could discover its purpose.

Not this morning. She felt the grief wash over her as she thought of the contents of the letter's that lay before her.

This horrific thing that had come upon her family! What would she do if it were her child? The tears spilled from her eyes even as she wiped at her face. She should go. She should be there. There, with her family, her parents.

What would Jamie have her do? *Oh, God…oh, Jamie, I miss you so. Lord, protect him! Be grateful, Elisabeth—he is alive!* That grief, that sadness—that overwhelming sense of loss rose in her with a despair she could scarcely contain, yet again, as in the preceding months, she fought it down.

It had been months since she had heard from him. Months without a telegraph, months without a letter! She knew he was not dead. She could feel it. She would *know* if he were dead. She *would*—for a piece of *her* would have died, or would he remain within her soul for all time? She would not think of that now… She simply would not!

She ran her hands through her hair and paced the floor. What would she say? How would one begin? The thought that she would never again see her brother—or her husband! *Lord! Lord! Please, please, I beg of you…*

She searched within her for the anger and the determination that had brought her through the difficulties in her life, the acceptance, the *surrender*…and found there to be none. She felt no determination, nor surrender to the strife and sorrow of this world. She could not find the will—the *need*!

A vision of her daughters rose in her mind and in her heart… She could do *this* for them! For *her daughters*, she would and could survive! She *would summon the courage to withstand this and whatever was to come in the future.*

How did one deal with the loss of a child? Why had this happened? Why? Of all the mean-spirited persons in the world, why would God chose to take someone as kind, as lighthearted, as innocent…

She thought of Eleanor and Ma Parsons and all the children whose parents had buried them on the Oregon Trail. She found she could not bear the emotions that rose in her. She raised her head to the heavens and felt the tears spill over her face, and saw only the aging rafters of her home, the sod roof sprinkling its dust upon the floors. She smiled and a small, bewildered, mordant chuckle surfaced. *You have a very strange sense of instruction Lord!* Was this, as Sally Susanne said, *her very own plan for her life… My,* had she been brave—*whence she had formulated such a plan as this!*

She would write to Mama first. That would be the most difficult. Then to Papa, the thought of Papa causing the sobs to rise yet again… *he* had been his favorite, she knew that—his favorite son—of that she was certain, so alike they had been. *Oh, Papa, I am so very sorry.*

She rose and carefully pulled the large plank from its placement across her ornate door. The sight of it—a reminder of the Crows visit to her and Jamie just before he had left the last time. *The last time. Lord, tell me that he is alive—tell me he is well.*

Standing on the stoop, she looked out over the vastness of the land. She heard the whiny of Mercy, Trésor, and Danny, of Blackie and Fleur, as the girls had named the newest offspring of Danny and Mercy. She smiled, for the excess of the many horses and cattle made their home on the land; though like royalty, these five horses were given provisions like no other.

A mere hint of Papa's crocus' struggled to push their way through the leisurely thawing ground as the sun rose over the Big and Little Belt mountains in the east, and to the south she could see the Absaroka Range; she shuddered at the thought of the Bozeman Trail. The golden rays of sunshine shimmered on the snows that were a perpetual blanket to the mountainous ranges. The twitter of birds could be heard, and she watched a large herd of elk as they crossed to the river below. Peace. Peace and order seemed to pervade in this world outside her heart. She turned and went back into the house.

The letters lay startlingly white against the table. There had been none from Mama, though she was not surprised. Mama rarely wrote to her.

She sighed and sat down, taking pen in hand, the ink well a safe distance away. She would say nothing to Mama of Jamie; it would be a slight matter of consideration within Mama's mind and heart.

The year of our Lord; 1865, 6 April

My Dearest Mama,

I have struggled for the words of comfort you need Mama, for I find none that will convey my sorrow for the loss of your and my Jeremiah. I daresay I have no thought of what you must be feeling; yet I do know of the tremendous grief that must set upon your heart.

I have watched so very many parents lose their children and to know that you, Mama... are to join in that horrific pain is overwhelming.

I picture him now in my minds eye; his curling blonde locks as a young boy, his laughter, as he raced through the house, our home. His heart so pure and innocent. I shan't say my grief is the equivalent of yours, for I know not what you feel, but I shall miss him so very much. Do you recall? He was to visit me.

I, who have caused you grief as well, I could not be more dreadfully grievous at that thought Mama. There is no consolation, of that I am certain and yet he did what he wished. To join in the war and to fight for his country is indeed an honor. To be laid to rest at the young age of sixteen years, is more than I can comprehend. I feel I cannot express my grief or my sorrow for you and Papa and Grandmère. Know how very much I love you and how very much I loved Jeremiah. He shall always be in my prayers and in my thoughts and I shall always tell my children of their brave Uncle Jeremiah.

Please know—I would desire nothing more than to be there with you at this time to help you in any manner afforded me.

Elisabeth held the envelope in her hand, looked again at Papa's handwriting in the lower left corner; it was marked "Urgent!" She took the contents from the envelope and once again unfolded the many pages. Perhaps reading it yet again would afford her the proper words to reply to Papa. Perchance she would find he had *not* said those things, had not written those words—those words that were so very final, words that wrenched at her heart, words that shattered her heart. How *could* she bear this—how could her parents?

Her hand trembled as she unfolded the many pages, the paper, thin and fine, the family crest engraved on each page. Papa's hand indeed must have trembled as he began, as his usually perfect penmanship ran decidedly downhill, the scroll left strokes that scribbled downward, rather than the articulate and brave strokes so very prolific throughout his many previous letters to her.

> *The Year of Our Lord, 1865–15 February,*
>
> *My most Darling Daughter~Elisabeth,*
>
> *As I take pen in hand I take note that it trembles—for the news I have is profoundly difficult for me to write, as if the writing of it will indeed prove the truth of it. With all you have had to bear, I regret most hardily to add to your most grievous circumstances—and yet you must be told.*

She had read the letter so very many times and yet her body shook, as she reached for the chair to steady herself.

> *It is our Jeremiah, Elisabeth, it is our Jeremiah—we received word this past week that they had identified his body. My young son, your brother; is dead Elisabeth, Jeremiah is gone. As I write these words I find I must pause for I am overwhelmed by grief—both for you and myself.*
>
> *With the greatest love for you,*
> *Your Papa*

20—February

My Dear Elisabeth,

My most humble apologies for My untoward display of emotion and yet, you of all persons I know will be forgiving. I shall attempt to relay to you the information we were given. But first I must address your own concerns for your husband, James Prescott, information that gives me little less pleasure than the announcement of Jeremiahs' passing. I would be remiss in my responsibilities as your father should I not do so. Oh but I wish I would be by your side at this moment for such horrendously grievous news to come in one letter. Please, call on our Lord Elisabeth, be strong, come home with your daughters, you will be welcomed with open arms.

As I write this I pray that you have someone there to help you deal with this news. I have contacted the list of persons that I received from you and it is with great remorse I must inform you that your James, our James, has been captured—or so it would seem.

She breathed a sigh of relief, for she had not swooned, nor screamed, nor felt the blackness envelope her mind, as had happened upon the first reading of the letter. Yet she felt the trembling of her entire body as she continued to read the letter.

General Piedmont has been given this information by what he termed a reliable source and has given me every consideration and reassurances that every effort to extract James from this oppressive situation is being done. There is an exchange of prisoner agreement between the factions and should that not come to fruition he informs me he shall himself make every attempt to rescue him. However, as I am certain you are aware; the war escalates at an alarming rate as Sherman has determined that it is necessary to break the very backbone of the Confederates, to disarm them with a vengeance not previously executed, in an effort to end this abominable circumstance of our own making. The newspapers have quoted him as saying "Citizens will raise a howl against my barbarity and cruelty; I will answer that war is war and not popularity seeking." I find it difficult that I, once so entrenched in the ideological outcome of the effort~ I now find I am uncertain as to the truth of our convictions.

Josiah sends his love to you and begs your forgiveness that he is unable to be at your side—his effort to rescue James from Andersonville is foremost in his mind. As well, I have been informed of a woman; Clara Barton that is a most determined and dedicated woman who has taken on the struggle to find prisoners and to go from camp to camp in an effort to care for their wounds and to notify those that love them. It seems her father convinced her that it was her duty as a Christian to help the soldiers. Following his death, Miss Barton returned to Washington to gather medical supplies. Ladies' Aid societies helped in sending bandages, food, and clothing. Miss Barton has finally gained permission from Quartermaster Daniel Rucker to work at the front lines. I shall make every effort to contact her and ascertain any and all information obtainable. Again, I would make a plea to you to bring your children and return to your home my dear Elisabeth.

I can imagine the breaking of your heart yet I must go on—as to our Jeremiah…Mama—your grand-mère, is taking Jeremiah's death in her stead and able to help with your dear mama, I thank the Lord for her. Her own experience's, as well, the excessive grief she has suffered and the many trials she had been made to bare in this life, Grand-mère is somewhat philosophical concerning the disastrous nature of this tremendous grief and despair. My Clarisse, your mama, does not fare well, for she claims she has now lost two of her children … if this statement is hurtful, please excuse my abruptness, yet from her point of view she has indeed lost you as well. She has taken to her bed, will not eat, nor communicate… I fear for her health as the grief has debilitated her beyond my expectations, and yet I can ascertain the depth of her emotions.

The young man, who came to inform us, was with Jeremiah on that fateful day and he described the most frightful of experiences. An occurrence beyond what I would have endeavored to imagine.

Please I beg of you, forgive me, indulge an old man my dear, for I am heartily sorry for your loss, and news of your James, yet I find I must remain stalwart for all but you. I find in you a brave and fine servant of the Lord and shall call on your courage and fearlessness, as I am most certain a father ought not do.

The young man, his name being Sargent Gabriel Bond, the most sincere and kind man, relayed to me, as your mama was unable to bear the details; understandably, yet, I felt I must know— I simply had to know the details of my sons death. Are you able to comprehend that Elisabeth? Your mama believes it will but add to my pain. And yet...

I digress—it occurred at the battle of Franklin; a very small township in Tennessee. Jeremiah was under the command of Brigadier General Emerson Opdycke, of the 41st Ohio. These men of Opdycke were said to have fought like tigers. Young Sargent Gabriel Bond proclaims that Opdycke disobeyed orders to move his men to a position of safety; he argued it was indefensible. Instead, he positioned his brigade behind the fortifications at the home of a Mr. F. B Carter. Sargent Bond said the Carter's were most kind and offered breakfast that first morning, as well as the use of their parlor. I cannot say I would have been so kind. Sargent Bond describes Mr. Carter as an aged man occupying his home with several grown children and near relatives. His son, a Confederate Officer, who had been taken prisoner, was at home on parole. They, —our men, the Union Soldiers— commenced with their battle preparations during that first day, digging breastworks; young Gabriel said the shovel had become as important as his rifle, the young man laughed at that. They established a battery on the summit at the right of the Carter's brick smoke house, making it possible to fire over the heads of the infantry in the front line and sweep the approaches...and they then waited for the Confederates' should they indeed come.

At near 4 p.m., a Confederate signal was dropped, bands played, the General's and Staff officers and couriers came forward, riding in from the south with a hundred battle flags waving. There were more that 20,000 men marching behind them. Young Gabriel said, "I—Jeremiah and I were excited! It was a grand sight sir,

A glorious sight sir, one I shall remember forever. They fired on us...we—we, all of us were so entranced at the sight of the gray and butternut uniform's, the flags, the band... we for a moment... well, then we heard the command. To fire! But, but sir, we...one of us; I didn't know then who, but I think it to have been Jeremiah shouted 'Captain for God sake, let us get behind the works'! Why, just see them coming! Enough to swallow us up!'"

In the telling of it I could somehow grasp the enthusiasm of the moment as the Sargent continued. "'Bout 7 p.m., someone killed General Granbury and General Cleburne and wounded Gordon— it was then that we knew the Confederates had no leadership! Yet they came on, the color bearers; they planted their Confederate flags upon the breastworks of the Union, our ground! But we killed them sir."

Young Gabriel does not recall when first he was aware that Jeremiah was not at his side, the battle lasted until 9p.m. that night. He said that "The Johnny Reb's just kept up the vain struggle until long after dark, when finally they put their hats on the ends of their muskets to signal to us, then called over that if we would stop shooting, they would surrender.

"The 'Detail's' were called in to collect the wounded and they were carried into the Carter's house where Union and Confederate doctors alike cut off limbs and threw them out the window..." He exclaimed, "'by morning the limbs they had sawed off rose to the upper story window of the home. There was a large thicket of locust trees to our right and the next mornin' it appeared as nothing more than toothpicks from the artillery. Then that night it rained...just awful sir, the water ran bloodied."

I cannot imagine such as that. I asked if the men suffered greatly and he said, "No sir 'seems Bayer has a new medicine that takes pain away instantly, they call it morphine. Why, the men be lickin' it off the Doc's hands."

I feared to ask the Sargent if Jeremiah died immediately or if he suffered terribly, yet I found I must know that as well. Gabriel said to me, "No sir, your son died heroically with a cannonball through his heart."

My Daughter, again I must apologize for the difficulty and additional grief I have caused you, it does give me strength to have struggled through the telling of it and somehow gives some minor acclaim for the death of my son and your brother.

As for your James~ Dear heart, have no fear—as I have spent some lengthy hours with the man and I know him to be resilient and strong willed—to say nothing of his great physical strength, as well, his profound and undying love for you, my daughter.

I end this abhorrent letter with a plea for you to call on Joseph Prescott, or go to Mrs. Sullivan; you should not remain alone at such a time as this... I beg of you.

I hold you in Highest Esteem My Elisabeth,

Much Love,
Your Papa

Elisabeth heard the creak of the door and Charlie suddenly stood at her side. "You startled me, Charlie."

"Should'a laid down the plank 'cross the door, Miz Prescott." He saw the tears that glistened in her green eyes, the puffiness of her face and reached out tentatively to touch her shoulder. "I'm right sorry for yur bothers passin', Miz Prescott. I am that. And Jamie, ya musn't worry none, ma'am. He's a tough bugger, ya know thet now, don't ya?"

Elisabeth reached up and laid her hand on that of his own. "I know, Charlie, I know. *He is alive!* I can feel it. Does that sound strange to you?"

"No, ma'am, it don't. I figure he's likely given them some grief theirselves. Be sorry they done captured the likes o' James Prescott. I rode line this mornin' everthing' appears fine. Snows melting. Went on up ta Joseph's, I done told him about yur brother an' 'bout what yur papa said 'bout Jamie, said he'd be down shortly, ma'am."

"Thank you, Charlie, I have no idea what I would do without you. Thank you."

She felt the squeeze of his fingers on her shoulder. "No need ma'am no need, I'll be here whenever ya need me. Too, I been thinkin' maybe it would be a good idea fer ya to go on back east, ya know—jus' till…"

"No, Charlie…thank you, but no. Jamie would want to know where I was. Where he could find the children and me. No, I am not going any place. Josiah will find him. I trust *Jamie* and I trust Josiah." She found she was surprised by her own words. She had considered going to her parents—but *home* was here, where Jamie had been, where he would return.

Spring 1865

The pain radiated throughout his body as he struggled to right himself. The sounds around him distant, the intense heat of his body pulsating with pain at each interval of time.

His nostrils filled with the pungent stench of *chickens* and *pigs*? The straw of the pallet he lay upon prickly. His body heavy and heated, the sweat ran in rivulets down his brow. Agony wracked his body with a weakness he found to be unfathomable, still, he willed himself to sit upright, all to no avail. He seemed unable to move, paralyzed in pain, a pain so intense, it was unimaginable. Where was he?

He could feel the bones that protruded at his hips as his hands fell away from them. *He was naked*! Fear gripped his heart, and he could hear the beat of it accelerate. *Where the hell was he? If he could just open his eyes*! His body refused to obey his commands. Was that water he heard? Once again, he struggled to rise, the nausea overwhelming, his sweat profuse. He could hear the sounds of animals, a cow, horses. How long had he been here?

Blackness seemed to slide like a blind, extinguishing the pain and the panic that overwhelmed him. A feeling of gratitude came over him as he welcomed the void. *Dreams pursued him.* He sat upon a valiant black stallion, the horse dancing with excitement. He could see land forever—mountains, rivers. Fields dotted with horses and cattle.

"Chil' don' touch thet, man…" The words of a woman leaning over him, the cool feel of water on his brow, his chest. "Youse gonna be fine, mista, jus' be still now, hear me. Run on, git them biscuits chil'."

He heard her, felt the coolness of the water with which she bathed his face. He felt his eyes flutter in a moment of recognition...a young Negro knelt over him. He heard the sound of small footfalls—a child...running. Rays of sunlight, dappled rays of sunlight that filtered through the spaces of the height of the roof. Once again the smell of animals pungent to his nostrils—that *and the filth of his own body*, the smell of the woman, warm with sweat.

"Kin you eat a bite, mista`? Take a sip now, it do ya good." He felt the moistness of her arm, as she slid it beneath his neck to raise his head.

Oh God, the ache was excruciating. *Where?* He couldn't identify *where* it hurt, more realistically he couldn't identify where it *did not* hurt. He felt the weakness shroud him, dipping him once more into darkness. His mind drifted from one avenue of thought to another, without substance, without clarity.

The sounds of rifle fire, colliding with the face of the most beautiful woman he had ever seen, her eyes green and flashing, the lashes black as night, the fall of her ebony hair about her ivory flesh, luxurious. The images vivid in their detail; flashes of her nakedness, her body smooth and lovely, her breasts taunt with perfection, as desirable as anything he could imagine. Now a child held in her arms. A massive kitchen stove. The sense of safety, of being loved, flooded his being.

Now came dreams of filth, the filth of men, the smell of offal, the screams of terror that reverberated within his very soul.

Within the obscurity of his mind, he felt his body tremble. The bones grating against the pallet of straw and earth he lay upon, the heat of his body seeming to accelerate. *Was he in hell?* Surely, there would be no kind words or water offered him in hell.

Within the darkness of his mind, the men he had killed stood before him. As far as his eyes could see, they stood. He watched as they fell, smelled the ripeness of their blood, tasted it in the back of his throat, watched with detachment as they dropped, gazed with wonder at the look of shock, the whiteness of their eyes. Strange...*few shown fear.*

He felt his head rolling from side to side, unable to stop the motion that caused such agony and nausea. He drifted once more into the nothingness of who he had become.

He saw a giant of a man riding toward him, the hair and beard of the giant, as red as fire. He heard him call out to him. "Aye, an' yer gonna be fine, lad."

Where was he, Scotland...surely the man's speech was of Scottish descent.

Again the sounds of moaning, screams of agony rose within the darkness of his mind. Walls of timber stood about him, a sea of men stood before him, their clothing hung in rags about their skeletal forms, many naked, their bodies emaciated beyond imagination, their buttocks excoriated from dysentery, the flesh hung in folds along their wasted frames. Their hair and beards matted, filled with crawling creatures. *Their eyes vacant, devoid of emotion,* they wander aimlessly at the edge of a small river, crouch cowardly, or from sheer exhaustion, along the perimeters of the enclosure. Men too beaten to cry out, too hungry to know hunger, too spent to wish to survive. Thirst a constant companion, as the water is dank and smells of excrement, of vomit.

Again, blessed darkness ensued. Within the darkness came the face of the woman. *Her name,* in the depths of his mind; he searched for her name. He knew her, he loved her, she loved him! *Why couldn't he remember?* Ineffable sadness filled his dream and once more the shroud fell over his mind, once again—lifting to reveal unmitigated panic. Heavy ropes tied about his hands and waist—the thud of the man in front of him as he fell, the horrific hole in the back of his head. He felt the whip as it cracked upon his back, as he was bid to pull the fallen man along. The strength of his anger...*the cost of that anger*...the dreaded whip...

the endless fatigue. Exhaustion and pain beyond anything he had experienced.

He watched the blood as it ran from his wrists, the blue black of the blowfly that crawled to lay its eggs in his torn flesh, the sweat that stung at his eyes, the sound of insects that skittered across his skin. He heard the rifle fire as it bounced around the feet of those walking in single file, each tied to another. Dependent upon each other to stand—to walk. His mind pushed at the dream…for surely it was but a dream—*a nightmare.*

The woman again…astride a white horse…flying across the flat of desolate land, a ghostly aberration of surreal beauty.

He envisioned herds of buffalo, of Indians. Their lances raised in pursuit. He felt moved by the sight. The woman sat beside him on the great white horse… Peace, he felt only peace. Peace that choked him, peace that caused inexplicable sadness. The woman smiled at him, spoke his name, *Jamie…* the sadness suddenly replaced by drifts of snow, a blazing fire by the rivers edge. The sounds of the river as it thundered about them, a sound that was serene. Laughter. He felt the softness of her skin, the fire of their embrace…

"Mista, mista, ya'll need ta drink an' have a bite. Y'all wake now." He heard the voice and anger welled in him that he should be pulled from the vision of the woman… He struggled to the surface of his delusional mind…the instinct for survival prevalent, a feeling unfamiliar, an emotion he thought having long vanished. For the first time that he could remember… *He thought of survival.*

"I's Magnolia, mista, does y'all have a name? Kin ya take some vittles?"

Her voice soft—but a whisper. He struggled to open his eyes, to rise from the discomfort of his position. *Every bone, every sinew, possessed of pain.*

He felt the coolness of the cloth she wiped across his brow and swallowed hard, biting back tears. Where was he, who was this woman, how did he get here? What did she say her name was,

Magnolia? He thought that was a tree. He heard the sniffling of a child, heard the small young voice.

"I's scart Mammie."

"Run along chil'. Do as I say, 'member not a word...skedaddle now. Drink this now, mista," The water dribbled from his lips. A spoon now held to his mouth...rice—no, grits. The south. He was in the south. *Magnolia*, a Negro.

His eyes fluttered open and the blue of the sky could be seen through the cracks of the roof. Twelve by twos, heavy timber to put on a roof. *A strange observation.*

He looked into the round blue/gray eyes of Magnolia, the lashes curled tightly, her skin a rich dark chocolate, her lips full and pink. He watched as they spread into a smile. "I's be grateful you be awake, mista. Y'all musta bin' a right purdy man."

He felt the crack of his lips as he smiled back at her. Felt the gurgling noise coming from deep within his chest.

"Jus' swallow, just swallow. It do ya good to eat, mista." She gently lay his head against the hardness of the ground. The grits seemed to flow down into his stomach with the rapidity of a rivers flow, landing there in the emptiness of it. The shock rising to form bile in his throat. "Sick. I think I am..."

"No's, ya not. Y'all lie down now. And keep thet food. I's been givin' ya sugar water. I's think ya gonna live. Does ya have a name, mista?"

"I, I...how long..."

"Y'all rest now, sleep be best."

He felt the void as it closed once more within his mind, felt the dreams surface and surrendered to them. Here there was no physical pain. He was so very tired—perhaps *the woman* waited for him in the darkness of his mind. He drifted deep within the void that he was certain would bring her to him, only to find a young boy in his arms.

The sobbing of the young man wrenched at his heart. The peaceful look within his clear blue eyes incongruent with the hole in his chest, the blood and guts that oozed from within his youthful body. He heard the sound of his own voice as he called the young man's name... *Tommy*. He felt he had known this boy for a very long time. Was it his son, a relative? Had he killed the boy? The boy wore a Confederate soldier's cap.

He looked down at his own blue jacket, a Yankees jacket—covered in the bodily fluids of *Tommy*. What would he tell this young mans mother? The grief he felt was profound. Cannon fire razed all about him. He lay the young man down and closed the lifeless eyes and ran. Anguish and shame pulling him deeper into the abyss of his mind. The blackness welcome. Even desired. A coward he was, he had left that child to die alone.

Within the darkness of his mind, he felt the sand on the hot wind of the desert, the gold of it glimmering from horizon to horizon, rippling across the earth like the waves of the ocean. The regal horse stood at his side, his ebony coat glistening in the brilliant sunlight. The white of the Tuareg wrapped about his head and shoulders, the native cloak, or jubbah—covering him from head to foot. His knife sheathed, his rifle slung over his shoulder. A small band of men on camels stood before him, the lyrical sounds of Aramaic and French coming to him on the winds of the desert. He was young and strong. He could see the strength in his well-formed hands. He could feel the bulk of muscle that lay in perfect symmetry upon his body, the breadth and depth of his shoulders and chest, the strength of his legs, the straightness of his broad back.

He heard the strength and purpose of his voice as the language of the French came from his lips, heard the laughter of the men on camels, the weight of the gold in the pouch at his waist. He felt the moistness of his body in the blistering sun, knew the length of his long thick mane of hair, as dark as that of the horse that stood beside him, his hoof pawing at the gold of the sand. His hair, *her hair*. His heart beat in anticipation. She was before him again, an oasis of love in the open desert. Smiling, perfect white teeth, the image of her floating just beyond reach.

Again he felt the incredible heat of his body. The pressure of the earth beneath him, and was roused by the soft mulling sounds of the Negro woman, the coolness of the water as she bathed his flesh.

"Is ya feelin' betta, mista? Youse not be so hot now. Ya gotta eat now."

He felt the spoon against his lips and willed them to part, to open his mouth, again, the food causing only nausea.

He struggled against the tremendous desire to fall back into the abyss of his dreams. For indeed; *they must be dreams.*

"Shoo, shoo. Filthy varmint! Theys eatin' at ya, mista." The drone of her voice, a distant colloquy within his battered mind. "They's comin'. Them varmints git ya dead…I's talk ta my man. May be he talk ta the massa'."

Who was coming? Dead! He would be dead. Would the dreams stop? Would he lose the woman, the redhaired giant? *Death…* The word seemed to cause only relief—a release from the pain that ravaged his body. *Varmints*, what did she mean? He had heard the sounds of critters in moments of lucidity, felt the nips upon his flesh. The incidental pain, long associated with his life—insignificant in comparison. Rats perhaps, he had thought this to be a barn in which he lay. But *who* was coming?

"My man done give me this, jus' swalla now." It was Magnolia's voice that roused him in the darkness. In his mind the burning liquid had substance and the color of gold, it stung his lips and burned its way down his throat, to lay like a warm blanket in the pit of his stomach. Whisky? Bittersweet. The taste bringing with it memories. The sting and burn dredging pain, then, pushing it away.

His lips moved to say what was on his mind. "Thank you, thank you," he heard nothing of his voice…only looked into the smiling eyes of Magnolia.

"They's gonna move ya up ta the big house in ta mornin'… soldiers, them boys be lookin' fer ya. Hankerin' ta see ya died, mista. This here moonshine—it git ya 'til mornin'."

The pain was excruciating, yet a precursor of lucidity entered with it, still certain he dreamt, unwilling to climb the heights of his mind for fear of losing *her*. He could feel the warmth of her body, as it lay curled, spooned to his back, removing the desire to change his position. Never had he felt this safe, this cocooned in the love this woman held for him, and he for her. The glow that seemed to emanate from their love seemed to fill the small room they occupied. *Oh, if he could stay here, with her*…with this feeling of love and security. He felt her small hand as it rested on his waist, fearing to touch it, afraid it was not real. *Lord, let him not awaken*, if indeed he was dreaming, let this not end.

He felt his eyes open, felt the horrifying sadness that *she* was gone. That he still lay on a pallet of straw on the earthen floor. The reality threatened to tumble him to the depths of his grief… He lay on his side, a position he was certain had not been entertained prior. A position that was the cause of his increased pain, the bones creaking within his wasted body. The sharpness of his shoulder and hip bones threatening to tear at his flesh, to grind together on their decent to the earth he lay upon. With great effort, he willed his body to return to its prone condition.

He looked up at the night sky and saw the twinkling of the stars, the moon shown brightly through the spaces within the heavy planks. Venus hung below the moon and he felt a tear slid down his face; if he could remember that was Venus, why couldn't he remember who *she* was, who *he* was. He swallowed hard, fighting back the uselessness of tears, fighting down the nausea that seemed to be his constant companion. Where was he, what had happened? Who was he? How did he get here?

Sikes Plantation

The sharp grating of his bones as they clashed against one another woke him. Someone was lifting him. He struggled to open his eyes, only to look into vivid blue eyes surrounded by thinning locks of gray hair that hung about his face. The odor of tobacco strong, his teeth yellowed. "Take him, Jonas."

This would be his demise. Did they think he was dying, so near death as to dispose of him now? The woman—Magnolia was it?—had said, *they* were coming... Who were *they*? Were they going to bury him? He doubted he could dig out from beneath the ground. Perhaps they had a pyre.

The effort involved concerning what had happened to him seemed to ebb and flow within his mind. Did he care if he lived or died?

Within the depths of his subconscious mind, he heard the screams of the men they had burned or buried alive. *Ta keep the stench down.* Oh my God, give me strength. He fought to give voice to his emotions and found he had none. He pushed against the giant that held him in his arms, carrying him like a child. The arms, thick and strong, the color of coffee, slick with the sweat of heat and humidity, his body odor strong and pungent.

"Be still." The white man shushed him. The void rose once more and he succumbed to it, welcomed it. Better to be unconscious if you were to be burned or buried alive.

He heard the voice of the woman called Magnolia, heard the groan that came from deep within his chest, as he struggled for words. "Massa, these here is all was with the man. I done saved 'em."

"Fine, fine, Magnolia, give them to me, won't go well should they ta find 'em on him."

Again he struggled to free himself from the giants embrace, sought the depths of his mind for words that would stop this.

"Quiet, fella, ya'll git us all kilt'," the white man whispered.

He could see the sky. The moon, a single hazy orb of marble, the smattering of ginger colored sunlight as it rose over the treetops. The sound of water rushing. The foot falls of the black man that carried him. Feel the pain of jostling. He welcomed the emptiness that came, fearing the moments of lucidity.

"Jonas, carry him on up ta the house, put him in Jackson's bed."

"Yes, sir, Massa'"

His eyes scanned the room around him. Had he been in this room before? No, this was darker; the room that he had seen in his mind was the color of gold, of honey. These logs were of darker wood, the wadding—the color of iron. His eyes followed the lines within the room, across the end of the bed he lay upon, a dark, ornate footboard, a large matching bureau stood at the far wall. A bed of feathers, *he lay upon a bed of feathers.* He felt the single tear as it slid down his face; *they didn't bury him, they weren't going to ignite his body.* The room was cast in shadows, the only light an ornate lantern. He was in someone's home.

"No! Deddy how could you! I'll not have him here. *Take him away!* Deddy! *Please.*" A woman's voice he had not heard before, a young woman. The pain and anguish in her voice unmistakable. If he could just rise, perhaps he could make her understand. Sobs rumbled in his chest. He fought to push them back.

Allan Sikes looked at his daughter, her hair disheveled from sleep, the toe of her bare foot circling in the dust of the maple floors. Floors now old and scarred.

This had been his fathers dream, *his* plantation… Allan just didn't have the stomach for it, or the ambition, such a damned lot of work. From sun up to sundown, they toiled. Depending on the slaves and Mother Nature to be kind; to rain, *not to rain.* The tobacco and cotton threatened by any manner of disease, and critter. *And now this, this ungodly war.* It had been five years! Five years of daily devastation. He was so damned tired he could cry. *One hell of a lot of good that would do!* Perhaps he was beyond tears, weary to the bone—of the bloodshed, of the hatred of those that thought they knew what was best for all of them. A government for the people, of the people—w*hat a lot of bull that was!*

Allan crooked his finger and gently pulled Abigail's chin up, tears filled her eyes, but he recognized the anger that flew behind them. Those blue eyes that looked back at him were his very own. But for an instant, he thought of the day she had been born; some, what, sixteen perhaps seventeen years ago. He had been so disappointed. He had wanted a son more than anything. *Someone to hunt with, someone to talk with, a man of principal and faith.* Yet this lovely child had weaseled her way into his heart, her nature; so like that of his mother. A little spitfire she was. Independent as all get out! She chewed on her bottom lip now. Crushing back words, he was certain. That, too, his mother had done.

He thought of Lydia who lay upstairs in bed; he had been a disappointment to her he was certain, but he didn't care anymore…couldn't care. His parents were gone now. His Lydia's family home had been burned out by the Union Army, their mansion and barns off the Stones River gone. His mother-in-law lay frail and waiting for her Maker in another room in the house of his plantation. The many bedrooms of the house empty of his sons, his beautiful boys dead, or gone to fight the damned men of Lincoln's war. *For what?* The younger children, frightened to death, now cloistered in but one room. He'd never understand. God, how much was one man to abide. If he took just this one small step to save one man, perhaps, just maybe, the Lord would see and approve, save his son's lives. He thought of the brutality with which they had killed Nathanial and felt his stomach churn.

"Daughter, Abigail, look at me. Think of y'all's brothers, it would be seemly should someone be lookin' after the likes o' them. Y'all know thet, Abigail. Ya do now."

"But what of Mama? This will jus' kill her, Deddy." She thought of her mother. She had not come from out of her room since *they* had been here. *The damned blue coats.* She had watched as they had pranced on their fine horses, aimed their rifles and killed her small brother. Watched as her mother had stood on the porch, wringing her hands and screaming in agony. Watched as she had fallen on her knees, sobbing. Could hear again the pleading grief within her voice. "*Allan, do somethin'. For the sake of God, do somethin'. Stop them! Please!*"

She had watched as her father had lifted the ten-year-old Nathanial into his arms sobbing, felt the grief and anger as they had all watched, as his life seemed to slowly ebb away. She heard again, the laughter of the man on the horse, the wicked satanic sound of his mocking amusement, his words, as he threatened to burn their house, the barns, the slave's quarters. Felt the shame and anger as her father had pleaded with them, *to leave. To go.* The information he had given them; she bit her lip and swallowed hard, thinking of the words her father had said. "Best we limit their killin' daughter. Tend to yer mama."

They had not heard from Jackson for months, or since *that* day. He had rode off, saying he would kill as many of the bastards as he could. Maybe join the Mississippi Militia—the grievous hatred in his young voice, *horrifying.* Her older brothers long ago having joined in the fight.

She watched now as Deddy fumbled with the papers Magnolia had given him. Did she want to deprive this man of care, of life? He was perhaps but a pawn in this game of war these men were playing. Should there be a woman in charge it would have been over long ago. *Men and their silly games!* Burning Atlanta, killing their brothers, burning plantations, killing innocent children, devastating a country.

They were destitute; she knew that. And if the slaves left... well, best she not consider that as yet.

Her father was a kind, decent man. Weak perhaps, or perhaps she simply didn't understand. She *would* want someone to care for her brothers—for Jackson, in particular—he was her friend, her playmate. Should this have been him, she would wish someone to give him life, to save him from the torments of fear and pain.

She looked at the man that lay on the bed, so ghostly pale against the once white linen. His form too long for the bed he lay upon, the gauntness of his face and body looking much like that of a corpse, his blue-black hair stringy and filled with crawling creatures. His skin covered with raw purulent sores and bloody wounds of what were surely rat bites. He could be sick beyond anything they could do for him.

Again she thought of Mama, in truth; her mother need never know.

Allan's voice was thoughtful. "So he's Lincoln's man."

Abigail watched as her father perused the papers. Were they letters? "Do y'all think thet's true, Deddy?"

"From the looks of these here letters, I'd say so...but..." He folded the papers and placed them in his pocket. "Take the children. Take 'em to the cellar. Jonas said them Yankees were at the Carter Plantation yesterday. They'll more'n' likely be here today. Likely at dawn. Go, Abigail. Do as you're told."

"But, Deddy, the war is over. I, I don't understand."

"Yes, well, that is all well an' good but Davis don't seem ta see it thet away. Till he does, we're at war."

The war was over. Did he hear that clearly? Davis...Davis. That name meant something to him. He heard the moan that came rippling through his body. Felt the arm of Magnolia as the burning hot liquid coursed over his lips, he was grateful she had given it to him. The burning liquid eased the pain, pushed at the panic that filled his mind with darkness and fear. Fear, the last thing to fall within man, his greatest enemy... Where had he heard that? *Fear*...he felt he had had many conversations concerning fear.

"It be best ya'll sleep, mista."

But sleep did not come. His consciousness did not tumble into the black abyss of nothingness. He fought to hold on to the lucidity that had so long escaped him. Was it the kindness of these people, or the fact that he could indeed identify the culprit? It was his *fear*, a fear that he could identify. *Fear that was like a fire that permeated his entire being*—that held him in this darkness, this terror, this cavern of loss. With a coherent mind came reality. He struggled to hold on to the cohesiveness of his thoughts. He had no name, no family, no talents, nor roots; he simply existed. Today, this very moment in time, was the first day of his life. He had no idea where he came from, what abilities he had. *Who were his people?* He clung to reality, a reality that was elusive, that brought with it startling truths, unimagined terror.

His mind fought to maintain clarity. Struggled to accept what in truth his reality was. These were sobering thoughts, still *it need not bring with it fear*. It made no difference if he knew his name, if he had a life other than today, perhaps what he had thought to be dreams, nightmares, were memories, what if that were the truth?

Emotion welled within his chest, and he felt the trembling of his bones. A memory, *the woman...the Scotsman...the land*. Oh, God, let that be so.

Rebels Not Yanks

Abigail struggled to execute her father's orders. She had long ago run out of entertainment for the children while in the cellar. If it were up to her she would wait to hear the thunder of hooves as they rode up to the plantation.

Waking each child in turn, she thought of her mother. *Lord, she would never have this many children;* no wonder the woman had taken to her bed. And what was she to do about them, Mama and Granny? Just let the soldiers ravage them? *Would they do that to old women?* She knew they would do it to her! She had fought them off more than a time or two. 'Damned men, with their endless lust and their joy in fighting! "Y'all come now, we must once again go ta the cellar."

She looked at the sleeping figures of her brothers and sisters. Five still left. Nathaniel now dead; perhaps the two older boys as well, Jackson gone, *nine* chil'ren her mama had birthed. She could smell the foul odor of dirty bodies as she hovered over the large bed where all the children had taken up sleeping...too frightened to go to their own rooms. All of them in need of bathing! The last soldiers had blown up the well, the river was now their only source of water. She would take them to the river...after... She had counted three bars of soap left, one more thing that needed replenishing. That *and candles*.

She heard the chickens as they scurried in the yard below. Purty little things; she would need the eggs, perhaps Jonas could kill a couple of wild turkey's today, she had flour and milk; some lard that was a bit rancid, but it'd do. She'd have Bertha make biscuits and boiled turkey...some greens; she had seen dandelions in the yard and the turnips had sprouted tops.

Abigail turned from the sleeping children, upon leaving the room she once more commanded, "Come y'all get your sorry selves up, and come climb down ta the cellar, I'll be comin' shortly."

She passed through the dogtrot to the building that housed the kitchens, looked at the ash bucket that stood in the back. She would have to speak to the Negras 'bout that. Why was it empty? It wasn't like they had not been burning wood in the cook stove. *Lordy, it is hot*, she thought as she traversed the small area between the main house and the kitchens. *Need ta have them Negras to bring up water to do the wash...* her thoughts colliding. *Lord, what a bushel of things to do.*

"Bertha. Bertha, Deddy thinks the soldiers are on their way. Get up now y'all an' get to the cellar. Tell the others, too, send Sean to help Deddy with the loading."

Perhaps her father had already sent for Sean—made no difference. He *would* need help. For a moment her heart skipped a beat, fear sliding close to it. *Surely the damn Yankees would jus' go on home and leave them be.*

Flashes of the Yankees raced through her mind. The rifle raised, the sound, the smell of the fire that had propelled the bullet straight into the heart of young Nathaniel, his marbles spilling from his hand, she had watched with detached fascination as they had bounced on the ground around his falling body.

She stopped and placed her hand on the doorframe. *Girl it be no differen' than a twister...* she heard Bertha's voice in her mind. Bertha was right; both killed without compassion or thought. Destruction the only thing they sought.

Where was she? Bertha was always up at this time of a morning. "Bertha?" she hollered.

"I's comin', Miss Abby. I's here chil'."

"Oh, praise the Lord, I was worried..."

"No need, chil'. Now, what you want, girl?"

Abigail quickly recounted the needs for the day and turned to run to the dining room. Turning she said, "Do y'all have something to feed the children whilst we wait?"

"I's got hush puppies, thet's all I's got this mornin'."

"Bertha, did y'all know of the man Magnolia has been nursin'?" She watched as Bertha turned her back to her, gathering the hard hush puppies from yesterdays meal, as she did so, she stoked the fire in the big flatiron stove. "Bertha?"

"Well now chil', guess I did all right. Jus' thought the fella'd pass."

"How long has he been here? Where did she find him?"

"I's don't rightly know chil'. Days…a week…Jonas. He done foun' him lyin' by the other side ta river. Only knowed him to be livin' when he throwed him over his shoulder ta bury him…heard the mangy fella moan like."

"And Magnolia has been caring for him all this time?"

"'Guess so, you know Magnolia, ken'nt stand fer even the chickens ta suffer none. Youse think he live?"

Abigail shook her head. "I…I am not certain. I have never seen anyone so starved and live. It's well, I find him…" She paused and swallowed hard. "Bertha, ah know it ta be unkindly of me… *He makes my skin crawl*, seems such a large man, and there is absolutely no meat on his bones, and well, he is far to filthy to be lyin' in a bed of linen. An' Deddy thinks he might be a *Yankee*."

"I do believe they got a soul too chil', gowan' see ta them chil'ren."

"You best come to the cellar too."

"I's be there, soon as I hear them soldier's comin on up the hill. Y'all g'wan now."

Abigail placed the hush puppies in her pockets and ran to the dining room.

Crawling beneath the table she lifted the door that was built into the floor. A twister room…thunder, lighting, wind, and rain—the precursor of twisters. Twisters that took there own sweet time to rip apart your lives. Once, when she was very young, the rain and wind had lasted for days, and the river had risen to the small knoll surrounding their house. The slaves' quarters had looked as if they had been built in the middle of the river. When at last it had receded, they had simply picked up fish, turtles and frogs from the ground.

She thought of the turtle soup Bertha made and her mouth watered. That, and fried pickles where her favorite thing…well, other than strawberry pie.

Allan stood now with Sean, his overseer. They rapidly loaded the rifles and pistols that lined the wall of the library. The pungent smell of gun oil and wadding, as prevalent as that of cigars and the leather binding on the many books. Finished loading, Allan wiped his hands on his filthy trousers. "Sean, take this rifle and pistol to Abigail…and tell her to use it if she must. Too, see to it Jonas is armed. Tell the other slaves to hide in the fields." Allan knew Sean did not approve of arming Jonas, but what the hell, the man was still here. Hadn't run off like the slaves of many of the plantation owners, and Allan trusted Jonas, often more than he trusted Sean.

Sean merely nodded his head. He hadn't said a word all the while they had worked. He seldom did. And now, well he had as many things to lose as Allan himself. Without the Negras, they had no need of an overseer. Allan shook his head. If it was really over…the war…what the hell was he to do? *Lord, don't y'all push a man to his knees.*

His grandeddy and his deddy had built this house and farmed this land for over a hundred years, and he had an inkling it would stand for another hundred. Now why the hell he thought that, he had no idea. He looked around at the room in which he stood and thought of the hours he had spent here. Reading. Thinking. Rocking in that old rocker. He could hear his deddy's voice now, hollering at him, "Get out here, boy. Get on that horse of yours and see how to run this place. I ain't gonna be around forever to help your sorry ass."

Allan felt the bulge of the man's papers in his pockets, rightly didn't know what to do about them. Oh, he'd read them all right, whilst in the privy this morning. General James Martin Prescott the papers had said. He was, just as Allan had thought, a damned Yankee and a damned *general* at that. Said the man was six-foot-two and weighed some hundred an' eighty pounds, now what the hell could have caused this emaciation in a man that size? But it did look as though it were the same fella, eyes the color of golden honey, hair that might be black, hard ta tell, tangled and filthy as it was. Hailed from Montana. Just where the hell Montana was he wasn't quite certain, but he figured the Oregon Territories most likely. A wife and two children. The small card folded and refolded within the personal letters so often the ink was near gone, the penmanship of the letters fluid and downright purty.

He hadn't had time to read the letters. Soon as the fella gained some sense, he'd give them to him. But now, he couldn't take the chance of the confederacy knowin' he had a Union soldier lying abed within his house, though, with the slaves always talkin', it was doubtful it was a secret.

Allan looked around the library and picked up his rifle; checked that his knife was in its sheath and climbed the stairs to the third floor; hotter than hell it was up here. He walked the hallway to where his mother-in-law lay. Still sleeping, the old lady was. What was she, somewhere's near eighty years old now?

The room was small and the odor of it fetid. The old lady had most likely soiled herself again...*old age*...Allan didn't look forward to such as that. Perhaps being killed by the union army was preferable.

The sun would be up damned soon; he had no time to waste. Check on Lydia and get on down to the porch. Best get on with it...the waiting being the worst.

Opening the door to Lydia's room was like opening the door to the past. It had been his mama's room before—crystal chandeliers, heavy velvet draperies now faded by the morning sunlight that streamed from the east of a mornin'. Ladies things rested on the dressing table; mirrors and face powder, some perfume from France. He remembered the day he had bought it. Gone all the way to Atlanta, taken Lydia an' a house slave. He had bought her grand things, frills an' lace—perfumes. They had gone to the theatre there.

The theatre, a thing of ashes now, along with the once burgeoning city of Atlanta, that too was gone, along with everything he was familiar with, as well as his future, if indeed what he had heard was correct. *The North had won!*

He looked at the carpet beneath his feet, worn near threadbare now and thought of the hours he had sat on it as a child playing marbles, his mama reading to him. The door to his room glared back at him. That door had not been used in years, Lydia wouldn't abide it, certainly not since Nathaniel passed...*the marbles*—made his gut clench. The memory of marbles now associated only with Nathaniel. The marbles rolling willy nilly as they fell from his sons hand, the dust, the smell of gun powder and the blood of his son as he lay dying in his arms.

"Lydia, you awake?"

"Yes, Allan, I'm awake. What do y'all want now?"

"Jus' to say we've heard the soldiers are coming. 'Thought I'd take y'all to the cellar with Abigail and the children. Come I'll help you."

"No, Allan, I'll not be goin' to the cellar. If they wish to kill me, I believe I'll just stay here and wait. I have no purpose now to you, or the children."

"Lydia…please. The children need you."

"I think not, Allan. Please Allan, please leave my room. If y'all could send my maid, the chamber pot needs emptyin'."

Allan looked at the face of his wife. He saw the years of disappointment on her face, the purse of her lips, the lack of luster on her once smooth skin, the crease of her forehead, the frown that bridged her nose. It had been his father's idea to marry her. He was then and now, in love with Magnolia's mother. Sinful he knew, but you can't always control *who* you love. He pushed the thought from his mind. He and Lydia had been married for twenty-five years and he did care for her, but he was tired of arguing with her, tired of trying to live up to her gaud awful expectations. "As you wish, Lydia."

He felt the heavy chains around his hands, the rope at his neck, the heat, as the sun beat upon his clothing. The dust as it rose in his nostrils. The men's footsteps as they pounded the ground; they marched in single file, perhaps fifty, perhaps one hundred men.

In his peripheral vision, he could see the horizon to the west, the sun sinking. His hat was gone. Yet he was grateful for the uniform he wore; although dark navy blue, it would keep him warm in the early morning and protect him from the sunlight during these long days. They had been marching for days now, perhaps four. His last memories were of battle, of Tennessee; the Stones River was it? Before that the Carter plantation…his thoughts were unclear. The desert sands rose before his eyes in the dream…and he rode a camel…

Hallucinations. His mind was filled with them! He felt the sting of the whip on his back. Christ. He had to pay attention if he was to survive. He knew he was dreaming…but his rational mind knew there was important information there, in his subconscious mind; *he must fight the terror that reigned there.* Yet once again…he succumbed to the darkness of oblivion…

Allan and Sean, along with Jonas sat in the old rocking chairs on the long sweeping porch, the sun was setting to the west and purple hues of color formed across the rolling hills, covered with the green of hackberry and walnut trees. *A wondrous sight to behold, should you not be waiting for the Union Army to kill you,* Allan thought to himself. He heard the squeak of the rocker as it stopped and watched the length of Sean as he rose from the rocker.

"Miss Abigail, she be right, they ain't coming. I got plenty to do."

Allan watched the back of his overseer as he took the steps down from the porch. "Ah, guess that be it then. But stay clost, ya never know, they may come this evening. I'll go speak to the house slaves, you tell the field slaves to come on in."

"I will."

Allan watched as Sean headed down towards the fields. What a wasted day…damned Yankees… At every turn, they cost him money… Nathaniel and his other sons rose to cloud his mind. He shook his head as if that would clear it. "Jonas, go on down and tell Bertha, too, you might want to tell Magnolia and Lila." After all these years, her name on his tongue brought a tightness to his trousers.

"Yes, Massa'…here be y'er weapon."

"Naw, Jonas, y'all keep it until we know fer sure this is over… You won't be about shootin' me now, will ya?" He heard the chuckle from the big black man and smiled. "No, Massa', not today."

"Good." Allan turned and went into the house, going into the dining room he rapped on the floor three times with the butt of his rifle. The tousled blond head of his youngest son could be seen raising the trap door.

"Tell your sister it doesn't look as if they're coming…but be mindful."

"Yes, sir."

He'd been awake and aware of his surroundings several times throughout the day and yet he found it difficult to focus his thought processes. His mind would feel rational for a brief period of time and then the fatigue would simply seep in like a thief in the night. He sensed it to be late afternoon. Strange, he had not seen nor heard anyone the entire day. Perhaps he had dreamed he lay in a large home.

Perhaps that man and woman were but a dream…and yet, he felt the feather bed beneath him, the pillow his head rested on, felt the stirrings of hunger within his body. He felt the subtle urges to move his hands, to reposition his feet, and although these were minuet innuendos of thought he found them miraculous. Little by little his strength was returning…he felt the movement of his hands and was grateful beyond words.

Fatigue washed as a wave across his mind, like a fog that brought with it sleep. Sleep that brought the dreams he thought to be the answer to his dilemma. Who was he? How did he get here?

Reverberating about the small room where he lay, he heard the shot ring out. His eyes flew open to see the muzzle blast, to hear another shot.

My God, they were firing at him.

The acrid smell of gunpowder filled the air and he felt the sweat as it poured from his body, the trembling that followed— *the crushing weight of,* the breath knocked out of him, the blow so intense. The warm stench of blood as it poured over him. He felt the sharp movement of his hand and arm as they flew to the area of the crushing blow to his chest… *Why wasn't he dead?*

The lifeless blue eyes that lay in white freckled skin stared back into his own eyes of amber.

The red hair of the man lay fanned across his own bony chest. His jacket of gray, giving no doubt as to who he was.

Raising his head he looked up at the muzzle of the gun that rested upon the back of the man that lay dead upon his chest. The blue/green eyes of Magnolia stared back at him. "Mista, youse all right?"

"Yes, thank you, Magnolia, I believe I am."

"Y'all kin talk?"

He grinned at her and lay his head down.

Suddenly the room was alive with persons—male and female. "My God, Magnolia, what have you done? Where did you get that gun?" The voice belonged to the man called Allan.

"Magnolia! What in tarnation have y'all done? Ah declare, we shall surely all be killed by our own now!" The young woman, *Abigail*...

"Girl...give me that! Jonas!" Allan's voice again.

Strange, his world had expanded exponentially in a very brief period of time.

He desperately tried to raise himself. Only to slump under the weight of the man that Magnolia had shot and killed. He heard the shouts of Allan. "Lila. Lila! Where the devil did she get this gun?"

"I's done stole it, Massa... I sawd thet' man and knowed what he was lookin' fer. I's did Massa. I heard him askin' y'all 'bout thet mista man and I's just couldn't let him kill him or take him off to do..."

He could hear the sobs that reverberated from her chest. Once again he raised his head from the pillow. "Thank you, Magnolia, thank you."

Behind Magnolia stood a tall lithe black woman; the color of deep, rich honey. Eyes that slanted in the most intriguing way... shots of silver slid through her thick hair, cheekbones jutted from beneath her eyes, her lips full and ripe. Her nose regal, perhaps Egyptian? He watched as Allan rested his hand upon the woman's shoulder.

"Lila, take the girl. Jonas, take the gun and put it back in the library. Quickly, come back and help me. Abigail, girl, fetch soap and water—lye."

His head fell once more to the pillow, the strength he had so recently possessed, gone...the darkness threatening once more to envelope his mind. He felt the weight of the man being lifted from him. Heard the murmurings of Allan, as he and Jonas stripped the man of clothing and papers. Listened as Allan instructed Jonas "to burn the man."

"Won't be good should they find his body here on the plantation. Here, burn these with him."

He opened his eyes to see Allan pull papers apart, giving some of them to Jonas. Folding the ones he had found on the Confederate soldiers body with the remaining papers and placing them in the confederate uniform.

"These will be his...y'all understand, this is the man and this here's his name. MacRegan, it says here. Sargent Michael MacRegan. Y'all understand?"

"Yes, Massa'."

"So *he* has a name now. Michael MacRegan. Now, off with y'all. Abigail, did ya hear me?"

"I did, Deddy, I did."

He felt the cool, soapy water as Abigail sponged his face and neck. The stench of warm blood replaced by the odor of lye.

A fragrance he remembered...

Miss Abigail

Coming from the kitchens, Abigail entered the once sumptuous dining room, seeing the man that sat at the table she stopped and stood watching the stranger that sat before her. His hands folded at his forehead, his elbows on the table. She though of Mama's words: "Abigail, Abigail, young and able, get your elbows off the table…" a silly, inane thought.

She missed Mama…their lives…*before*.

Obviously he hadn't heard her come into the room. He appeared to be deep in thought. She knew him to be confused; this man knew nothing of his life before, only the nightmare of his incarceration at Andersonville—*Fort Sumter*. For but a brief moment, guilt rose in her, guilt that *her* people should be responsible for the ungodly wickedness that had come upon this man. And yet she understood much of it. The Southern families had themselves, but little to eat. The *billy yank* had devastated the South—the land, the grand Southern plantations, both large and small. Why indeed, would those in charge feed and clothe those prisoners who were responsible for demolishing their very way of life? Grief quickly pervaded her heart and mind, the grief swiftly shifting to that of anger.

She looked about her—the once opulent and graceful room. Tarnished silver servers sat upon lovely darkened sterling trays. Elegant brocade draperies adorned the windows, festooned with silk fringe that lay against the silk-papered walls. The soft aqua hue of the southern sea giving the room a feeling of peace and tranquility.

The bullet holes in the walls, the shattered glazing—a reminder of things that she could do nothing of. The missing Chippendale chairs that had matched the table gave credence to the anger she felt. The fools had burned them! Used them for firewood! She sighed and the man looked up at her.

He had gained a substantial amount of weight and still he looked gaunt and ill. His eyes haunted—as if he still resided in the world of Andersonville. His stunningly handsome face continued to be shrouded in disbelief. The throes of agony and despair of those that have been shattered, etched deeply and hauntingly within his eyes.

"Pardon me, ma'am."

She watched as he attempted to rise. So she had been correct; *he was a gentleman.* "Please, you may remain seated."

"Tell me again—your name? I seem unable to recall." He gave a slight chuckle. "In fact, I still do not recall my own."

She walked to the table and pulled the chair out and seated herself opposite him. "Miss Abigail. Miss Abigail Simpson Sikes."

"Of course. Abigail. I apologize for not having the ability to retain your name, *for...for...so many things.*" His voice was husky with emotion. Once again he hung his head. Breathing deeply, he looked up at her. "I am so bitterly apologetic for my intrusion on your lives. I find it difficult to believe that this, this, this despicable thing that has occurred here is the fault of who I am, or a part of. I seem to find it difficult to remember things. What did you say my name was?"

She sighed and looked into the eyes of the enemy. She found no malice there, no hatred. Only disbelief. Had he but forgotten the reason he fought, or was he but one of the many who simply found it *his duty?* Men and their *despicable duty!* The mere thought made her wish to scream. She thought of Daniel and pushed the thought from her mind. *They were to have been married!*

She quickly turned her head from the man's sight, brushing at the tears that rushed from her eyes. Again her mama's words: "*Excessive tears are as vulgar as a lack of compassion.*" She *had shown compassion for this man!* She must admit it to be feigned in the beginning—however…

Although he was obviously not a *Southern man*, he was well spoken and polite. As he had fought for his life here in her father's house, in his delirium, she had heard him muttering in the language of the French, as well as some genus of Asian language.

He was not a young man, perhaps in his mid thirties, certainly not as old as her father. But then her father had aged dramatically during the dreadful years of war. *This war!* They had lost everything! She sighed and looked again at the man that sat across the table from her.

"Yes, Abigail. Miss Abigail." Abigail's thoughts ran to the day her father had taken the man's papers and replaced them with the dead Confederate soldiers—to care for and feed a Union soldier would have certainly seen them all dead. *Treason*, they would be found guilty of. It was no wonder he was confused. They had given him the history and the name of the Confederate soldier who had come looking for the Union soldiers said to have been in the area.

They had killed one of their own! In truth not to save *him*, but to save themselves! Save themselves from the tyranny of being branded a spy, a co-conspirator of the *Blue Coats*. Union bastards they were! What other despicable thing could happen to them!

She knew his name to be James Prescott, *General J*ames Prescott; his only memories, that of Andersonville. A prison for the enemy of the man they said him to be. It made no sense… not even to her.

"Sargent Michael MacRegan, that is as Deddy said shown on your papers." Once again guilt suffused her heart. Was she to be complicit in this fabrication of lies?

She watched as he ran his damaged, gnarled hand through the glossy thickness of his hair, the silver that brushed through it shown in the sunlight that crept through the windows. The hand obviously had been shattered in a most harsh manner. The scars of manacles grazed his wrists.

"Would y'all like something to eat, Mista MacRegan? Perhaps a glass of sweet tea?"

"No. Thank you, no. Please excuse me, I have intruded into your home and now into your dining room…"

She found her own actions to be out of character as she reached the expanse of the table and rested her hand upon his own. "I declare, I would not say it has been a pleasurable experience for any of us, Mr. MacRegan, however, Deddy insisted we bring y'all back to health. Please consider yourself to be welcome in our home as well as our dinin' room." She knew it to be forward of her to touch this man, but it certainly was not something she had not done in the past, he simply was naught to have memory of it. Why—in her most remote imaginin's she would not have thought it possible that she, Abigail Simpson Sikes would have found it within her to treat this man's body and mind. Deddy had been *most insistent.*

Perhaps his hands would heal, the abrasions on his wrists and ankles from the manacles, yet the holes from the musket balls she had dug out, the lashings from the whips—they would endure for the remainder of his life. Her very hands had explored his body and probed into his flesh.

He sat before her, near healed of body. *His mind—Lord—do take this burden from me!* She knew she was doing this man a grave disservice. She would continue this charade for a time, as her deddy had requested; however, at some point, she would gather his papers from Deddy and give them to him. Again her musings strayed to Daniel, should he be in the home of a woman of the North, she would like to think he would be cared for as well.

His voice interrupted her considerations. "Tell me of your life…before, I apparently have no recall of what my life was like."

So…she was to be the source of his memories. Again she felt the tight grip of deception clutch at her heart.

"Do you have a husband? Did I live here?" his voice soft and inquiring.

Her thoughts ran before her, and she knew in time he would remember. He was not of the South and would surely ascertain that in the months to come. His speech, his mannerisms; it would soon become apparent they were most unlike those of the southerners, or would they be learned—as he had no other memories. In his delirium, she had heard him shout out the name of *Danny*, of *Mack*. Heard the soft moanings of longing and the name of a woman—*Elisabeth*…

She rose from the table; once more he made an attempt to rise. "No, please, y'all may remain seated." She paced the floor, felt the softness of the Persian carpet beneath her feet, the creaking of the age-old wood. Turning she looked at him. *Lord, be with me.* "I declare, Mista MacRegan, I have no sense of where to begin."

He listened in deep concentration to the Southern drawl of her words.

"Please, call me Michael, if that indeed is my name—I must admit it does not feel—*familiar*."

His words did not fall on deaf ears; she too thought it did not suit him. "Verra well, Mista Michael. No, y'all did not reside here. And no, I'm as yet unmarried, my beau—Daniel has yet to return." She hated the wistful sound in her voice.

"I am very sorry."

"Yes, well, be that as it may…" She heard the terseness within her voice.

He could feel the anger that permeated her words, yet instinctively he wished to know all he could of his surroundings. Perhaps he soon would be strong enough to venture out of doors. "Tell me of your life here, here on this lovely plantation."

It had been nearly five years, this damnable war! Five years of devastation, starvation, and fear! Five years since she had allowed her mind to wander to the years previous, years that they had led an idyllic life of comfort and fortune. She thought of the elaborate dinner parties, she could hear the sounds of music and laughter, the smells that had emanated from the kitchens and the gleam of sterling and crystal on the table in this very room. The clink of glasses raised in toasts to this person or endeavor. To the success of crops and children born. Of her engagement, yet again, Daniel's face flashed before her minds eye and she breathed deeply. His hair, blond and tousled, his evening dress immaculate. Should he not return she would remain a spinster; the thought caused her bitter grief.

She found herself to be pacing the carpeted floors. Looking through the tall paladin windows, she could see the drive before her, the lovely old magnolias that lined the broad entrance to Magnolia Plantation. She smiled and thought of the stylish carriages and the finely dressed gentlemen and ladies that had arrived at an evening soiree so many years ago. She could hear the laughter and the gaiety, could envision her fine clothing. She felt now her hand as it reached to touch the pearls that rested at her neck, touched her soft ash blonde locks, envisioned the once whiteness of her unblemished skin; knew it to be spotted now from hours in the fields.

She could smell the fields, hear the chatter of their slaves, the warmth of the summer air, the feel of it against her skin. Hot and damp. The softness of the lawn fabric of her clothing as it had clung to her body. Heard the fans that wafted throughout the house. Jonas, as he appeared in the dining room with his uniform of white, the whiteness of his gloved hands as he served the claret and scotch. The blackness of his skin, a most startling contrast.

"Miss Abigail? I have intruded..." He once more attempted to rise.

"No, yes...no, not in the least." Turning to look at him, she now saw how lovely his amber eyes were. The raw-boned features, the clothing that belonged to one of her brother's, hung loosely from his emaciated, large frame. His shoulders, broad and hunched forward over the table.

She began, her voice soft and wistful, "It was lovely. We raise cotton and tobacco, here on this plantation."

"And may I ask, why do you call them plantations?"

"Why, kind sir, that is what they are. But yes, sir, I understand, it is from the word *plant*—that is what we southerners do, we plant. Tobacco, cotton, some plantations grow rice and sugarcane, corn, wheat, oats, rye, flax, and hemp, often indigo. Although many a gentlemen find it more enticing to raise horses, swine, and cattle. We are—*we were...*" Her voice faltered… "An agrarian society, and I declare, we are quite paternalist compared to y'all up north. However, unlike y'all in the north we have had a rarity of immigrants over the years. Our very society is one of old and viable families with deep origins in southern culture. We Southerners have dissimilar music, religion, literature, and recreation, in particular our men folk. Politeness is the very epitome of our culture. Why, ah declare, it is said that a southern gentlemen shall remain polite until his dagger strikes your very heart. *Of course there is our speech.*

"Ah'm quite certain the south is far dissimilar from that of the northern peoples. I do believe it is due to the weather here. We are warm and hot, the humidity giving you a feelin' of comfort. The vegetation…the soft moss that hangs upon the old oak trees, the softness of the breeze, *why*—Mista Michael, I declare we can smell the sea from our very homes.

"We altogetha' love to entertain, to have grand parties, but y'all up there know nothing of the terrible work and toil of the gentlemen and the southern ladies, of the managin' of a great plantation. Why my deddy does work so verra' hard. Southern men are the very epitome of masculine chivalry and strive for honor and maintaining our verra' *old* cultcha'. But then y'all know thet' now don't ya."

Abigail found she was clasping her hands so tightly they pained her. She heard her words and knew she had betrayed her deddy...she had referred to *him* as a *Northerner!* She could not go on! Had he heard the words, had they registered in his battered mind? "Ah do apologize, Mr. MacRegan, ah seem to have lost my composure. Please, pardon me." She heard him rise from the table as she walked purposefully to the staircase.

He could feel her anger, sense her disdain for him, *for what he represented*. Never before had he experienced this feeling, but then he could remember very little. He felt vulnerable, exposed, unworthy of—of what? These emotions that arose in him felt unfamiliar. He supposed every man was worthy of love, appreciation—of understanding.

He sat once again and dropped his head over the table, his hands raised to his head. He had a profound desire to pull at his hair, to scream in agony and despair! To make this all go away. Who the hell was he anyway? How did he get here? *Why was he here?*

Minuet memories, flashes of images raged within his mind—as quickly as they came, he reached for them, finding them gone, vanished within the recesses of what? Fear? What man, what person is so terrified of what lurks in the depths of his subconscious that he cannot stand to view it. Was it his injuries or something more profound that caused such detrimental capacity? He found little solace in the fact that he was physically improved. For without a mind, without memories, what did life hold for him? He could discern from her conversation he was indeed a blue coat... The *Union soldier* they had rescued...the man who had caused them a *not entirely pleasurable experience...* in the words of Miss Abigail. What other reason had he given her to feel such loathing for him? He drew his hands down over his face. Not surprised to find them wet with tears. Truth be known, tears were welcome, for the pain he felt ran much deeper than those of tears. A pain that retched at his very heart, his very soul.

He looked about at the tattered remnants of this once elegant room, a room that echoed money, privilege, high society, and knew that he was the reason for its demise. *He and his kind.* He knew by her implication, by her inference to his being a *Northerner*. He looked at the shattered glazing of the windows, the bullets and musket balls lodged within the costly wall-coverings.

A chill ran through his very being. If he could just think! "Deddy said..." He heard her words. "Deddy said..."

So Allan Sikes knew the answer—*knew who he was!* Would that be a beginning? Would that indeed facilitate the return of his memories? Why didn't the man simply come forward with the information... or simply ask him to leave?

He pushed at the table to rise from the chair and found he was shaking—weak and spent. The sweat of the exertion lay upon his entire body. He was indeed unwell. Once again he seated himself in the chair.

Think! If he could just think—of what? What did he know? He felt certain *Michael* was not his name. Micah—Micah was a name that he felt he knew...was it his name? *That was not correct either.* Once again he ran his hands through his hair. He could feel the indentation in his skull. Had it pierced his brain? Would he never recover his memory? He looked at the scarring on his wrists. He could feel the pain in his leg and the ache that radiated up to his hip. He knew there to be welts across his back, his legs, they too, burned in pain. The memories of the prison were as a red-hot agony that surged through him, he had not lost *those* memories. The one thing he needed to forget... Those thoughts, bringing with them fear and terror unlike any he had known. He could smell the odor, the foulness of the air. See the men that wandered aimlessly. Unclothed, most of them, or with rags that clung to their emaciated bodies. He saw sticks of wood and a terror rose in him so profound that he would not be granted articulation. *He was afraid of sticks*...of a simple pole that crossed a yard...inane thoughts rushed at him. The perspiration rose within him to cover the surface of his body; all from the fear the strange fence brought.

Suddenly he could envision men that stood by his sides, those that had any semblance of tattered clothing—*these men had on blue coats*! Uniforms! He *was* a union soldier! The tears welled from deep within him and he was grateful for the memory. He felt the sobs and they shook his frail body—felt the heat of the tears as they spilled down his cheeks. *Thank you, Lord*... if he could remember *that*... He would remember the rest; it was fear that had locked his life so tightly in a small box...*a box he could and would open*!

He shook his head as if to clear it, wiping his nose with the back of his hand. It was something! A beginning! He was grateful!

He understood Miss Abigail's loathsome attitude towards him, her anger. He could never express his gratitude to these people. He needed to talk to Allan...but not now, not yet. He must be stronger. He must retrieve his memories, his abilities to think, to concentrate. Time...he must allow his body to heal. He trusted these people would allow him to stay here while he did so. The war was over; he had heard them say so repeatedly. He was not certain who had won...Lincoln?

Ah...another memory! Once again his body shook with tears of gratitude and joy! He *did* remember the *war*, over the secession of the Southern States, of slavery. A woman... *Elisabeth*... Who was she to him? He could see her. The most beautiful woman he could ever imagine! He had seen her in his dreams—her on a white horse, in a drawing room... *Who was she?* The grief that filled his heart, the joy that filled that same heart came unbidden with the images of this woman, yet, he could not place her.

"Mista! Mista, youse need ta eat. Come now."

He looked up to see the cook. *Oh, Lord, help me remember her name.* He felt the faint smile that crossed his face. He had remembered more in the last hour than he had in weeks—perhaps months! *Thank you, Lord!*

His mind wandered again as he rose to do the black woman's bidding... Was he a religious man? He noticed in his thoughts he often *gave thanks.*

Jonas

Mick stood from his position of kneeling at the huge columns that once supported what he thought to have been a fine gate. With the heel of his hand, he pushed the sweat that ran from his forehead, threating to fill his eyes. Not that that small gesture had a great influence, the sweat trickled behind his ears and down his back. It was six o'clock in the morning and devilishly hot. He was pulling weeds and thought perhaps he would hang the gate, *if* he was able find it in the plethora of items Allan had stored in the barn.

He had rehung doors within the house, patching bayonet holes and bullet holes, had replaced flooring that had been ripped up in an attempt to find hidden gold or silver—or men—*Union men*! Confederate soldiers had randomly searched the southern plantations—for food, gold, anything that would sustain their fight. They looked for Union soldiers that the owners would take pity on, giving them safe harbor. To find a Union man within the home of Southern gentry was reason enough to have the Confederates kill you, your children, your slaves, and burn your house. It was treason! Pure and simple!

Miss Abigail had shooed him from the house, —exclaiming, "It ta' be quite disquieting to have y'all lurkin' "bout. With the infernal squabblin' of the youngster's, I surely do not require y'all's presence interferin' with my sense of peacefulness. It is up to myself to be polishin' silver and makin' an attempt ta' restore what all *can* be restored ta' it's former glory. Y'all surely done accomplished a mighty fine amount of work. Y'all go now, an' take some sunshine an' rest a bit, Michael MacRegan!"

He found rest was not something he was proficient at. He had looked at the grand entrance to the plantation. A road that was not unlike those in France... *How the hell did he know that? Had he been to France?* Visions of marketplaces and a river...not like the Stones River but wide and very deep, seemed to dance through his mind, leaving him with neither a clear memory of the image, or from whence it had arisen.

The heat of the sun seared his back, the scares of the leaded whips stung like hell. They had healed and then festered, only to repeat the cycle. Etched deeply within the flesh of his back, they had been penetrating and deep. As they had healed, the wounds had left great welts that crisscrossed his back in intricate patterns. *Perhaps he should put a shirt on, yet he was nearly finished here.* His leg and his shoulder pained him, though should you consider the many wounds he had suffered, his physical body was in fine fashion. The near-mortal wound lay within his mind. He shook his head, and swallowed. *This was not where he belonged. This was not who he was. Was he a traitor to these fine people?* He did not know... He could not recall.

He took a deep breath and continued pulling up the weeds. He had started at the stairway of the once grand mansion and progressed the half mile or so to the pillars at the end of the long entrance to the plantation, in truth, it continued for nearly two miles along the river. Enormous trees with small long, lace like leaves glistened in the early morning sunlight. The breeze that drifted off the river was cool and subtle. He stood to watch the vibrant crimson cardinals as they flitted from one branch to another of honey suckle that grew wild and dense, its fragrance floating softly, filling the humid air with the scent of a woman. He smiled. *The scent of a woman.* What did that mean to him? His mind wandered to the dream he had had last night... The woman of implausible beauty ran naked through the woods. The sound of her laughter...the ebony of her hair shone as it fell down her back, floating with each step she had taken, her bare feet skittering through the copse of trees. He was behind her, stark naked, stalking her, without malice; *they were playing.* She had stopped and turned toward him, her breasts heaving, their fullness, the tautness of her nipples, the small ribcage, the slender waist. The brush hiding her mound of Venus, the coal black bush that covered it, barely visible. He had felt his heart swell in love and anticipation; he had looked to see her face. This was *her*, this was the woman that came to him in his dreams. Her face, unclear, as she turned, laughed and ran on. Suddenly he had awakened. Unreserved anguish swept through him, he had clasped his hand over his mouth to keep from crying out. Try as he might he could not go back to sleep...sleep; that was where *she* was. He wanted desperately to go there to be with her...to sleep, to dream.

There were many other visions, other dreams, that held such fear, such abject terror—terror that coursed throughout his body, terror that left him soaked in cold sweat, terror that lived on through the next days. It was then he fought *not to sleep.* Visions of men...visions of *sticks*—of naked men. Starving men. Emaciated men, open wounds that covered the entirety of their bodies. In one such dream he had been eating bugs and worms. Another, more fearful, was the sound of the whip as it cracked across his body... on those nights he would awaken to his own screams of fear. Often Abigail, Lila or Magnolia would appear, shushing him... trying to comfort him...of late they came less frequently, they had all agreed—*it did no good.* He had no memory of where these events had transpired or who had inflicted them, worse by far—he could not confront what was visceral—what was real! Hopeful his mind would heal...hope that lay with the woman in his dreams, the *presence of her* within those dreams drove him to fight!

"It lookin' mighty fine, Mista Mick." He heard the voice of Allan's Nigra, Jonas. He could feel the footsteps of the big black man pulsating from the earth as he came more closely. Standing, he reached out to shake Jonas' hand. "Fine morning, Jonas, I should be in the fields."

"No, siree' Massa' Allan, he done say you not ta work in them fields til' ya on the mend! This be lookin' fine, Mista Mick, sure 'nough do!"

"I thought I would go, look in the barn for the gate and put it back up."

"'Ain't no gate, Mista Mick. Ain't no gate. They done used all them gates in the south fer bullets an' cannonballs. Done run out of thet—just like the food stuff."

Mick looked at the big man. They were the same size—the two of them. Both lean and worn, both broad of shoulder, with thick muscles that rippled across their backs and torsos, the sheen of sweat upon their bodies gave them the appearance of lustrous jewels, one the color of onyx, the other of burnished gold. The thighs of the black man gigantic, his pants stretched tightly across them, he, like *Mick* had ripped them off below the knees, the heat so oppressive as to make clothing optional.

"How are the crops, Jonas?" From his vantage point, he could see nothing but fields of cotton, small white clouds, abundantly adhering to plants of emerald green.

"Oh, they be fine. Not like afore, but then I don't guess they be no one wantin' ta buy 'em anyways. Them French and Englis' done quit on the south."

"Jonas, my God...how the hell did all this happen? Can you tell me some of it? I have so many questions... Were you there? Where did I come from, how did I get here? Do you know my name? Christ, man, I need to know...and why are you here? Aren't you free now?"

"Was always free, Mista Mick... This here's my home...my chillun' is here, my woman's here...Massa' Allan the bestest friend I done got...This is home, Mista. Mick. Thet's whys I here. Massa' Allan, he done got old...the war...it done ruin't ever thin'... Miss

Lydia gone... Them boys gone. Massa' Allan he don't know if they dead 'er not...could be buried out there in some dirt with no name...no...I's not gonna leave 'im..."

He could feel the care and loyalty within Jonas' words. These people were wise beyond...wiser than the men that had written the books that he had read in Allan's sizeable library. He thought of Bertha's words to him just this morning. "I's don' knows yus name, Mista Mick...but iffna' I was you, I'd be a thinkin' not so much on who I was, but 'whose' I was...it'd be heppin' more." She had turned, picked up the cornbread, and left the dining room. Profound words they were. He daresay, she was more than likely right. He hadn't thought of that—of asking for help from the Father. He had only struggled to help himself, that and badgered those around him to answer the many questions that proliferated his thoughts. They were all most likely tired of his asking those same questions, for it came out of his mouth at least weekly, try as he might to stifle it. He knew he was not *Michael MacRegan*; it simply provided him with no anchor, no feeling of familiarity. Wouldn't he be fair and ruddy, perhaps redheaded, or was Michael MacRegan a black Irishman? He took a long deep breath and rubbed his sweat soaked head. "Jonas, do you know who found me?"

"I's did. I's carried youse all the way from thet river over yonder."

"You did! Do you know how I got there, when I got there?"

"No, sir, don't rightly know. I be thinkin' yu be dead for I got y'all ta thet there barn. Iffin' it not fer Magnolia youse be dead fer sure."

"Jonas, do you know my *real name*? Would you tell me? *Mick, Michael, MacRegan*—it...it just doesn't feel right. If I could just remember *something*, anything, I believe it would improve my health substantially... I read books in Allan's, *Mr.* Allan's library and I know who some of those people are...I've read those books. I have seen that country...*I know I have!* Please, if you know my name..."

"Massa' Allan, he'd…" Jonas looked into the eyes of the man that had been dumped from the train, or *perhaps a wagon*, thought of his emaciated body, this man whose bones shone through his beaten, oozing flesh. His hair long and matted—filled with lice, the massive dent in his head.

"Trust me. Jonas, have I given you any reason to mistrust me? I simply believe that if I knew *my name* the rest would come in time." He watched as Jonas ran his great black toe around the pea size golden stones of the drive. "Massa' Allan…"

"Please, I beg of you, man."

"Youse' had on an' ole blue…the Massa', I's think he got's youse papers." He felt the Lord woulda wanted him ta tell this man. "Mista Mick…iff'n the Massa' fin' out, he be thinkin' I not be his best nigger…an I is." Jonas watched the man, not knowing what to do for him.

His body shook from the depth of his emotion; he felt the dirge of tears come and turned his face from Jonas.

"Come up now, Mista Mick. Git ahol' yerself. Miss Abigail she done watch fer everthin'. It don't change nothin'. Youse gotta promise, Mista Mick, youse gotta promise."

Mick rose, trying desperately to control his emotions. It was a small bit of information in truth, but it was a beginning! "Jonas, do you know how long I've been here?"

"I's don't rightly know, Mista Mick, them buttercups they be right to poppin'."

"Buttercups? What in the devil are buttercups?" It was a beginning. Still tears traced his face, as he embraced Jonas. "Jonas, are you able to read?"

"I's kin sure 'nough. Massa', he done teach all us niggers ta read and write some…but it not be a thin' to say of. Against ta law to teach us niggers…most folks think we don't got ta same hed'."

Pulling away from Jonas, *Mick* began to laugh, joy suffused him.

"Wha' y'all laughin' at? It not a bit funny!"

"It's joy, Jonas, unmitigated Joy! Joy for you, for Bertha! She told me to look to the Lord! It's Bertha and the Lord! I'll not breathe a word, I promise! If ever you need anything! Anything I can do for you—I will always be in your debt. *Always.* Thank you, Jonas! Thank you!"

"Yes, sir, Mista Mick, yes, sir. I's got ta git back ta them fields. Youse 'member, Mista Mick, youse 'member, I's never say'd a thin'."

Mick reached out and took the man's hand in both of his own, pumping it up and down. "I will never betray you—never!"

Diagnoses

Dr. Elam Coyle stood before the man known to the Sikes' family as Michael MacRegan, *Mick* he preferred to be addressed. Elam Coyle was clothed in a three-piece gray-stripped suit, a black silk tie hugged his neck beneath the white starched rounded collar, with pince-nez glasses perched upon a straight patrician nose. His eyes glittered a clear blue, showing humor and intelligence, his hair and beard were a silvery white. In this unbearable heat, not a drop of sweat could be seen on his brow. He held his thumbs tucked into the pockets of the vest he wore; Mick could see the sparkle of the gold watch fob and chain.

Mick was seated in the library of Allan Sikes. Allan, as well as Jonas, stood at the far side of the room, the wall behind them held shelf upon shelf of leather-bound books, volumes of geography, poetry, architecture, horticulture, and the works of great writers. The ceiling fan rotated above them in whispers of squeaking gists.

Jonas stood tall and muscular, his great black forearms crossed in front of his massive chest. Allan Sikes, the master of the plantation stood stoic, cigar held in his hand, the ash falling on the worn Persian carpet, the smoke curling in aromatic wisps. The men waited patiently while the doctor conducted his examination.

"Y'all look to be a fine specimen, though a might boney. That bullet hole in yur arm an' leg healed agreeably…fine extraction I might add. Now, those wounds on your backside…" The doctor swallowed hard and sighed, carefully running his hand over the welted scar tissue of Mick's back, the lashing wounds extending well down his buttocks, *musta done this with the man buck naked*. The doctor's mind having great difficulty absorbing the atrocities men imposed upon one another. *The pain that had been endured during such barbarism*...he could only imagine. He could see and feel the lead ball marks that had been tied to the lashings of leather that had been used to whip this man. "They're a might deep, most likely to fester from time to time...I figure they give y'all some discomfiture." He cleared his throat and rubbed at his chin whiskers, "Are your private parts workin', did they castrate ya, son? Looks to me as if they whipped y'all the... Stand up, Mista MacRegan, pull down your drawers."

Mick did as he was asked, he knew full well that both Jonas and Allan had seen what he was about to reveal to Dr. Coyle, he, himself had felt the wounds, the pus that had run from them. He could readily envision what the doctor would find.

Dr. Elam Coyle looked at the wounds that wrapped around this once male perfection, he examined the wounds that extended often to the areas around his ankles. He'd seen slaves whipped to this extent; *they had been dead*. How this man had survived such brutality he would never know. Without looking up from his examination he queried Allan Sikes, "How long he been here with y'all, Allan?"

Allan thought for a moment and looked at Jonas for clarification... "Think it was April, not quite certain...'bout six months time." He thought of the time that had transpired during which he had known nothing of the man's presence in the barn whilst Magnolia had nursed him. "I declare, I think that ta be 'bout right."

"It pain ya some, son, does it?"

Mick could sense the doctors concern in his voice, in his touch. He nodded his head. "On occasion, though the pain seems to lessen each day."

Dr. Coyle stood back and looked at Mick, desperate for control of his emotions. "Yes, well now, y'all get dressed. Now, it is only my own opinion—but sunlight is good to heal damn near anything—vitamin D they're declarin' it to be. Mind now, like all good things, tis to be taken in small doses, also said to be good for what ails you." He chuckled. "Thet bullet that entered your leg. Well, I suppose it might have chipped a bone...y'all might continue with that limp for a bit, but given your apparent physical endurance and appearance, y'all's age—that too, perhaps will heal. Now then, as far as your memory...well, I reason Allan here is more than willing to help you with that...aren't ya now, Allan?"

Allan coughed and inhaled deeply of his cigar. "Well, yes, indeed, if'n y'all think it be proper and no harm come ta my family."

"The war is over, Allan! Damn'it! They killt' Lincoln...let this be done! We Southerners must get on with our lives, and I might add, judgment and bitterness will cause more damage to y'all's health then them there bullets! Now then, son, I figure—as far as your memory, I think, now I have no way of bein' certain, y'all understand?"

Mick looked at him, he felt the man to be a fine man doing the very best he could under the circumstances. He buckled his belt and nodded his head. "Yes, sir, I understand. Any help you can afford me, any information as to how to deal with this——with this uncertainty, —would be very much appreciated— . Allan, Jonas, I am beholden to both of you and your women, Miss Abigail, Miss Lila, Miss Magnolia, and Bertha too. Please understand, I know whatever you did, you did to save your family."

"So now, Allan, perchance we can have your word—you shall indeed provide this man with whatever possession's he had with him upon his arrival, as well, details concerning where and when y'all found him?"

"Yes, of course, Elam...we meant no harm!"

"Course not, war is hell on earth, but we must get on with the task of livin' now mustn't we."

Mick watched Allan run his hands through the sparseness of his graying, sweating hair, watched Jonas lay his great hand upon the shoulder of what was once his master, now his friend and employer.

"Now then, with that settled, I believe you to be suffering from retrograde amnesia, that's as I would term it. I find no bullet holes, only a depression of the skull. Do you recall when this event occurred?"

"No, no…"

"Do you recollect anything at all of your past—before your arrival here?"

"No, but I have vivid dreams and a sense of…of that… I am not the person they say I am." Mick looked at Allan and Jonas apologetically.

"Any vomiting, hallucinations, nausea?"

"I do vomit, but it is never accompanied by nausea, and I do find that strange."

"Isn't strange atol'. What *can* you remember?"

"Strange things…I am able to speak several languages and can recall poetry."

"Do you have headaches, vision problems, convulsions?"

"Headaches, terrible headaches."

"Yes, yes…well, I believe, and we can clearly see y'all been beat near ta death, I believe it's the hippocampus, the left frontal hemisphere. Y'all see…that affects long-term memory. It's the temporal lobe, above your left ear. An' the symptom's y'all tellin' me of, it seems clear to me that a great blow to the head or likely many blows, have created this."

Mick looked at the shorter man, this kind man that was so affected by the inhumane treatment he had been subjected to. "Will I heal, will I be able to remember?"

"Well, I can't say for certain. I believe your memory will return in time. As we, us doctors, think the part of your brain that has language is located in an extremely small space under, and within the temporal lobe. If you can speak several languages, then I would interpret that to mean it's but bruised and swollen yet.

"We know so little about the brain. There was some exploration into ancient sites around France that revealed hundreds of skulls with the tell-tale signs of trepanation. Skulls discovered in the Cavern de l'Homme-Mort, the sepulchral grottoes of Baye and in the dolmen of Lozère, that all date back to the Neolithic era some four to five thousand years ago. If I recollect proper, there was one burial site in France where 120 prehistoric skulls were found, forty of which had had trepanation performed."

"I had heard that."

"You know what that means?" Utter shock lay in his voice, with wide clear eyes he looked at the man before him.

"Yes! Yes, I do…" Surprise was in Mick's voice as well.

"Tell them," the doctor said, his head stirring in the direction of Allan and Jonas.

"Why, why, it is the boring of a hole in the skull much like the Egyptians…"

The room stilled—silence filled it. Only the gentle whirring of the fan could be heard.

The doctor looked at Mick quizzically… "You can remember hearin' that?"

Still as shocked as the doctor, Mick nearly stammered… "Yes, yes, I attended University in Paris, France." His body shook—*how could this be?* "How is that possible—that I am able to remember such details randomly?"

"Well, son." He looked at the silver in the jet black hair of this handsome man and chuckled. "Well, sir, I would say you have had severe blows to the head, perhaps several, that and great, might I say, *numerous* emotional trauma's *you do not wish* to remember. *Perhaps you are ashamed to remember…*"

Mick started to speak…

Elam Coyle raised his hand to silence him. "I know, shame is not something a man cares to admit, but the war…and I suspect a prisoner of that war—had many indecencies *that were put upon him*, despicable acts performed *to* him…shame and fear is a most powerful weapon, particularly in the case of proud and honorable men. Strong, capable men, men that are honorable enough to go to war… Perhaps you are hiding from the ones you love with your inability to remember. War, *this war*, has had profound effects on the lives of everyone in the country, not simply its soldiers. However, in light of the examination, I would say, given enough time you shall regain your memory and your identity. And with courage, Allan here could be of some help.

"Bring those dreams of yours to the forefront, examine them—push them forward an' backward within your mind and your emotions. Use that same courage that got y'all in this damnable mess. Pull it from the depths of your bowels—or chose to simply forget the past and move onward." Dr. Coyle looked at his patient. "However, I do declare, from what y'all have relayed to me, you shall do yourself a grave injustice should you chose the latter.

"In the meantime…do not become overly heated, work with caution, query every circumference within your mind, and above all, rest. I believe you shall heal. I would say—by winter, y'all shall have attained a degree of the health y'all obviously, previously enjoyed."

Mick reached out to grasp the man's hand, fighting a losing battle against the emotions that welled within him. "I cannot tell you how grateful I am for this, this insight! Thank you! Thank you! I will never be able to repay you… Thank you!" Mick clasped the doctors' arms, to pull him to him, to embrace him.

Elam Coyle chuckled. "No need, no need. I'm dreadful sorry for what you have suffered and judging by your speech I expect it was at the hands of those tryin' to protect our Southern culture… I am sorry for that sir. We did what we must, each of us… It shall never transpire again. I shall leave you now. Allan, I believe you have some papers that belong to this man."

"Yes. Yes." Allan looked at Jonas.

Mick strongly suspected Jonas had had a great deal to do with the doctor having been called upon, as well as the papers Allan Sikes was about to provide him. He found his hand literally to be shaking, with perspiration forming on the entirety of his body. Papers…what information did they hold. Could he bear the knowing…did they have anything at all to do with his dreams… with his nightmares? *Get ahold of yourself, man…* He heard Allan's voice.

"Yes, of course, it is just…I must say *a relief*, well y'all most certainly are not from the south. We kin' tell by y'all's discourse."

Mick looked carefully at Allan, he was visibly trembling. "Yes, my speech," through tear-filled eyes, Mick smiled.

"Believe it or not, it is said we speak the King's English down here in the south, but you sir, use no conjunctions—ain't heard *ain't or y'all* come out of yer mouth, not oncet." The doctor laughed a great belly laugh, his own speech now filled with that of the Deep South.

Mick rose and shook hands with the man. "I wish to thank you once again." He looked into the twinkling blue eyes and the white-whiskered face of the jovial doctor.

"'Come get me Jonas should y'all be in need. He'll come around."

Mick realized he was holding his breath; his hands were trembling as he watched Allan go to his desk drawer and unlock it. Suddenly he was aware that Jonas had left the room.

"Would y'all be havin' some whisky now?"

"Yes, thank you, I believe this calls for a celebration of sorts. You have been most kind and I shall never be able to repay you, Allan."

"Hell's fire, tweren't me that had the stones to do such as thet'. Twer' Magnolia, Lila an Jonas, them Negras have more courage then most white folks. Most o' them's had a hard, hard way."

Mick watched as the golden liquid spilled into the crystal tumblers, watched as Allan lifted the documents from beneath a false bottom in the drawer of his desk. He reached for the amber liquid and raised his glass to Allan. "To you, sir. Thank you…"

Allan pursed his lips hard together…looking at the papers with new eyes. The danger now over… *He hoped like hell that was true…* "Ah well, if it ain't over—the war I mean ta say, *I do have a friend* in the north…General James Martin Prescott, that's y'all's real name."

He didn't know why; he did not expect Allan to say those words, and he certainly didn't expect to have them mean anything to him. And yet—and yet, he wanted to fall on his knees in gratitude, to cry, to shout for joy, and laugh! *That was his name. He knew now, he felt the rightness of it within his very bones.*

Allan looked at the emotions that rose and fell over the face of this man he had come to call his friend; suddenly he was ashamed of having not had the courage to give him his rightful due. "Jim, do they call you?"

"No…no. Jamie or James or James Martin." He heard the voice of a woman in his head…*Jamie—James Martin…his mother, his…his wife?*

"Sorry…Mick…James…but well, I had Jonas burn the clothes y'all was wearin'."

"No. No, Massa'. I done got 'em…right here."

Allan looked at Jonas.

"Sorry, Massa…just figered, it be a sorrowful thing fer a man ta not be knowin' his rightful place in this world."

"No. No, Jonas y'all did the right thing."

Jamie looked at the Union Army uniform…what was left of it, *filthy, foul, frayed, and worn.* "Thank you, Jonas…thank you!"

"Mista James, there be some papers sewn tiny like—in here." Jonas opened the trousers and Jamie felt the waistband…far too thick—far too lumpy… He reached for the foul clothing and quite suddenly found he must sit down. Emotions raced through him and he felt the tears well in his eyes.

"We be leavin' y'all now… Take yer time…Bertha'll bring ya a bite ta eat."

Jamie could not even raise his head. Sensations filled him to overflowing—excitement, fear, *hope*; for the first time since he could remember he felt *hope*! He wished like hell it was fear and shame as Elam Coyle had said… *Fear and shame* perhaps he could overcome… *Could he?* Would he find within these pages, within the waistband of his trousers… *Were they even his trousers…* something that would give him the courage to…*to fight*! Yes, he needed to find that courage within him to fight; just as the doctor had said.

He looked at his enlistment documents; worn and stained with every thing from blood to coffee. His hand trembled as he unfolded the page, grateful for the thickness of the document. A document intended to survive the trials and tribulations of war…but for five long years? His heart skipped a beat, then thudded within his great chest, *General James Martin Prescott… two children.* He saw her name—*wife: Elisabeth…Montana Territory…volunteer…* The sobs welled from so deep within him he feared they could be heard throughout the house.

He dropped his head and whispered through heart-rending sobs. *"Father, thank you!"*

James Martin Prescott

Without the benevolence of this fine family he would not exist, of that he was certain. Time stood still as he struggled to remove the minuet stitches that encased the lump within the waistband of his tattered trousers; what would he find? Anxiety tugged at his heart.

The aromatic fragrance of gardenias wafted through the open windows, the scent lifted upon the hot, humid breeze and he felt the sweat upon his brow. Was it the heat or fear? Fear, his constant companion, leaving him only during times of toil, hours spent in the fields with the Negroes, time spent in the company of the horses, of long hours of labor to repair the devastation to Allan Sikes's plantation. In truth he felt at home here, here within the quiet gentleness of the southern culture. Or was it mere safety he felt.

He hesitated as the last of the stiches revealed the much sought after paper. Paper folded in minuscule squares. He felt the bile rise within him, the panic that engulfed him. *Would it be, could it be...* He willed his fingers to proceed. With hands that trembled at the touch, he removed the document, at first befuddled by the script. *French*...the letter was written in French.

He swallowed hard and fought for control over the shaking of his hands least he tear the aged paper. Fear, once more raised its head. *Would the missive belong to him?* What if these were not his trousers? They held a rope, not a belt, or buckle, but only that of frayed, filthy hemp. Trousers once the color of the Union blue, nearly indiscernible by the filth and foul odor. *Lord...please...* He felt the sweat upon his palms and the racing of his heart. Could he do this, did he wish to know what lie within these words. *Could he read French?*

His mind raged with uncertainty and dread. He lay the trousers on the threadbare carpet and rose to pour himself a whisky. Fire shot down his throat and he felt the burn as it rested dramatically within his gut. He ran his hands through the dark, thick tresses of his hair and paced the floor, his breathing rapid and halting. Again he sat...the paper now held within his hands...the folds so tight he feared they would tear upon his touch.

Would this letter provide him with his person, his ambitions, would it restore his sense of self, of his individuality, all those characteristics that made a man an individual. All those minuet innuendos of life, of growth, of a capacity to love and be loved... *Was he prepared to acknowledge those things—to embrace them?*

He held the battered parchment gently; he paced the floor yet again. His mind racing through the events of the last several hours; of the examination, of the information they had relayed to him concerning the most defiled of all prisons. *A prisoner* of the war camp they called *Andersonville.* Of the men the doctor had seen, of the news that had traveled from the South and from the North, of the cruelty and the disease, of the beatings and starvation.

Dr. Elam Coyle had said, "It be more than a bit obvious ta me that y'all from Andersonville. It's said, they merely opened the gates of the prison when Lee had surrendered...some thirty thousand men ran fer trains an' wagons, some lingered inside ta die, their minds bein' so befuddled they knew not to run, didn't understand that they were free. One such prison in the north said ta be as bad...you must give yerself credit for survivin' such as that, it took great courage, of that ya kin' be certain. Courage an' the memory of somthin' more powerful ta survive fer, now don't y'all think...'"

Jonas had said, "I's done found y'all 'sides the river. Me be thinkin' youse be dead, fer sure... Miss Magnolia, she ... 'y'all dinn't weigh but thet' of a chil'—only be bones. Y'all's head bashed in. 'Youse skin stretched tight "cross them big bones of yeran'...God awful sores, blood an' pus...y'all smelled real bad!" The sound of Jonas's voice rang in his ears.

He looked at the remainder of his uniform, now certain it was his... He could feel the sense of love within the fragility of the letter he held... Was there perhaps another letter sewn within the folds and linings? Would that be more than he was worthy? He sat down and cautiously opened the pages—three front and back, the ink smeared in places, the words often indiscernible at a glance, for the paper had disappeared. His hands shook, his eyes blurred from tears that threatened to fall, he looked up at the ceiling; willing God, *begging God* to give him strength and courage.

1864, The month indiscernible...

L'amour de ma vie, la raison de mon existence, Pour mon mari, Jamie,

I write this in French for then you shall always know it is me who writes. I write as minuet as is afforded me, for I have so very much to inform you. My heart gives me great pain Jamie my love, truly physical pain, of anguish, of joy, of grief and hope; a fullness that causes' me to contemplate my body is not sufficient to shelter it. I believe it to be love Jamie, unconditional love that causes this pain, this joy. This, which we all long for, this, which the Lord has given to both of us. Are we not blessed!

Jamie my love, we are to have another child, once again you have left me with the gift of a child. Petra thinks I shall deliver in some seven months time...I know you wish for a boy, I shall be happy to have a healthy child. My health is exemplary; you are not to be concerned. Ellie is growing, as is Jesse, both are wonderfully intelligent. Jesse is talking now...much like her mother—(you shall laugh) it is non-stop chatter causing me to laugh. Of course they are beautiful children. Jesse is kind and considerate and quite effusive, Ellie remains quiet and contemplative, even through the chatter.

Oh Jamie, I miss you so very much, so much I am often angry with you—of course I then recall those are the very things I so deeply fell in love with as a very young girl—your courage, your patriotism, your sense of adventure.

I dream of you and awake to find the bed cold and empty beside me. I dream of illicit things my darling...most lascivious games of play and lovemaking.

As I ride line in the mornings I long for your presence beside me. To speak of the life that rises and falls, to view the splendor of the mountains and the colors that unfurl as the sun rises in the east. Danny misses you, he searches for you with his eyes and perks his ears at the sound of someone coming...like myself; he awaits your return.

The grains and grasses grow well this year, the weather having been conducive to warrant a tremendous crop. I have, as you have instructed me—recorded all those things you find so necessary; the numbers on the new cattle; those that are from the King ranch, the Santa Gertrudis and our own white face and those that have interbred. The mustangs become more plentiful each day and Charlie continues to be of great and infinite assistance.

With sadness I must inform you that my Jeremiah was killed at the battle of Franklin in Tennessee...did I already tell you of that? It has nearly broken my heart, were it not for you and the children...Jamie. stay safe, my darling, know that I love you more than life itself, that I long for the devastation this war has caused to be done with! To have you home with me, with our daughters! I long to hear the sound of your voice, to feel the strength of your arms as they hold me, to feel the oneness of our souls, to have conversations that need not be finished—as we think as one. I miss the touch of your hand on my face and the longing I see in your eyes, the love, the lust, the laughter. I miss the fragrance of you, the dreams and the enthusiasm that is you! I miss our joining; our lovemaking. My heart breaks with passion and loneliness Jamie. Knowing I will see you again is the only reason for my survival.

I have returned...I found I must stop and control my emotions, for there are some things I must be advised of...do you wish me to make arrangements for the railroad persons to purchase the cattle and what of the transportation? I think they could be herded to the site down the Western Trail, over the Powder River to Fort Laramie, with the help of but three hired hands. The idea is mine, but I have consulted with Joseph and Charlie, and they concur that it should be accomplished by the end of summer? What are your wishes? As to your question in your letter of last, I have very able hands, and Charlie is very good at handling them...I laugh as he says, "they are an ornery lot, bad trouble!"

Because of the war, there are ever more persons coming west, although none have settled near us as yet. I believe they are traveling to the west coast.

What is taking place within the war now? Where are you? Are you well? Do you have food to eat, water to drink? I read the papers, though they are old by the time they reach us here and I shudder with fear for your safety. Knowing how courageous and capable you are is the only reason I remain with the ability to rest—to let go of the fear. Sally Susanne has been a tremendous comfort as well as Ma and Ilene. Joseph, Mack and Charlie have been here near daily to inquire as to my well being, as well as to help with the ranch. Jamie you have achieved that which you set out to achieve...for you have land as far as the eye can see. Now my darling, I beseech you, come home to us.

Write as soon and as often as is afforded...I wait quite impatiently for your letters and your poetry...I shall not become maudlin—just please know how very much you are a part of me; and Survive! James Martin! Survive! Come home to us, I beg you!

Your loving wife,
Elisabeth Parthena Prescott

He had read the letter repeatedly, placing it on the table and once more reaching out to read it yet again. He had torn apart the remainder of his uniform, finding fragments of folded illegible letters—all with the name *Elisabeth* at the end of them. He could not identify his emotions other than that of great joy, grief and sadness. He felt the swelling of his chest as the sorrow became unbearable. Did this man she so ardently loved still exist in him, could he find the strength to go to her, to love her, to remember her. His body shook with the tremendous depth of his desolation, racked with his sobs. Where would he begin? Certainly this was the woman in his dreams, there, in his dreams, he had known that love as well, he must bring those dreams to the forefront of his mind!

Should he have to endure the brutality of prison, of disgrace, it seemed but a small price to pay.

He had failed as a man, as a soldier and more importantly—as a husband, as a father. The dreams, the *dreams* were but *memories* that had surfaced within his defenseless, sleeping mind, his heart crying out for love and acceptance. He knew them now for what they were—*truth*. Shame, disgrace, his lack of courage evident; exposed before these honorable men…even that of Allan Sikes. He felt vulnerable and embarrassed, the elation of having discovered his name, his history of sorts, his own distinctiveness, having departed rapidly. Rather than joy and jubilation he was now left with shamefulness that was his to own, *to acknowledge as belonging to him*. Would he have chosen this, would he have sought after his identity should he have known that it came with *unendurable humiliation*?

Nausea erupted within him, neither from sickness nor injuries, but from the worthlessness of his being, a soil upon his God, his own very nature. Others had risen above this. He…he found it unbearable to accept, his lack of courage, his inability to cope.

He was but the remnant of a man of courage and adventure, of the man this woman thought him to be. A man that had traveled to Europe and the Arab nation's rose in him, contrasting, judging him in contradiction of the man that sat huddled within the darkness of Allan Sikes's barn. A man that trembled in fear and loathing of the emotions he felt—for the vileness of his own countenance rose with profundity within his very soul. He must remember! He must relive each and every moment, each and every blow—each and every demeaning punishment that had befallen him. He must come to terms with his fear and find departure from this—this despicable weakness that had become a part of *who* he was.

Shame, the doctor had said, *shame*, as if he were found naked in the Garden of Eden. Shame that was so intense he could not face his God—his loved ones.

Of all the emotions that rampaged through him, shame was more powerful than fear. Perhaps it was the precursor of fear—of doubt and helplessness. *Shame* that brought him to his knees, *shame* that allowed him to sit within the corner with the rats and creeping things in the darkness—to hide from his God, to hide from those who professed to love him. Broken by Satan, or the archangel... Strange, he could remember passages within the bible yet...

No! He *could* remember all of it! He must remember! He must acknowledge *who he had become!* They had stripped him; they had broken him—with what? Pain, starvation, humiliation—were these reasons enough to give up his identity, his ego, his family?

"Oh, God!" Jamie heard the cry of his own words as they echoed throughout the darkness of the barn. Cries of terror and remorse—of hopelessness and despair.

If those that loved him could see *who* he truly was—would they love him? There was, in his estimation nothing about him to love. He was a broken man, a man without honor—a shell of *whom* the Lord had given him. Emptiness pervaded him. Was his soul intact? *Lord* is it? Fear enfolded him as he asked, for what would the reply be? Could he hear the Lord? Where was his humility before the God he had so treasured...only fear surfaced—the void within his visage looming large and infinite, and yet without consideration.

Where would he begin? Where would one be instructed? Who would instruct him to place the pieces of his memory into the light of day, to bring them out of the depths of darkness and cruelty?

"Forgiveness." The word rose in his mind and he grasped at it. "*Forgiveness—begin by forgiving those who have trespassed against you. Forgive yourself for your inequities for you are but a man...*"

He swallowed hard, the lump in his throat was of enormous proportions; as though he must swallow his pride...was pride what had placed him here, here in this desolate place within his mind. *Courage.* The word came...from what source? *He knew it to be his God*...for what other person could it be? These were not his thoughts. He had not the inclination for forgiveness, nor the valor to go forward with his healing. At this moment, it appeared an insurmountable task he was ill equipped to embark upon. Again he heard the voice. *Trust—prayer...as in the beginning you were without sin.* Did he even understand the meaning of these mere words...was he a religious man? He knew he was a man of faith. Memories of words and poetry rose from his heart; *God is all around me, Elisabeth, I feel Him in the sounds of the earth...the gentle breeze on the air, the birds of the sky.*

> Man is imbued with pride...the precursor of all other emotions...
> A still small voice spake unto me,
> Thou art so full of misery,
> Were not it better not to be?

He found he could recite the entirety of the poem "The Two Voices" by Alfred Lord Tennyson.

As if external from his body, reliving a memory of a long ago time, in his mind's eye, he saw her again, the young exquisite woman, as she knelt before the altar, at the iconostasis to receive communion. There was no ring on her finger and he could sense that it was *her* family to his right. He stood in a cathedral of ornate gothic beauty; he watched as she rose and turned, the lace veil that covered her head did nothing to hide the luxuriant tresses of onyx. Her eyes lifted to meet his own, eyes of the greatest beauty he had ever seen, green with the light of the world in them, the light of love…

Revelation

Jamie had not been granted the relief of sleep. Nights had been a tortuous time. Toil and long hours in the fields gave him no respite from the soulless journey he had begun.

Had it been hours—minutes? Time seemed to have stood still in the pain, anguish, and darkness of the barn, his soul exposed before his Maker, his physical and psychological expression of humanity having left. There appeared no recourse but to die—or to surrender—a surreal feeling seemed to transfix the atmosphere about and within him. How long had it been since last he had felt that profound surrender—*surrender to his Maker, to his God?*

The feeling of tightness in his chest the emptiness that had left a blackness in his heart and on his soul, had been replaced with a sensation, a manifestation of love, of...yes...of forgiveness, of transparency. Emotions rose in him of praise, of thanks, of profound peace. The tears shed now were tears of joy, of transgressions not taken, of forgiveness for things he had *not* done. He felt the weight as it lifted from his heart, from his mind, from his physical body.

Words came to him, words *given to him*, for he himself was incapable of rational thought. He envisioned the image of the Christ, or was He in truth before him? His eyes flew open and he raised them to look heavenward... *Oh, but would that be truth!*

The light filtered through the cracks in the ceiling of the barn, the dawn of day was rising, the dust motes of straw floating upon the air, imparting a golden attendance. He felt the tears of joy as they traveled along his face to drip upon his bare chest, to trickle among the dark hairs there, hot tears of joy and thanksgiving.

He heard the words of his own voice from a distant time; a man of his memories—Josiah; Josiah…Josiah…who was that? *His brother*…it seemed he had a brother…the man looked a great deal like he himself, with the exception of his startling intense blue eyes, eyes that were not truly blue; but the color of the southern seas.

They were sitting, rather squatting, on the sun burnt grasses of open, arid plains, the golden hues of mustards, yellows. Purples and pinks of the boundless crenelated bluffs stood regal behind them. He heard Josiah's voice, within his reminiscences—the sadness in his voice, the torturous agony, the pain, as he had bared his suffering soul to Jamie. He had wanted no comfort, he sought no solace, Jamie had but reached out to this very private man and hugged him, a moment in time when neither of them had felt ill at ease in the intimacy of the embrace. Jamie had very much wished to tell him of what he had read, what the esteemed philosopher of ages gone by had said, and now those words came to *him* in consolation.

"It is a fear, and it is only fitting in the young, who live by feeling, but are held back by the feeling of shame. We would not praise older people for such a sense of shame." Aristotle had thus continued, "Since shame should concern acts done voluntarily, and a decent person would not voluntarily do something shameful. A sense of shame is not a virtue, but more like a feeling than a stable character trait." Jamie smiled to himself, for now he was to admonish himself for feeling shame…

His thoughts ran to the man Josiah who rose in his memories, recollections of their conversation on that day came in a flourish of images; an image of coffins floating, bouncing on a ocean of navy blue, the waves crashing against them, the sharks, as their noses banged at the pine coffins, shattering them. Of Josiah, his eyes filled with heart felt grief and shame—for *he* had determined they leave Austria. *His wife and his children…gone.*

Again Jamie's thoughts turned inward, he had not *volunteered for brutality!* He had *not inflicted it! He was not to blame*! He doubtless had made a grave error in judgment to have put himself in danger, perhaps he was at fault for that, perhaps he had led his men into…the mere thought caused him extreme sorrow, *yet* this was a *war*, a war like no other he had experienced.

His thoughts came with crystal clarity now. Memories surged; images filled his mind's eye…images of the great pyramids of Egypt, of tall date palms and the River Nile. The hot, golden sands and fragrances of Morocco, the sweltering heat. The French men he had fought for, the Arabs he had fought against—then to join their ranks.

He let his mind wander, let it explore, to revisit the life he had lived and found the richness of it, the joy of his many experiences. He could feel and sense the excitement of the streets of Paris, smell the slightly musty odor of the Seine River, the scent of the flowers that hung in baskets from the shelter of sidewalk cafes. He heard once more the sounds of children playing on the banks of the river. He could smell the aroma of the coffee, could feel the sunshine on his face. In his mind's eye, he watched as his hand reached for the espresso. He remembered the gazes from the women passersby, as he sat at the sidewalk café, his long legs stretched to their maximum along the cobblestones.

None of those women looked like the raven-haired beauty in the church, *or* that same woman on the back of the great white horse. Had his betrayal been the most extreme to that of the black haired woman? The green eyes flashed before him. His betrayal of her…was that the reason it was so intolerably difficult for him to remember her? He sought out the dreams, the aberrations he had had. He once more heard the sound of his own voice, the horrific scream of her name that had arisen from his very soul during those tormented delusions. His heart leapt!

Elisabeth, Elisabeth, Elisabeth! He felt the heat of the tears, and joy that filled his heart! *Elisabeth!* He saw her now—among a field of daisies, struggling beneath him with a knife, and he remembered; *he remembered*! He saw the mighty river. He could hear its thunder and looked from it to a small log house that sat upon the precipice of a knoll; the smoke curling from the chimney. He remembered he had built that house. Within his memories rose the whinnying of horses and the fragrance of tall grasses being cut.

He heard the laughter of this elegant woman, the charm of her childlike giggle. He could remember the sound of the clatter of a buckboard as they rode into a small dirty mining town; his mind searched for the name... Butte, *Butte, Montana!*

His senses were filled with memories, memories that flooded his mind, his senses responding to each and every one, reacting with joy.

New recollections assaulted his mind—he heard a rifle shot and smelled the powder. He saw Joseph's wife fall before him and for a brief moment thought he had killed her. The image of Joseph—*his brother* rose before his minds eye. Great, joyous, homely Joseph! Tears of joy spilled from his eyes. He saw *Mack* the giant Scotsman, the man who rivaled only that of Joseph and Josiah in his heart, and knew the great Scotsman had been with him throughout the trials of the early part of this war, this fight for the country he loved!

He could envision his horse, Danny, black as night, with loyalty and swiftness and beauty that was uncompromised. He remembered the purchase of Mercy, the great white horse he had seen in his dreams... He had purchased her for *his wife, Elisabeth,* for a wedding gift.

His body trembled as sobs of joy overwhelmed him... *Thank you, Lord! Thank you!*

The sweat poured from his body from the great exertion of the memories, of the emotions brought about by those memories—of the grief and longing! His chest heaved with sobs that he reasoned would strangle the breath from him.

The image of Gettysburg rose within him and he fought it; he shuddered and swallowed the fear and the bile that rose at the memories... *Too much! Too much... Lord, please give me the courage! I beseech you...give me the valor to rise above this this fear—this trembling at the truth...* The battle at the Stones River... *Oh, God!* Of Columbia...

He felt the shackles, felt the abrasiveness of the rope and chain that tied all of them together...the blood that dripped from his wrists, the wound in his leg...the bullet lodged there...he heard the whistle of the train. The heat assaulted his memories, the *stench of humanity*! His mind filled with the sounds and moans; the shrieks of the many men imprisoned within the tall timbers of the arid, massive pen of men. His senses relived and felt the horrific fear; as he, in his mind, looked upon the straggled small fence—*that should they cross—they would surely be shot* or beaten. He again could taste the bugs and dirt, the bark and leaves that they had eaten to survive. He again felt the dysentery that had continuously run down his legs, felt the pain of the many sores on his body, a body that had grown weak and frail from starvation, from beatings. The beating's not only by guards, but also by other prisoners, prisoner's that would work in gangs of the most insane, the most distraught, themselves fighting to survive the brutality, the endless, unmerciful, minute by minute struggle to simply survive. These were his compatriots. These men were all Union men, yet they would kill one another for the right to drink the furthest upstream, the trickle of water often indiscernible...fight to the death for a small piece of cloth, or the right to lay out of the suns blistering heat. He envisioned a man, the man who had helped him to survive. The wily look of insanity that lay within his eyes, his words; "Starvation lad, you will not be minding it so very much *soon*...similar to sex; go long enough without either—food for the mind, the body, you cease the thought of it. Both to decline in a slow and might I add, a most painful death...*with it your very soul.*"

Jamie's mind struggled for memories *of peace, of tranquility, of joy!*

He heard the laughter of a small dark haired child—*his daughter*, Ellie, as she ran to him! "Papa! Papa!" He saw the infant in the cradle. Jesse! He heard the happy, joyous giggles that came from her cradle. *The letter...Elisabeth's letter—he had three children!*

He watched, within his mind's eye, the figure of Elisabeth, the same image of beauty, yet with trousers and a western hat covering her hair, making her face even more remarkable for all its visibility.

He heard the sound of a man's laughter and the sight of Pa Parsons's great ears, and Jamie chuckled.

He heard his own voice whisper into the solitude of the old barn. *"Thank you! Thank you!"* and felt the dirt beneath him, as he lay prostrate on the ground. *Surrender, forgiveness, knowledge* had been given him. "Lord, I beg of you, let me never forget this moment!"

He took a deep breath and pushed himself from the earth, his eyes resting on Bertha, the cook.

"I's sorry, mista. I's sorry, come ta git eggs...I's sorry. I see youse 'membered now *whose* y'all b'long ta. I's happy fer y'all! Sure nough I's be. When y'all git done speakin' wiff' the Lord, the Massa' wants y'all."

With that, she was gone.

He viewed his surroundings with astonishment... It had been weeks since Dr. Elam Coyle, had examined him, weeks of further torment, for now he knew; *it was he* that must find the courage to recall who he was, or as Bertha had pointed out, *to remember whose he was...* He smiled. This was the same barn Jonas had brought him too, the same barn Magnolia and Lila had nursed him. He would not forget this barn. He had indeed been blessed.

Jamie's Last Letter

Elisabeth looked in on the children; they lay fast asleep. Lord, how she wished to rest, to sleep a deep child like sleep, *a dirt nap,* as Ma termed it.

Carrying the lantern, she sat down at the table, perhaps if she read his letters once again. It had been so long since his last letter, she often felt no connection with him whatsoever. The depths of emptiness within her heart left an unbearable darkness. *Lord, protect him. Lord, surround him in your light.*

She was so tired, *tired* of the loneliness and worry, tired of the dreadful responsibility of the ranch, tired of trying to keep her daughters cognizant that indeed *they had a father.* She looked at the stack of letters, each stack tied in thin red and white ribbon she had indulged on at Sally Susanne's shop. The red and white, making her think of St. Valentine's Day—of all things! She thought of her history lessons at Miss Priscilla's, and how this had come about, recalling with vividness the outrage she had felt at such a young age:

> Valentine was a Roman Priest, during the time of the emperor Claudius. Claudius persecuted the church at that particular time and passed an edict that prohibited the marriage of young people; his basis for this was on the hypothesis that unmarried soldiers fought better than married soldiers because married soldiers would be afraid of what might happen to their wives or families if they died.

Elisabeth most certainly understood that! Look what had beset her, Jamie, her parents, as well as Ma and Pa Parsons! This war had affected the lives of each person in America.

Did she wish she had not married Jamie, had not run away with him? She smiled at the thought, for to live without Jamie—was to be only a portion of who she truly was. He was her heart, her soul, the reason she awoke in the morning.

> Valentine secretly married them because of the edict. The Priest Valentine was eventually caught, imprisoned, and tortured for performing marriage ceremonies against the command of Emperor Claudius the second.

If indeed, she lived in that time she would wish for the Priest Valentine to marry her as well. Her mind wandered to his punishment…

> It was in 269 AD that Valentine was sentenced to a three-part execution of beatings, stonings, and finally decapitation, all because of his stand for Christian marriage. The story goes that the last words he wrote were in a note to Asterius's daughter who was blind, with whom he had prayed with and healed. He had signed the note, "from your Valentine."

What a strange thing to think of, yet love was often all she thought of, as if she were once again that vivacious fourteen-year-old, waiting on the day she would become sixteen, thus she might abscond from Papa's home with James Martin Prescott.

She looked at the clock—2:00 am. *The dream* had awoken her, a dream that was a constant companion to her nights. The dream of him leaving her, his kisses, his promise to return…promises he had not kept. Was he dead? If indeed that were true, what would she do? For the thousandth time—she quite simply refused to admit that! *She would know, she would feel his loss!* Would he for all eternity be part of *whom* she was? Sally Susanne thought that to be true…that souls were united for all eternity.

Self-pity she was indeed wallowing in, within its dark and selfish cloud. In the years since last Jamie had left to serve his damnable country, she had read some of Grandmère's journal, the journal she had found sequestered among her trunk bearing Mama's wedding dress. If Grandmère could suffer such—*such despicable trials and tribulation*—certainly she, Elisabeth should be capable of bearing this!

Many were far more deserving of Gods grace…she thought once more of Ma Parsons, of all the children she had lost. Tommy had been killed in a battle in Tennessee, much like Jeremiah, although Papa had gone to retrieve Jeremiah, Tommy's body had never been sent home to Ma and Pa—the distance, far too great. He had died in Jamie's arms. Their Micah; having come home with the "soldiers' sickness"; now often incoherent and unable to work his gold mine, with Ben having to manage both that and his own store.

"Count your blessings, Elisabeth," Grandmère's words rang in her ears. The thought of Grandmère as near to the loss of Jamie as one could attain.

Had Jamie received any of her letters? Did he know he had another daughter; *Sylvia Belle* she had named her. Did he know that?

Was this the dream? Would she wake up and find she had only dreamt of loving and being loved, of her daughters, of the trek west, the land of Montana? She often thought she had dreamed a life of luxury and privilege, of Philadelphia, of *Jeremiah's death—of Jamie's capture.*

She reached for the stack of letters from Jamie, the last one dated June 1, 1864, the pages fragile and tear-stained. Yet she could feel his presence within them, feel the love and longing, feel the regret of his decision to leave her. The words were imbedded on her heart and mind, to again read them, seemed superfluous;

without opening the page's she could envision the writing. The letter being in French, as he had always written, "Should it fall in the hands of the enemy…"

She knew in her heart he wrote to her in French because it was the language they spoke most frequently, for it was the language of love. She thought how strange it was that he spoke languages so easily; Latin would pour from him, Arabic, and Spanish as well, the language of the Flathead Indians.

Carefully unfolding the pages, the words rang out from her memory—from her heart.

> *Ce jour de notre Seigneur 16 Mai 1864*
>
> *Ma chérie Elisabeth, ma femme, mon ami, mon amant, la mère de mes enfants, c'est avec une grande sorrow that I say these words, for I have been most foolhardy to have left you for a country that is dissolving before my very eyes. The battles rage on and on, the dead lie at my every turn. I have left you for this—this despicable quest that has reached a momentum that even Grant and Sherman appear unable to end. Bobby Lee and Jefferson Davis have no intention of surrender; on they fight as if they were indeed imbued of the Holy Spirit. Not unlike the Arabs and the French. Mankind seems to be filled with arrogance and hubris…*
>
> *Sherman has been injured so frequently as to leave him with but one leg, having lost it at Chickamauga, one arm has been crippled by a bullet at Gettysburg. We often must strap him to his horse. I greatly admire his dedication and his "mind over matter" attitude, as we have all suffered wounds of some import (not to worry, my darling, there have been none I cannot bear).*
>
> *These two factions—the Union and the Confederates, no longer care for their original motives, or of the idealistic nature of their cause, but fight on now as a way of life.*
>
> *My enlistment shall be up at the end of July, and I shall again return to you, and there I shall stay! I find that I, like commanders before me find in my heart a great distress at the constant killing and mutilation of my brothers. Poetry of pain and sadness consume my heart and mind, and I am shocked at*

these revelations, as I would have deemed myself a great warrior. Being physically and mentally proficient in war does not provide the heart with the strength needed to endure the brutality and the murder of one's human family.

She pushed the letter aside and dropped her head to rest on her folded arms, letting the tears spill. To a great degree, the tears were a comfort, a release, for so long she had been unable to cry. With that thought, she envisioned Eleanor; perhaps that indeed was the depths of her pain.

Dear God, where was he? That letter was over a year old; the war had been over since April! Lord, what do you wish of me? I surrender, Lord. I surrender! For I can bear no more…

Instantaneously she could feel His presence—as tangible as anything she had experienced. The words unspoken, yet the thoughts, and yes, instructions, came clear and concise to her mind and rested within her heart. Was it a vision out of her imagination? *He* was not! *The Lord stood in her home!* If but an instant, an instant that seemed an eternity, an eternity of peace and purpose, of solutions, of self-abnegation, and yes, visions. Visions of green fields with small white flowers, of warmth and sunshine, long moss draped massive old trees…and *Jamie.*

She dropped to the floor and praised God—the Lord in all his glory! The tears, the sobs—now ones of overwhelming gratitude, of praise, and yes, *complete and utter surrender.*

"Stand, my child," she heard *Him* say, and she stood before his outstretched hand. Was He going to take her, was she going to die now, this very minute? She thought of her daughters and lowered her eyes from the intensity of *His*. "No, my child, you have many things yet to do."

When she looked again He was gone. The aberration was gone. She thanked *Him* and again kneeled on the floor, the sobs came freely now, sobs of clarity and relief. "Thank you, thank you! Thank you, Lord, for Sally Susanne. I would not have believed it possible without her *Voices*. Without her teachings."

She breathed deeply and reached for pen and paper. She must write this down perchance it be lost forever. The list—the visions—the instructions, had come so clearly and yet so rapidly. *Thank you Lord. He* had been in her home...was He in everyone's home...and they took no notice?

She heard the thoughts again. "*I am here always. Waiting for the surrender of the heart, the mind, the physical being. Always, keep your heart open to Me; trust in Me. You, like all, will have many trials in this life. Listen to that voice in your heart, in your mind, that is where I reside.*"

She had felt that presence, *His* presence in Ilene and Mack's home, in Sally Susanne's. "Thank you, Lord, thank you." What a meager insignificant means of gratitude—*words*...she would give her life for that feeling of divine love, of acceptance, of purity, of selflessness that had filled her being at that moment.

It was clear, beyond doubt; she was to go to Philadelphia. She was to contact Josiah and Sally Susanne. She was to search for Jamie amidst the South... She thought of the vision, the Spanish moss, the huge old trees, the fields of green, the white flowers. She must consult Uncle Percy's geography books.

She was to go now! That was indeed clear! Was the railroad finished...how was she to get there?

The vision of Jamie rose in her mind, and yet again, the tears of joy streamed... She had seen him! The Lord had shown him to her! He was alive! He was thin and browned by the sun, his body bare with the exception of extremely short pants. His hair dark and damp hung about the striking chiseled features of his face. A massive brick pillar stood behind where he stood, beyond it a row of immense deciduous trees, the subtle green of Spanish moss, pendant upon them. She could sense within him a sense of loss, of confusion, of defeat. Was it defeat? That was not *her* Jamie! She had never known him to be defeated! Whatever could have transpired to cause him to feel thus? It broke her heart!

What was she to do first? "Lord, if You can hear me..." She smiled, for the answer lay in her mind, as *He* had said it would.

She would talk to Charlie this morning as they rode line. It was a busy time of the year to leave the ranch, the fields were ripe with grain; there were foods to store and candles and soap to make. Charlie would need to care for the ranch. She would speak to Mack and Ilene, Joseph and Eleanor concerning the rest. She thought of Eleanor and knew what her thoughts would be concerning adding to Joseph's workload, she didn't give a mite… not one!

Money, she would need to use some of the gold… She would count it tonight.

Tomorrow she would send a wire to Josiah…and go to see Sally Susanne.

Thank you, Lord! She crossed herself and genuflected in the direction *He* had stood.

Read next; *Ancestral Bonz IV; The Journey*

Also by Carroll Silvera:

Ancestral Bonz I: The Prescotts

Ancestral Bonz II: Montana

Ancestral Bonz III: Civil War

Silver Threads…to Gold

…Every Nine seconds

What Doesn't Kill You

CPSIA information can be obtained
at www.ICGtesting.com
Printed in the USA
LVOW11s0219060517
533362LV00001B/1/P

9 781942 451983